# Mindfulness and the Psychology of Oppression



This book offers a comprehensive, evidence-based, and engaging inquiry into women's oppression and its mitigation through contemplative practices like meditation. It combines scholarly depth with embodied experiences and practices that interweave individual, interpersonal, and public relationships.

Locating oppression as an internalized psychological response to toxic social messaging, the author distils research from multiple sources – cognitive science, philosophy, psychology, feminism, and Buddhist psychology – to consider how mindfulness might be deployed to help women navigate misogyny. The book draws on cross-cultural data from historical and contemporary sources supplemented with accounts from the author's own life to illustrate misogyny through cases ranging in severity from overt violence to covert micro-aggressions and gaslighting. Introducing new theories and insights on the role of emotions and consciousness in oppression, the author proposes an anti-oppressive mindfulness agenda to help women navigate misogyny and recover from the aftermath of oppression.

Mapping out a vision for how meditation might become a more effective path for women's liberation and wellbeing, this book is an invaluable resource for educators, social workers, clinicians, and contemplative practitioners alike. It will also be highly relevant reading for students, educators, clinicians, and researchers of psychology, mindfulness, and gender studies.

**Seonaigh MacPherson** is a professor of adult and higher education with a specialization in diversity and mindfulness-based teaching and learning (MBTL) in the Faculty of Education, Community, and Human Development at the University of the Fraser Valley in British Columbia, Canada.

**Women and Psychology**
Series Editor: Jane Ussher
*Professor of Women's Health Psychology, University of Western Sydney*

This series brings together current theory and research on women and psychology. Drawing on scholarship from a number of different areas of psychology, it bridges the gap between abstract research and the reality of women's lives by integrating theory and practice, research and policy.

Each book addresses a 'cutting edge' issue of research, covering topics such as postnatal depression and eating disorders, and addressing a wide range of theories and methodologies.

The series provides accessible and concise accounts of key issues in the study of women and psychology, and clearly demonstrates the centrality of psychology debates within women's studies or feminism.

Other titles in this series:

**Postfeminism and Body Image**
*Sarah Riley, Adrienne Evans and Martine Robson*

**Trans Reproductive and Sexual Health: Justice, Embodiment and Agency**
*Damien W. Riggs, Jane M. Ussher, Kerry H. Robinson, Shoshana Rosenberg*

**Reframing Trauma Through Social Justice: Resisting the Politics of Mainstream Trauma Discourse**
*Catrina Brown*

**Narratives of Childhood Domestic Violence: Epistemic Justice, Young Women and Transitions to Young Adulthood**
*Tanya Frances*

**Mindfulness and the Psychology of Oppression: Navigating Misogyny**
*Seonaigh MacPherson*

For more information about this series, please visit: https://www.routledge.com/Women-and-Psychology/book-series/SE0263

# Mindfulness and the Psychology of Oppression

## Navigating Misogyny

Seonaigh MacPherson

Routledge
Taylor & Francis Group
NEW YORK AND LONDON

Designed cover image: Getty Images

First published 2026
by Routledge
605 Third Avenue, New York, NY 10158

and by Routledge
4 Park Square, Milton Park, Abingdon, Oxon, OX14 4RN

*Routledge is an imprint of the Taylor & Francis Group, an informa business*



ISBN: 978-1-032-58267-2 (hbk)
ISBN: 978-1-032-58266-5 (pbk)
ISBN: 978-1-003-44935-5 (ebk)

DOI: 10.4324/9781003449355

Typeset in Sabon
by SPi Technologies India Pvt Ltd (Straive)

# Contents

# Acknowledgements

I would like to thank Routledge, first and foremost, for continuing to champion critical research and scholarship directed at global equity and justice. In particular, I would like to thank my editor, Emilie Coin, and the series editor, Jane Ussher. I am grateful for their patience and multiple extensions to complete the research and writing, which went well beyond the dates I originally projected. So too, their suggested edits were invaluable in helping me to feel more satisfied with the final quality of the work.

I would like to acknowledge friends who helped inspire and improve the book while easing the burden of writing. My mindfulness community in Canada helped motivate and refine the orientation of this book, including Jackie Seidel, Rosemina Munjee, Ron Plowright, Faye Martin, and Kulli Yee. Carole Roy encouraged me to keep writing when I was on the brink of giving up, so she deserves credit for this book getting finished. Natasha van Bentum has been a steady support throughout and contributed directly to aspects of the theory, notably and significantly, the seventh attribute of consciousness, *affiliation*, with implications for compassion. Not coincidentally, our own affiliation continues to support my consciousness to overcome the slings and arrows of outrageous fortune! My dear friend and retired social worker Joanna Carson discussed anti-oppressive mindfulness with me on many occasions. Zeporah Richards Horodezky helped ground me with her friendship while she navigated the challenges of coming to terms with oppression as we age. Worthy of thanks, too, are my beautiful canine friends, Karma and Tashi (RIP).

Last but not least, I would like to acknowledge the lifelong contributions of teachers and mentors. The first group is composed of mindfulness and meditation teachers – notably the Ven. Namgyal Rinpoche, Tarchin Hearn, Cecile Kwiat, Ven. Tara Rinpoche, and HH Dalai Lama. The other group is composed of those women whose bravery, intelligence, compassion, and suffering have inspired my own search for liberation from oppression and misogyny: my mother, Beverly; my aunts, Marion and Joanne; and the nuns of Dolma Ling, as well as my aforementioned community and friends. Finally, deserving of acknowledgement are those feminists who taught me at a distance through their scholarship and writing, including Shulamith Firestone, Simone de Beauvoir, Sara Ahmed, and Kate Manne.

# Preface

This book was far more difficult to write than I anticipated when I first proposed it to Routledge. As I prepare the final manuscript now, the morning news is preoccupied with the current US administration's latest assaults on anti-oppressive initiatives, referred to as "DEI" (signifying diversity, equity and inclusion policies and practices) or "wokeness." These assaults have explicitly targeted women, African-Americans, and migrants by defunding and silencing research, policies, and programming in government, universities, museums, the media, and schools.

Though perhaps an outmoded term, "civilization" is an ideal I'd like to invoke as a context for this book. It is worth reclaiming with both broadened and narrower significance. If we whittle the construct down to its root, that is, to what is "civil," it conveys the civility defended and developed through civilizing movements across time and space. What all civilizations inculcate is the attempt to refine both what is humane and what is variously experienced as the good life, namely, wellbeing, and the scope of persons able to access to it. Since the Second World War, this has manifested in global development initiatives that reflect a shared sense of what civilization may be, symbolically beginning with the *UN Declaration of Human Rights*. It is perhaps not surprising that one of the first acts of this current US administration was to remove the USA from the UN Human Rights Agency.

These are not merely modern trends. Mindfulness derives from a method originating in 500 BCE in South Asia within early Buddhism. Even such a long time ago, the Buddha contested caste and gender distinctions to articulate a path and form communities organized around the pursuit of liberation from oppression, variously perceived. Most cultures in the world have pathways to find and cultivate kindness, compassion, and respect, not only for those on whom we depend as family and friends but also for those more distant to us as strangers or even enemies.

I locate the origins of this study of oppression and anti-oppressive mindfulness within such noble beginnings in the hopes that it might contribute, however modestly, to the civilizing of humanity and so help realize our potential as a caretaker species of one another and the Earth. This millennial-long journey to "civilize" humanity from its self-interested and violent inclinations is the project of the best of religious, secular, educational, and cultural life globally.

Yet, in these troubling times, rather than "civilizing," these expanding expressions of social justice are disparagingly referred to by some populist conservative voices as "wokeness." Were this now-pejorative term analysed by how it is used, it would seem to signify compassion, human rights, equality, and anti-oppressive practices well beyond any seemingly justifiable critiques of "political correctness" or affirmative action policies. These purported conservatives misconstrue and debase freedom of speech as the freedom to speak hate, as if speaking hate were itself a virtue, while all the while silencing dissent through the coarsest abuses of power. Perhaps it is an example of Freud's *return of the repressed*, evidence of the pent-up rage of White male entitlement expressing itself to claim what it is they believe that they are owed.

After the 2024 US election, Elon Musk repeated his view that empathy is the "fundamental weakness of Western civilization" (Happyscribe, 2025). Describing what he called "the empathy exploit," he referred to an unspecified "they" enacting a conspiracy of kindness: "They're exploiting a bug in Western civilization, which is the empathy response." This use of the word "bug" aligns with his reference to a "woke-virus," equating life with a computer game. In his biography of Musk, Isaacson (2023) reports how Elon came to this conclusion about empathy after addictively playing the video game *Polytopia*. Elon's brother recounted to Isaacson Elon's eight "*Polytopia* Life Lessons," the first two being that *Empathy is not an asset* and *Play life like a game*:

> *Empathy is not an asset.* "He knows that I have an empathy gene, unlike him, and it has hurt me in business," Kimbal says. "*Polytopia* taught me how he thinks when you remove empathy. When you're playing a video game, there is no empathy, right?"
>
> (p. 426)

This book is written against the beliefs that life is a game and empathy is a disadvantage. Instead, it is written on the premise that cooperation and compassion are the promise of humanity and of the world. Furthermore, these attacks on cooperation, empathy, and compassion are veiled attacks on women, for whom these values often dominate in practice if not in principle. I truly believe that the fate of the status of women is tied up with the fate of these values and vice versa. This is not to say that I believe that individual women are more compassionate than individual men. Regrettably, many women opt to undermine other women and suppress them as they were themselves suppressed.

Having taught undergraduate and graduate courses in mindfulness and mindfulness-based teaching and learning (MBTL), I am well aware of the gendering of mindfulness and compassion. Over 90% of my students have been women. I anticipate the same in you, my readers, but I welcome men who choose to traverse this path with us as practitioners, teachers, and allies alike. This gender imbalance was less true in Buddhist contexts, where many of the students and most of the teachers in my experience were male. The problem was that patriarchy went alongside this more balanced representation by men, leading to very few women being elevated or supported to teach (with too many being seduced instead).

Indeed, this book originated with my asking the question of why so many women are drawn to mindfulness and so many men aren't. I think the answer to that question is complex, but oppression is part of the story. Secular-scientific mindfulness seems to offer a safer space for women to learn mindfulness and to develop professionally as teachers and clinicians, free of both gender discrimination (GD) and the abuses of misogyny.

Ultimately, I write for those who struggle against oppression and its aftermath. That struggle has dominated my own life, both personally and professionally, a struggle that has paid off manifold in contributing to a life of meaning and flourishing. I realize there may be people for whom oppression is a distant and unrelatable concept, though I find it difficult to believe that any woman does not recognize some form of oppression within her past experience. Still, I celebrate women who may be living free of, or remain unfamiliar with, oppression. Indeed, I have encountered friends, family, neighbours, acquaintances, and community leaders who have resisted or overcome oppression and now enjoy free and flourishing lives. Fortunately, there are many liberated women who now live among us.

This is proudly a feminist book that is committed to the liberation of women. As such, it adheres to two fundamental tenets of the women's movement. First, it is constructivist in theoretical orientation, recognizing, as Simone de Beauvoir first reminded us, that "a woman is not born but made." Second is the related feminist principle that "the personal is political." Just as the social impacts the personal, so does the personal impact the social. The patterns of domination and hierarchy and oppression and liberation that we negotiate personally in our lives and minds echo the challenges to our collective liberation from domination and oppression. So, it is my belief that is an error to separate arbitrarily and favour more extraverted actions aimed at social or structural change over more introspective psychological change.

Oppression involves certain overlapping features, regardless of the identity of its victims or aggressors. Although there are distinctive causes and historical roots, the way oppression is internalized in the mind, its harms, and its remedies share some broad, even universal patterns. Therefore, I am confident that this book will be of interest to all of those who consider themselves to be anti-oppressive practitioners or who struggle against any form of oppression in their lives. My own radically uncertain yet boundless hope sees in this project the future of humanity, writ whole, liberated from psychological oppression and systems of domination, free to flourish and manifest the great potential nascent in our biology and our history.

Victoria, BC, Canada
May 2025

## References

Happyscribe. (2025). *#2281 Elon Musk. The Joe Rogan Experience.* Feb 28, 2025. https://www.happyscribe.com/public/the-joe-rogan-experience/2281-elon-musk

Isaacson, W. (2023). *Elon Musk.* Simon & Schuster.

# 1 Introduction

As I embark on this book, I am aware of the impulse to avoid what it is I am trying to hold onto at the centre of this project, that is, oppression. Like a centrifugal force pushing outwards to the limits of our conditioned awareness, oppression comes with an impulse to look away, to view it as an exception rather than a rule, as a singular event rather than an experience with social and even biological ramifications. The biblical story of Lot's wife comes to mind, who, unnamed, defies God by looking back at the destruction of Sodom and Gomorrah and so endures God's punishment when she is transformed into a pillar of salt. Resistance begins in that singular act of looking back and accepting the consequences of that compassionate gesture of curiosity.

This is a book about psychic wounds and what can be learned from observing them. More than learning about the wound, it is about learning *as* a wound. The encounter with oppression often leads to dysfunctional, maladaptive learning about oneself and the world in ways that perpetuate oppression. In this respect, this book is about *unlearning* oppression. It is about unlearning oppression to recover dignity, love, and meaning from the aftermath of shame, humiliation, and anger. "Lick your wounds and move on" comes to mind, but as anyone with a dog can attest to, licking wounds often does more harm than good. Consequently, healing from oppression must involve more than just revisiting memories of oppressive experiences. It entails mending wounds by recognizing and moving *through* oppression in the present, not merely being captive to its legacy in memories unearthed through therapeutic processes of disclosure.

In my case, I begin this journey as a woman. Whatever other identities and identifications I may have, it is as a woman that I come to this topic, naturally. I don't claim that all women experience the kinds of oppression I have known or faced, but I do know that many women do experience oppression in multiple forms and contexts, including women in other cultures and places in the world. I have lived, loved, and worked with many of these women.

Life in theory bears little resemblance to a life lived. To know a life in theory, we consider biology, psychology, sociology, economics, political science, or anthropology, or perhaps, more personally, we look to family trees,

DOI: 10.4324/9781003449355-1

to history, to the stories we inherit from others about how we came to be here or perhaps to the evidence of records, photographs, and videos. Yet, to comprehend a life *lived*, we turn to something very different; we turn to *experience*. The word embeds the Latin root *experientia*, meaning to try, to risk, to put to the test and sharing etymology with words like *experiment* and *expert*. By tracing these word origins, we discover something lost or eroded in its conventional sense: experience as proof or evidence, somehow surpassing theory, involving risk and, ultimately, leading to confidence and expertise.

So, I begin with experience: *In the beginning was?* Well, experience, but necessarily channelled into memory and *the word* as abstraction. That is the challenge we all face in working with experience: How to represent in language or imagery what was first known directly through the senses and perception and only then in memory or recollection so as to make it comprehensible both to ourselves, in reflection, and to others, in communication.

We might call such representations *biography*, literally life-writing, or perhaps *auto-biography* as self-life-writing. Writing about lived experiences involves moving beyond stories and theories about a life to the lived experience of *being alive* and inhabiting a consciousness, the heart of mindfulness itself. Mindful forms of representation try to render life experiences with more empirical details, often evoked and nuanced within more poetic and aesthetic forms. It is not information about life that is the point so much as the experience of life and of inhabiting a human body and mind. This entails, as Wordsworth suggested, "emotion recollected in tranquillity," while phenomenologically distilling ordinary conscious experience as free as possible of distortions from preconceptions and interpretations. Therefore, I choose to land somewhere between the two, to understand oppression both as an objective condition with clinical implications and as a quality of experience with phenomenological and aesthetic features.

In this type of inquiry into experience, I do not adhere to the conventional sequence, time, and structure of stories, to chronologies, to the "writing of/in time," as a linear trajectory of events. There is no beginning, middle, or end. Instead, I track the time of experience and the unfolding of memory in relation to it, as unfiltered by culture as possible: I wish to discern how oppression appears to the mind in experience, as more cyclical and circular, like a spiral repeating patterns and revolutions through time to extend what is known and knowable. Such *achronologies* begin with seemingly random, yet non-random, moments to situate the text in the chaotic midst of a life: a beginning which is itself an extension of what came before yet somehow marks a difference, a turning, a risk, a revolution. This singular experience was a bird singing, when, as a 19-year-old, I first learned *to sit*, mindful:

> And so it began with a birdsong. Hearing that bird sing outside a window seemed, however improbably, a way out. To hear a bird sing for the first time, despite inhabiting this world for over two decades, made me question what else I'd missed. It told me not to trust the education I was subjected to. The bird was out of view, but the song reached down

> and filled my attention with its presence, as a kind of bliss. I knew this was an experience I could revisit. Meditation could take me here to affiliate with a greater-than-human life. A kind of biological affiliation.

This book considers the intergenerational wounds inflicted by oppression on the psyches of women and other oppressed people. I took up this difficult topic to consider how mindfulness offers a path out of such affliction from my own experience, as a way to heal, protect, and liberate from these wounds. My motivation emerged from a slow, percolating recognition of the insidious nature of oppression in my own life and in the lives of women and others close to me.

The relationship between oppression and mindfulness is tricky. I once naively believed oppression derived from social and political harms that could persist *out there* without necessarily impinging on my self-confidence, personhood, and consciousness *in here*. I nurtured an optimistic assumption that, if sufficiently strong and trained up with mindfulness, my mind as *the inner world* could remain largely impervious to oppressive and discriminatory environments *out there*. My long-standing engagement in Buddhism, with its idealistic conception of liberation as an exclusively internal process of transformation, tended to bolster this misapprehension. Although I used mindfulness to conserve wellbeing, it also enabled me to filter out evidence of threats to that wellbeing so as to cope and endure a work environment that was becoming increasingly untenable.

Ultimately, a personal crisis dismantled the illusion underpinning this mistaken view. At the time, at the seeming apex of my life and career as a university professor, I thought myself content and well. During the previous two years, I had published a book, completed a sabbatical, won a leading faculty service award, and been promoted to the highest rank as full professor with tenure. Yet something was amiss, though I couldn't quite put my finger on it. I suffered from persistent fatigue and frustration, aggravated by the steady irritant of passive aggression coming from work colleagues and administrators. I worried that mindfulness may have been propping me up to cope within this veneer of adequacy, all the while masking obstacles that were preventing me from living well and flourishing.

Then, a bullying challenge with a colleague suddenly escalated out of the blue, or so it seemed at the time. As the military metaphor of *shock and awe* suggests, I was left unable to fight back in the ensuing confusion. Later, when I recovered some of my dignity and perspective, intense anger and self-defensiveness replaced what had been crippling shame and humiliation. This anger propelled me to seek justice within the institution and the systems that served it, without success: HR, union, workplace standards bodies, union oversite bodies, etc. When the manifold mechanisms designed to address such conflicts failed, through slow and deliberate attrition, I had little choice but to accept the superficial peace on offer in lieu of fairness, justice, and truth.

This personal crisis mirrors many accounts of the emotions of oppression reported in the research literature as documented in Chapter 4. My shame response, what Bartky (1990) refers to as "shame-attunement," is known to accompany protective impulses to inhibit and conceal (Deigh, 1983). These impulses to inhibit and conceal, in turn, reinforce states of anxiety, depression, repression, withdrawal, and silence, rendering the oppressed vulnerable to the extrinsic control of others and the loss of autonomy and wellbeing (e.g., Ryan et al., 2021). As the mind wrests itself from oppression through resistance and recovery, challenging transitional emotions often arise like anger, defensiveness, defiance, or irritability. These emotions involve more expressive forms of self-protection that can nonetheless pose a challenge to self-regulation and the capacity to conform to the emotional expectations of social situations. This is a paradox: While moving out of shame with its inhibiting and concealing impulses, the aftermath of oppression makes it difficult to self-regulate in the face of such strong emotions, which can exacerbate forms of discrimination and threats from antagonistic (social) environments.

This paradox has several implications. One is to recognize that these purportedly "negative" emotions play a natural and important role in the process of liberation. Yet they also reinforce the injustice of oppression in that it is very challenging to experience wellbeing when subjected to such negative emotions. The capacity to self-regulate and experience some degree of wellbeing, in turn, is often a precondition of effective social action. Studying the intellectuals and activists who furthered our understanding of oppression, what becomes clear is that there is a high cost exacted on anti-oppression activists for believing that social action trumps personal wellbeing. So many pioneers in anti-oppressive activism died tragically or prematurely. Franz Fanon, for example, a psychiatrist and pioneer in the study of oppression, died at only 36 years of age, the same year as the publication of his 1961 book, *The Wretched of the Earth*. More recently, Sarah Ahmed (2010), who critiqued the popular depiction of happiness in *The Promise of Happiness*, ended up leaving her prestigious professorial position at the University of London after realizing her struggles to counter institutional misogyny and discrimination were futile. Shulamith Firestone, author of the landmark (1970) feminist call to revolution, *The Dialectic of Sex*, died alone in 2012, impoverished after suffering repeated extended hospitalizations for schizophrenia. In the end, she was subjected to abuse and marginalization by the women within the organizations she created (Faladi, 2013). Paradoxically, she described post-oppression life in her earlier book as full of *play* and *love*, where freedom allows "love to flow unimpeded" (p. 216). This tragically resurfaces years later, in *Airless Spaces* (Firestone, 1998), when she describes (of a fictional character standing for herself) the loss of wellbeing as the loss of the possibility of love:

> Perhaps due to the medication, her biggest trouble was that she couldn't care about anything, and love was forgotten. That left getting through the blank days as comfortably as possible, trying not to sink under the boredom and total loss of hope. She was lucid, yes, at what price. She

> sometimes recognized on the faces of others joy and ambition and other emotions she could recall having had once, long ago. But her life was ruined, and she had no salvage plan.
>
> (p. 59)

Polar views of oppression as either exclusively an internalized psychological problem or a structural systemic social issue are both faulty. How we conduct our lives *is* social action, and to bring wellbeing and fairness to the world begins by bringing it to life and mind. This is the promise of mindfulness. Bartky (1990) claims that "feminist consciousness is consciousness of *victimization*" (p. 15). Yet the belief of oneself as a victim can be counterproductive to liberation, which is dependent on recovering agency and self-confidence from victimhood.

### Oppression as Consciousness

As I argue in this book, even more serious than the negative impacts of oppression on emotions and the capacity to regulate emotions are its negative impacts consciousness itself. Consciousness is constituted at the juncture of emotion and self-awareness. For consciousness to develop requires some degree of contentment and joy, enabling curiosity in both the self and the world. When the background emotion in consciousness is unspecified *shame* and humiliation arising from internalized oppression, or the intense anger and defensiveness as it is resisted, the capacity for a fuller, more conscious perspective is constrained.

As a biological phenomenon, consciousness is a recursive domain in which living beings represent and navigate environments through their felt experience, which is constructed via sensory-motor systems, cognition, and, for humans, symbolic language, culture, and thought. Consciousness can't be located entirely in the biology of the organism, however, or in its matter and physiology, nor is it located exclusively in the environment. Instead, consciousness exists in the ecological niche where the organism and environment intersect. The heart of consciousness is the experience of the self, the apparent navigator of the organism, poised to interpret and respond to the world. Consciousness is neither entirely personal nor collective but enmeshed between the two, a zone of experience involving shared structures and forms or expression and representation acquired through embodiment.

As an expression of consciousness, oppression can never be addressed solely within a narrow personal or political frame of reference. Oppression is something both done to us by the (social) world but also something we are complicit in co-constructing. Yet "complicity" needs to be qualified in that much of this process is neither intentional nor even conscious. The pre-conscious nature of oppression makes it difficult for victims, perpetrators, and bystanders alike to correct. Some oppression manifests as implicit bias, which can manifest as bias against one's own identity. Some is self-repression, reinforced by social stigma internalized as shame. In this way, oppression diminishes consciousness with its associated sense of personhood (self) and wellbeing (as flourishing), thereby diminishing agency as the power to realize our goals in the world. And as we experience oppression individually, it is necessarily experienced by others in our community who share the same oppressed social identity.

Oppression inhabits the invisible web in which the world becomes the self and the self, the world. This makes it tricky to know where to begin. Is it best to direct our efforts to change the self or the world? In either direction, we are prone to see through a glass, darkly. Mindfulness is a way to see across this seeming chasm between the psychology of the self and the suchness of the world. Mindfulness is noticing, recognizing, and acting with a more subtle awareness able to notice how the mind constitutes our experience of the world. In this way, mindfulness-based anti-oppressive practice is both a collective and personal path to wellbeing.

*Liberation* describes the state following the removal of oppression. As a construct, liberation has complex discursive histories burdened with markedly unfree ideological abuses. On the one hand, as freedom, liberation is tangible and personal, a process we struggle to maintain, as autonomy, even in the midst of our most intimate relations. In self-determination theory, such autonomy is defined as a natural intrinsic motivator for humans (Ryan et al., 2021). On the other hand, autonomy can be compromised in the very name of freedom, as, for example, in capitalism as *free* enterprise. The experience of most people shifting from agriculture or small business labour to industrial labour would not represent the change as an enhancement of autonomy and freedom.

Mindfulness is associated with liberation in some of the earliest Buddhist texts: liberation from suffering, broadly construed. The original term for mindfulness in Pali is *sati*. The English (Welsh) 19th/early-20th Pali scholar, T.W. Rhys David, first coined the term *mindfulness* to translate *sati*. Initially, he proposed *self-possession* but later settled on *mindfulness*; self-possession, however, better conveys this sense of mindfulness as a source of autonomy, self-determination, and, ultimately, freedom.

## Women's Oppression

Feminism and the "women's liberation" movement together constitute a type of praxis. Praxis describes activities where practice is closely informed by theory: Theory is applied in practice, and, reciprocally, practice is developed and guided by theory. Feminist theories about women's oppression became integrated, applied, and tested in social action through women's liberation movements. Over the past century and longer, four distinctive "waves" of feminist theories about women's oppression and freedom emerged.

First-wave feminism of the late 19th and early 20th centuries emphasized the basic political and social equality rights of women (e.g., Cady Stanton, 1848). The theory of equal rights informed the suffragette movement that culminated in women getting equal voting rights and more access to education and employment. In the 1950–1970s, second-wave feminism examined the impact of oppression on women's consciousness and psyches, arising out of the internalization of oppression and women's unequal reproductive and subservient social roles (e.g., de Beauvoir, 2011/1949b; Firestone, 1970). This gave rise to an associated social movement focused on women's solidarity and consciousness-raising. Third-wave feminism focused on the impacts of intersectional identities when race and class differences compounded and altered the experience of oppression (e.g., hooks, 1984/2015). This aligned with a period of integrated and generic "social justice" movements. Recently, the *#me-too* social movement emerged alongside fourth-wave feminism, which in turn emphasized the insidious and institutionalized nature of misogyny with its reliance on micro-aggressions and forms of marginalization used to obstruct and marginalize women who challenge patriarchal norms (Ahmed, 2021; Manne, 2018). Women's oppression uniquely arose from intersecting biological and social causes and conditions. This deep link between biology and culture suggests why theories about women's oppression have woven such a circuitous path. It is no small undertaking! These successive waves, furthermore, are not in conflict but represent successive and interconnected levels and layers, each necessary to remedy affliction.

## Wellbeing

Overriding all other sources of knowledge is knowledge about wellbeing – whether in the governance of states and institutions or in governance over our personal lives. Historically, wellbeing, variously defined, has been construed as the end to which all means are justifiably directed. From the Buddhist conception of nirvana dating back to 500 BCE to Aristotle's conception of eudaimonia (flourishing) to dominant contemporary theories of psychology and economics, wellbeing – whether as happiness, flourishing, peace, or satisfaction – has been recognized as the "meaning" or purpose of life.

What distinguishes wellbeing from mere subjective happiness, however, is the inclusion of a wider range of both objective and subjective criteria. Criteria for wellbeing have been developed to guide governance policies in states, such as those developed by the Organization for Economic Cooperation and Development (OECD) (n.d.). These criteria include indicators for subjective happiness or life satisfaction as well as for material conditions such as income, housing, and healthy environments and for social conditions reflected in literacy, education, and healthcare.

Evidence-based wellbeing criteria are applied to personal development, too, where it serves as a source of *em*powerment (vs. power). As *eudaimonia* or flourishing, wellbeing can be interpreted as a natural, biological state that we are intrinsically motivated to reach and sustain through self-regulation. In this sense, just as physiological properties interact to maintain homeostatic balances in living systems, such as body temperature, so too processes and properties of consciousness or mind work towards a comparable state of balance or equipoise that we call wellbeing (eudaimonic wellbeing or flourishing). Through the self-regulation of attention, affect, and sensorimotor and cognitive functions, we monitor and adjust choices and circumstances to maintain wellbeing in the midst of change. Deci & Ryan (2013) refers to this process in self-determination theory, describing three critical intrinsic "natural" motivations directing our pursuits of wellbeing: struggles for autonomy (feeling in control of actions and circumstances), competence (feeling capable), and relatedness (feeling connected).

Oppression challenges the wellbeing of those affected and their capacities to self-regulate. For women, generations of scholarship have elucidated the social and psychological restrictions to women's capacities to develop full competence and self-regulated autonomy. Because mindfulness enhances self-regulation, autonomy, and wellbeing (e.g., MacPherson & Rockman, 2022; Ryan et al., 2021), it offers strong potential as an anti-oppressive praxis for women. Mindfulness works to mitigate or overcome oppression by empowering women's agency rather than relying on changing social systems exclusively. Through women's empowerment, we become capable of navigating and ultimately changing misogynistic systems that continue to resurface to protect patriarchy and patriarchal norms. What protects us against these resurfacing cycles of oppression is wellbeing: Wellbeing is our protection.

Since its inception, scholars have defined oppression as the result of the *internalization* of dehumanizing social norms (e.g., de Beauvoir, 1949a, 1949b; Fanon, 1961; Freire, 1970). Yet, despite this tacit and pervasive acceptance of psychological causes, focus has tended to land on its socio-political rather than psychological manifestations; however, in the last decade or so, increased attention has shifted to the psychological impacts of oppression arising from adverse childhood experiences, sustained traumas, and implicit biases. This re-orientation on oppression's psychological impacts has led to corresponding calls to recognize mindfulness as an anti-oppressive praxis (Berila, 2015; MacPherson and Rockman, 2022; Magee, 2019; Munjee and MacPherson, 2025).

## Mindfulness

Jon Kabat Zinn (2013), founder of the mindfulness-based stress reduction (MBSR) programme, defined mindfulness as "paying attention in a particular way: on purpose, in the present moment, and non-judgementally." Other definitions emerged in the wake of this, including operationalized definitions that were used to design a range of tests and measurements of mindfulness. These varied definitions concur in representing mindfulness as attention or awareness, intentionally directed or applied, open and receptive, broadening and all-encompassing, and anchored to the present (Black, 2011).

The explicit anti-oppressive lens is new to mindfulness. Although historical accounts of the first Buddhists describe liberation from gender and caste discrimination as the rationale and fruits of practice, such oppression was subsumed as "suffering." Mindfulness was rationalized broadly as a way to "awaken" practitioners from the conditioned existential habits and delusions of mind, the ultimate roots of all suffering. In contrast to this elevated rationale, contemporary secular-scientific programmes like MBSR and mindfulness-based cognitive therapy (MBCT) tend to ascribe far more prosaic ends to mindfulness, focused on its health-promotional benefits (MacPherson and Rockman, 2022).

As a form of anti-oppressive praxis, mindfulness is both smaller (than Buddhist) and larger (than secular-scientific mindfulness) in its target scope, intention, and rationale. The inductive process of mindfulness makes it particularly effective as an anti-oppressive intervention. Knowledge is accrued through the close observation of experience, and only then deductively applied to infer and construct theories about reality. This "front loading of experience" makes it distinct from other forms of experiential learning, most of which involve the learning of theories that are then applied in practice, such as professional practicums. Given oppression originates in discriminatory stories or theories about the oppressed, this inductive process allows those struggling in the aftermath of oppression to side-step the potentially oppressive and colonizing impacts of further exposure to discriminatory theories or discourse. Mindfulness teaches how to observe and recognize experience prior to any attempts to describe, conceptualize, and generalize what was experienced in post-practice inquiry processes. Such inquiry is highly valuable, in turn, when practitioners are supported to engaged in naming and theorizing that derived strictly from such experience.

From a scientific perspective, mindfulness is theorized to enhance wellbeing principally by enhancing the capacity to self-regulate attention and emotion. Researchers posit two approaches to emotion regulation: One involves top-down cognitive control exerted by the prefrontal cortex (PFC) on the brain's emotion centre, the amygdala, while another involves bottom-up control through enhanced awareness of the peripheral nervous system leading to *embodied emotion regulation* (Guendelman et al., 2017). Top-down strategies involve cognitive reappraisal, whereas bottom-up strategies involve increased awareness of peripheral embodied experiences. Evidence supports mindfulness doing both.

The current view is that mindfulness enhances both bottom-up and top-down processing, making more inputs available to awareness with increased efficiency in exerting specific controls over emotions (e.g., the amygdala) (Chiesa et al., 2013; Nakamura et al., 2021). Kral et al. (2018) found that novice practitioners in a short mindfulness programmes were more effective than controls at regulating positive affect (linked to desire) but no differences were found in regulating negative affect emotions. Chiesa et al. found that expert practitioners were more effective at regulating negative emotions than controls using bottom-up controls. Ardi et al. (2021) similarly found that participants who did a short eight-week MBSR course showed significantly different emotion regulation strategies than controls. They used enhanced interoceptive signals (peripheral), cultivated through mindfulness (e.g., bottom-up), to redirect responses to intense negative stimuli to a reappraisal (e.g., top-down) response.

## The Four Foundations of Mindfulness

### *The Body*

As an intentional practice, mindfulness begins with attention and awareness of the body. Indeed, the body is used as an anchor for mindfulness to support its resurfacing from formal practice to the continuum of informal "remembrance," the traditional meaning of the Buddhist term for mindfulness: *sati*. To anchor mindfulness is to invite attention to rest in an ongoing way on the breath, the entire body, or particular places in the body like the hands and/or feet. The body holds this special status in part not only because it is always with us, readily accessible to awareness, but also because it provides an immediate immersion in the present moment. To be mindful of the body, as a whole or part, is to be in the present. It is where, we might say, the mind most closely approaches the biological reality of our existence. Just as our life, consciousness, and death transpire through the body, so does the coming back to life and the senses through mindfulness. In body awareness, the key sense is interoception, though all of the senses involve information from the world interacting with the body through sense receptors. In this respect, it is also about coming back to the world (from abstraction).

What people learn in this first formal gesture by attending to bodily experience is the difference between direct sensory awareness and abstract conceptual thought. In mindfulness practices, when we try to regulate attention on sensation, our efforts are commonly and frequently interrupted by thoughts, to the extent that novice practitioners can become discouraged. This is where the instruction is to remind practitioners that recognizingthat the mind is not on the object of attention (e.g., the body) is also mindfulness. In this sense, mindfulness is not holding the mind unwaveringly on an object of attention, which is concentration, but rather it is awareness of what is present in consciousness in any given moment. That notwithstanding, the turning from abstract conceptual thought towards direct, sense experience is critical in mindfulness training to ground consciousness in the felt reality of the present.

To anchor mindfulness in the body and to distinguish conceptual (thought) from sensed (direct) experience are crucial for oppression work. Oppression begins by encountering, accepting, and internalizing discriminatory concepts about ourselves, families, and communities or identity groups. Such harmful concepts are mediated socially through language and culture. They are not based on our direct experiences of our bodies or communities but on socially mediated ideas about them. Therefore, the process of reclaiming autonomy needs to begin with recognizing and separating our lived experiences from internalized ideas and stories about them.

In her essay, "Throwing like a Girl: A Phenomenology of Feminine Body Comportment, Motility, and Spatiality," Young (1990) considers how the internalization of oppression is expressed in the phenomenology of being in a women's body. She begins by critiquing Levi Strauss' assumption that biology explains observed differences between how boys and girls, as young as 5 years of age, throw a ball. Instead, she argued these differences are explained better by how our minds are situated in bodies that reflect our environments and social interactions. This ecological and social situatedness is expressed first and most concretely through the body – its comportment, manner of moving, and use of space. She points to the ways, for example, women tend to contract their bodies in space, crossing legs and making themselves smaller by hugging their torsos. This interpretation of the situated embodiment of the mind, building and improving on de Beauvoir's (2011/1949b) concept of gender as situated, without reducing it to mere physicality or anatomy, paves the way to understanding the potential of mindfulness in unpacking the negative effects of oppression on both the body and mind.

By returning attention to the lived rather than imagined body, the practitioner is able to loosen the bounds of oppression at its roots. In the process, mindfulness moves beyond the storying and narrative work of therapy or some critical feminist analysis. As important as this work may be, it cannot on its own free us from the preconscious conditioning that lies in the very comportment, motility, and spatiality of our body in the world. Mindfulness brings us to such awareness, without a sense of judgement of any experience being correct or incorrect, right or wrong. With awareness, it is more amenable to change. How or why an experience came into being is not that relevant in mindfulness. Ultimately, that is a story. What is important is to notice the "what" of the experience in its features and entirety, directly and without judgement.

### *Feeling Tones*

Feeling tones are an imperfect term for what is referred to here. In classical Pali texts dating back to early Buddhism, the object of the second foundation of mindfulness is *vedana*, which is translated more literally as *sensations*. As objects of mindfulness, feeling tones refer to the valence associated with sensory experience (and memory) as positive, negative, and neutral. These valences originate through conditioning and generate habitual ways of perceiving and responding to sensed experiences or memories as attraction, aversion, or neutrality. They are a feature of consciousness itself, not only human consciousness.

Positive feeling tones generate attraction, desire, and wanting; negative feeling tones generate avoidance, aversion, and not wanting; and neutral feeling tones generate in diffference, boredom, and ignoring. The purpose here is to notice the feeling tones as part of lived experience, which require a more refined form of attention as they often appear automatically below the threshold of awareness. They are not corrected or changed intentionally; rather, they are merely noticed with a kind of equal interest or curiosity. This equal application of mindfulness is described as equanimity – a kind of joyful, open, and receptive awareness. In this respect, mindfulness itself brings a more positive affective tone to all experience. This view aligns with some current theories of emotions in psychology, which recognized the same three basic universal "emotions" or affective tones (Barrett, 2017).

Awareness of feeling tones is helpful to recognize and recover from oppression. Oppression is a socially conditioned phenomenon in which negative implicit biases become associated with the self and identity (Devos & Banaji, 2003). These implicit biases are not apparent consciously, so the first step is to recognize them. For example, positive feeling tones may be preconsciously associated with images of women in traditional roles like nursing and teaching and negative feeling tones associated with images of women in non-traditional roles like science (e.g., see Project Implicit, n.d.). The key here is that these implicit biases and their associated affective tones do not necessarily reflect our conscious or explicit views; the bias may exist preconsciously even when we are ourselves members of the discriminated group.

### *Mind or Consciousness*

The third foundation refers to mindfulness of the mind or consciousness itself. This includes mindfulness of thoughts, images, and emotions, as well as a form of meta-awareness or self-awareness in which one is simultaneously aware of an experience and that it is transpiring in consciousness. This is identified as *decentring* in research studies on mindfulness and clinical depression (Segal et al., 2019). Decentring is a key theme of MBCT, for example, when it teaches that "thoughts are not facts." It presupposes that there is a tendency to mistake what arises in the mind as both permanent and existing in a way that it does not. In a sense, we step out of immersion in habitual experience to witness the mind by identifying with a greater self or super-awareness, seeing the object, the mind itself, the (former) self, and the conditioned nature of all phenomena as bound to consciousness.

I prepared specific chapters in this book on the topics of emotions and consciousness because these are crucial existential aspects of oppression. In helping us to recognize and regulate negative or challenging moods and emotions, mindfulness helps to recover consciousness and emotion from some of the enduring legacies of oppression. As I discuss in Chapter 5, mindfulness impacts seven key aspects of consciousness: awareness/attention, affect, attunement, anticipation, agency, autonomy, and affiliation. The meta-awareness arising from mindfulness not only helps awareness to decentre from self-centred and habitual experience, it also decentres awareness from a naive, preconscious perspective and acceptance of social messaging.

### *Phenomena*

The reason mindfulness of "phenomena" is the fourth and final foundation is that it is only possible with some degree of insight into the previous three, that is, from mindfulness of body, feeling tones, and mind or consciousness. In a sense, this fourth foundation is about seeing the world more clearly, including oneself and one's own mind. It involves the systematic observation and awareness of the phenomena of the world - inner and outer. In a very real sense, it involves cultivating enhanced "objectivity," though not in the strictly scientific uses of that term. "Oppression" is no different than any other phenomenon in this regard, except that the critical object is oneself and the identity dynamics that give rise to oppression. Accordingly, investigating oppression mindfully as both a scientific and lived phenomenon is an example of this fourth foundation.

As much as this book intends to apply mindfulness to address oppression, it also sustains a critical perspective of troublesome social or cultural practices, systems, or texts associated with mindfulness that have perpetuated oppression or prevented it from being fully recognized as a key source of suffering. Accordingly, this book attempts to hold in mind the ambiguities and challenges of mindfulness as a historical and cultural practice. These past limitations do not negate, however, the promise of mindfulness as a resource to help free the consciousness of the oppressed from the legacy of oppression.

## References

Ahmed, S. (2010). *The promise of happiness*. Duke University Press.

Ahmed, S. (2021). *Complaint!* Duke University Press.

Ardi, Z., Golland, Y., Shafir, R., Sheppes, G., & Levit-Binnun, N. (2021). The effects of mindfulness-based stress reduction on the association between autonomic interoceptive signals and emotion regulation selection. *Psychosomatic Medicine*, *83*, 852–862.

Barrett, L. (2017). *How emotions are made: The secret life of the brain*. Mariner Books.

Bartky, S. (1990). *Femininity and domination: Studies in the phenomenology of oppression*. Routledge.

Berila, B. (2015). *Integrating mindfulness into anti-oppressive pedagogy: Social justice in higher education*. Routledge.

Black, D. (2011). A brief definition of mindfulness. *Mindful research guide*. Accessed from https://citeseerx.ist.psu.edu/document?repid=rep1&type=pdf&doi=0fc600e719983013f69b352fdd94d3acd7b17c69

Cady Stanton, E. (1848). Declaration of Rights and Sentiments. *Document signed by 100 of 300 delegates (68 women and 32 men) at Seneca Falls Convention.*

Chiesa, A., Serretti, A., & Jakobsen, J. (2013). Mindfulness: Top-down or bottom-up emotion regulation strategy? *Clinical Psychological Review*, *33*, 82–96. http://dx.doi.org/10.1016/j.cpr.2012.10.006

de Beauvoir, S. (1949a). *The ethics of ambiguity*. [Trans. B. Frechtman]. Citadel Press.

de Beauvoir, S. (2011/1949b). *The second sex* (C. Borde & S. Malavany-Chevallier, Trans.). Vintage. (Originally published in 1949).

Deci, E. & Ryan, R. (2013). *Intrinsic motivation and self-determination in human behavior*. 2nd ed. Springer.

Deigh, J. (1983). Shame and self-esteem: A critique. *Ethics*, *93*, 225–245.

Devos, T., & Banaji, M. (2003). Implicit self and identity. In M.R. Leary & J.P. Tangney (Eds.), *Handbook of self and identity*, (pp. 153–175). Guilford Press.

Faladi, S. (2013). Death of a revolutionary. *The New Yorker*. https://www.newyorker.com/magazine/2013/04/15/death-of-a-revolutionary

Fanon, F. (1961). *The wretched of the earth*. Francois Maspero.

Firestone, S. (1970). *The dialectic of sex: The case for feminist revolution*. Farrar, Straus, Giroux.
Firestone, S. (1998). *Airless spaces*. Semiotext(e).
Freire, P. (1970). *Pedagogy of the oppressed*. [Trans. M.B. Ramos]. Herder & Herder.
Guendelman, S., Medeiros, S., & Rampes, H. (2017). Mindfulness and emotion regulation: Insights from neurological, psychological, and clinical studies. *Frontiers in Psychology*, *8*, 23. https://doi.org/10.3389/fpsyg.2017.00220
Hooks, B. (1984/2015). *Feminist theory: From margin to center*. Routledge. (Originally published in 1984).
Kabat Zinn, J. (2013). *Full catastrophe living: Using the wisdom of your body and mind to face stress, pain, and illness*. Bantam Books.
Kral, T., Schuyler, B., Mumford, J., Rosenkranz, M., Lutz, A, & Davidson, R. (2018). Impact of short-and long-term mindfulness meditation training on amygdala reactivity to emotional stimuli. *NeuroImage*, *181*, 301–318. https://doi.org/10.1016/j.neuroimage.2018.07.013
MacPherson, S., & Rockman, P. (2022). *Mindfulness-based teaching and learning: Preparing mindfulness specialists in education and clinical care*. Routledge.
Magee, R. (2019). *The inner work of racial justice: Healing ourselves and transforming our communities through mindfulness*. Tarcher Perigree.
Manne, K. (2018). *Down girl: The logic of misogyny*. Oxford University Press.
Munjee, R. & MacPherson, S. (2025). Mindfulness and compassion in response to racism. *Diaspora, Indigenous, and Minority Education*, *19*(2), 91–107. https://doi.org/10.1080/15595692.2023.2254873
Nakamura, H., Tawatsuji, Y., Fang, S., & Matsui, T. (2021). Explanation of emotion regulation mechanism of mindfulness using a brain function model. *Neural Networks*, *138*, 198–214. https://doi.org/10.1016/j.neunet.2021.01.029
Organization for Economic Cooperation and Development. (n.d.) Measuring well-being and progress. https://www.oecd.org/en/topics/sub-issues/measuring-well-being-and-progress.html
Project Implicit. (n.d.). Project implicit: Preliminary information. Accessed at https://implicit.harvard.edu/implicit/takeatest.html
Ryan, R., Donald, J., & Bradshaw, E. (2021). Mindfulness and motivation: A process view using self-determination theory. *Current Directions in Psychological Science*, *30*(4), https://doi.org/10.1177/09637214211009511
Segal, Z., Anderson, A., Gulamani, T, Dinh Williams, L., Desormeau, Pl, Ferguson, A., Walsh, K., & Farb, N. (2019). Practice of therapy acquired regulatory skills and depressive relapse/recurrence prophylaxis following cognitive therapy or mindfulness based therapy. *Journal of Consulting and Clinical Psychology*, *87*(2), 161–170. https://doi.org/10.1037/ccp0000351
Young, I.M. (1990). *Throwing like a girl and other essays in feminist philosophy and social theory*. Indiana University Press.

# 2 The Location of Oppression

For Simone de Beauvoir (1949/2011), "the body is not a thing, it is a *situation*: it is our grasp on the world and a sketch of our projects" (in Moi, 2005; p. 59). Woman's *embodied* situation is her agency, irreducible to either the anatomical body (her sex) or abstractions in mind (her gender), an agency that shapes her "grasp" of the world as knowledge and her "projects" as the interest she takes in that world. She is not a subject (mind) situated in a body, but rather her embodiment *is* the situation from which she experiences herself, the world, and all situations. This integrative body-mind view has features in common with the ecology of mind theory, an enactivist view of cognition to account for how the body and mind together enact our experience of the world in a way that is irreducible to either. As de Beauvoir famously reminded us: "One is not born, but rather becomes, woman." In the interaction between the organism (as body-mind) and the world (as environment), the identity of a woman is expressed, including her oppression:

> But her body is not enough to define her; it has a lived reality only as taken on by consciousness through actions and within a society; biology alone cannot provide an answer to the question that concerns us: why is woman the Other?
>
> (p. 48)

For de Beauvoir (1949/2011), women's oppression is rooted in her socialization as "Other" and her internalization of that status: "[In] order for the Other not to turn into the One, the Other has to submit to this foreign point of view. Where does this submission in women come from?" (p. 7). This submission to oppressive makes her an object (to herself and others), narrowing her purpose and projects to serve others and their desires. These others – men, children, parents, community members, or others – are cast to be more essential. In this, de Beauvoir locates ultimate responsibility for freedom on a woman herself: "If woman discovers herself to be inessential and never turns into the essential, it is because she does not bring about this transformation herself" (p. 8).

DOI: 10.4324/9781003449355-2

I also see oppression as a problem of agency, located in the embodied minds and experiences of the oppressed. And, also like de Beauvoir (1949/2011), I understand this embodied situation of woman to be an *effect* of unjust and abusive historical situations embedded within social systems, institutions, and discourses and more palpably within power inequities in interpersonal relations. Conceiving of oppression in this way, as a complex psycho-social process, is crucial to developing a coherent evidence-based recovery of wellbeing as a *liberatory* strategy, as I am proposing here with mindfulness.

## Theoretical Frames of Reference

Although theories may seem abstract and remote from the lived experience of oppression, they are vital to recognizing and drawing inferences about the causes and conditions of oppression. Theories make visible what is partially hidden and obscured, thereby helping to interpret and explain phenomena. This is particularly crucial for a topic like oppression that is susceptible to antagonistic and ideological counter-narratives. As Wendell (1990) reminds us, "The perspective of the observer/philosopher is the best perspective from which to see the full distribution of power and responsibility in an oppressive situation" (p. 43). I here outline nested theories framing *oppression* as a construct, including its ethical ends and how it functions as a field of research and practice. These theories are nested in line with the ecology of mind as they straddle body-mind, biological-social, and organism-environment distinctions.

## Theorizing "Oppression" as a Construct

I use a particular construct of "oppression" to examine mindfulness as an anti-oppressive praxis. This construct derives from two principal theoretical sources: constructivism and the internalization of oppression as a psycho-social phenomenon. I present both in some detail below.

### *Constructivist Perspectives of Identity and Oppression*

Constructivism considers all experience and knowledge as created by the body-mind interacting through sensed and social worlds. Unlike naive realism and the objectivity of positivism, ecological and post-structural constructivism consider oppression as arising from *social situations* of unequal and exploitative power that give rise to *psychological states* of oppression. A key figure in this reasoning was Foucault (1978/1990), who conceived of power as "pervasive of an entire social body" and exercised variously through sovereignty, disciplines, or biopower (e.g., self-regulatory systems) (p. 122). Said (1978) emphasized the two-directional nature of social power, whereby the agency of the oppressed opposed dominating powers so as to resist oppression. For Said, oppression was overcome in part by "unlearning the inherent dominative mode," (p. 81). Freire (1970/2000), who also advocated "unlearning" internalized oppression, viewed oppression as the result of a deficient "banking" system of education that deposited the world of the oppressors onto the consciousness of the oppressed. Feminist theorists shared constructivist views of identity and women's oppression, most aligning with de Beauvoir's (1949/2011) depiction of women: "One is not born, but rather becomes, woman." In his discussion of Franz Fanon, Bhabha (1994) depicted oppression as the result of the splitting of identity, arising from the split between the subject (psyche) and identification (in the social world): "The very place of identification, caught in the tension of demand and desire, is a space of splitting" (p. 44).

### *The Internalization of Oppression*

Internalization is a necessary and key feature of oppression. It is insufficient to suggest that the mere presence of unequal power and dominance in a social environment necessarily creates a state of oppression in those affected. There must be a mediating process, whereby the minds of the oppressed become subjected to the social discourses being used to dominate and exploit them. Even in the most egregious and violent forms of collective socio-political domination, such as colonization, oppression and its associated harms persist most palpably and harmfully in the minds of the colonized rather than in their institutions or societies. Franz Fanon (1925–1961), for example, a Caribbean-born psychiatrist trained in France, documented the humiliations and harms of France's colonial oppression on the Algerian people by observing traumatized survivors of torture and psychiatric patients at the Algerian hospital where he was employed (Fanon, 1961; Stanford Encyclopaedia of Philosophy, 2019). This led Fanon (1967) to view "madness" critically, as a symptom of unhealthy and oppressive social conditions:

> Madness is one of the means by which we can lose our freedom. ... If psychiatry is the medical technique that proposes to help human beings no longer be a stranger to their environment, I can only confirm that the Arabs – permanently alienated within their own country – live in a state of absolute depersonalization.
>
> (p. 53)

So, for Fanon, madness was an expression of oppressive and unjust social systems manifesting in the psyche of the person. In fact, he went so far as to suggest – radically for his time – that madness was rooted principally in social rather than organic biological or psychological causes. This is a perspective he had in common with Jacques Lacan, reporting on Lacan's views at length in his Ph.D. dissertation: "Personally, if we had to define Lacan's position, we would say that it is a fierce defense of the right of madness to inhabit the human being" (in Gibson & Beneduce, 2017, p. 42). If madness is a right, it is a right to reject altogether the oppressive environment thrust upon one, despite the loss of freedom that accompanies such madness. As estrangement or alienation from environments, such madness foreshadows an ecology of mind perspective that presupposes the inseparability of mind from the environment. Feminist scholars later expanded on the idea that madness was a symptom of oppression (e.g., Ussher, 2011), while feminist therapists concluded that distress and psychological dysfunction were often symptoms of resistance to oppression and powerlessness (Brown, 1994, 2008; Conlin, 2017).

Why does it matter to theorize oppression as an internalized phenomenon? As Freire (2000) argued, it is the internalization of oppression that explains its perpetuation across generations. This can lead, in turn, to *horizontal oppression*, whereby the oppressed turn on one another. Horizontal oppression helps to explain why so many women engage in misogyny (see next chapter) and why the incidence of domestic abuse in oppressed Indigenous communities can be high (Burnette, 2015). This suggests the need for interdisciplinary inquiry in the study of oppression to connect political and psychological contexts, factors, and conditions (Prilleltensky & Gonick, 1996). Also, because the internalization of oppression impairs agency, and because agency is critical for recovery from oppression, any theory of recovery needs to be grounded in the dynamics of internalization. Finally, the proposed use of mindfulness as an anti-oppressive praxis depends on locating oppression, even partially, in the minds of the oppressed.

McKinley et al. (2020) designed the Historical Oppression Scale to measure the internalization of oppression using "internalized" and "externalized" operational indicators. Internalized indicators involved adopting the dehumanizing beliefs and behaviours of oppressors, including desiring their wealth or status and/or inculcating their myths. Externalized indicators involved projecting oppressive internalized myths onto members of one's oppressed group or one's family, leading to horizontal oppression. The resulting ten operationalized indicators of internalized oppression were as follows:

> Took frustrations out on each other and hurt each other; kept each other down; jealous of others' successes; allowed outsiders to take advantage of us; used alcohol and drugs too much; been sad or depressed; not received adequate education or resources; had lower standards and expectations for each other; treated each other unfairly; and not speaking up when we experience injustice
>
> (p. 296)

I use the term "internalization" to accord with conventions in the field used to describe how oppressive systems come to impact personal agency, identity, and psychological and social wellbeing. Banks and Stephens (2018) preferred the term *appropriated* rather than *internalized* oppression to avoid "psychology's over-focus on individuals and/or their internal processes without taking the broader context into consideration" (p. 91). While I am sympathetic, I think that the psychological aspect is a strength. Also, the term "appropriation" suggests that there is intention and conscious choice involved in the development of oppression.

## Ethical Ends

It is worthwhile considering the ethical ends of an anti-oppressive mindfulness before recommending it as a pathway. Two key ends that dominate I revisit are liberation and wellbeing.

### *Liberation*

*Liberation* is the term used by philosophers, Marxists, and Buddhist psychology to describe the condition or state free of oppression. Theorized as the aftermath of radical personal or social *revolutions* or awakening, in the case of Buddhism, the ends of liberation have fallen short of their mark when sought amidst the messy ground of the living. Most political revolutions have invited only more tyranny, while many purportedly awakened people have proved sometimes egregiously flawed. The idea of the *liberation* of women and the associated sexual *revolution* of the 1970s did provoke change by eroding some excesses of patriarchy, sexism, and misogyny in work, reproductive rights, and education; however, few women felt *liberated* merely from such freedoms given the persistent expectation for them to carry uneven reproductive and childrearing responsibilities while still facing implicit biases, misogyny, micro-aggressions, and discriminating subcultures. Ecologically, liberation doesn't fit well as liberation from biological systems doesn't really make sense given biology constitutes a tangible limit to freedom.

### *Eudaimonic Wellbeing*

In lieu of liberation, the construct *wellbeing* may be better suited to represent the ultimate ends of an anti-oppressive praxis. In this context, the term wellbeing refers to more than merely subjective happiness but to *eudaimonic wellbeing*, from Aristotle, referencing a combined objective and subjective state of *flourishing*. To flourish is to *live well* (as in *wellbeing*), not merely to *be well* (as in *wellness*): *Eudaimonia*, literally "good spirit," implied classically that a life was well lived if it was virtuous, not merely healthy, cultivated by perfecting the (as many as 18) virtues.

The modern interpretation of eudaimonic wellbeing has lost some of these classical associations with *virtue* (Proctor & Tweed, 2016). The modern use of eudaimonic wellbeing is used to differentiate wellbeing from the constructs of *subjective wellbeing* or *hedonic wellbeing*, which are operationalized as positive affect, low negative affect, and life satisfaction. Martela and Sheldon (2019) found that eudaimonic wellbeing was operationalized, in contrast, "in at least 45 different ways with 63 different constructs" (p. 458), which led them to define it parsimoniously as autonomy, competence, and relatedness, the three natural motivators at the heart of self-determination theory (Ryan & Deci, 2000, 2020). Garland et al. (2015) used wellbeing to describe the ultimate ends of mindfulness in their mindfulness-to-meaning theory, which they operationalized as the capacities to savour experience and derive meaning. Finally, Ryff et al. (2021) identified six operationalized indicators of eudaimonic wellbeing: autonomy, environmental mastery, personal growth, positive relations with others, purpose in life, and self-acceptance.

## "Oppression" as a Field of Inquiry

The study of oppression shares common features – and distinctions – that make oppression both a pan-human and specific historical phenomenon. As de Beauvoir (1949/2011) and Firestone (1970) have argued, women are a key case in the study of oppression in that their oppression is *not* historical but extends out of unequal biological roles in reproduction. Another aspect of the study of oppression is how varied forms of oppression (or, conversely, privilege) intersect to intensify, mute, or nuance the experience of oppression based on intersectional identities or "intersectionality" (Collins & Bilge, 2020). Therefore, I like to use an ecology of mind theory to highlight the universal (biologically human), particular (woman), and constructivist bases of oppression. Also, the sign "woman" has been deployed as a rationale for familial and social inequalities based on biological "sex" distinctions and not merely abstract socialized "gender" distinctions, so it seemed critical to use a theory that accounts for the biological embeddedness of mind, given the integration of body-mind and organism-environment.

### *The Theory of the Ecology of Mind*

In evoking *an ecology of mind*, I am drawing on three closely aligned theories: Bateson's (1972) *ecology of mind*, Maturana and Varela's (1980) *autopoiesis* and *the biology of cognition*, and Varela et al.'s (1991/2016) *enactivism*. These theories recognize three co-inhering, non-reductive domains implicit in all human experience: biological systems (a non-conscious processes); the recursive phenomenal domain of consciousness (including unconscious, conscious, and self-awareness); and a third domain of social systems, abstracted from the biological and cognitive to function as symbolic social orders based on institutional, discursive, socio-cultural, and interpersonal environments. In this way, both biological and social become nested ecological niches for human beings. Just as consciousness is an emergent, recursive property of biological systems that allows us to gaze back, so too does the social order enable "us" as collectives to recursively gaze back on the social impacts on individual consciousness. All these theories are constructivist and view human cognition (experience) as the creative emergence of worlds created out of conditioned inclinations and habits of mind arising from our status as sentient life, human life, and individuals.

Below I discuss four key features of this ecological interpretation of mind: (i) the mind as an ecological niche; (ii) the seven attributes (7As) of consciousness; (iii) the oppressed mind as a problem of adaptation and wellbeing; and (iv) the significance of the autonomous self-regulation of the body-mind.

### *The Mind as Ecological Niche*

Ecological niches are situations of direct contact and exchange between organisms and their environments. In the case of human beings, our ecological niches are not merely physical but also social, emerging from our use of symbolic language and culture. This social environment-*cum*-niche is not merely interactional, involving direct relations with other human beings or cooperating/competing non-human organisms, which is true for many species. Instead, human social environments are also abstract and symbolic systems, which make them, in a very real sense, *imagined*. Yet these social environments can be as potent and palpable as physical habitats in their capacity to mobilize power to impact most human contacts and exchanges with the environment. As language and symbolic culture, these social environments include social discourses that can mobilize power in ways that impact individual choices, self-perception, and identity in ways that foster oppression, control, or autonomy.

Neither entirely inside nor outside of the organism, the ecological niche is where we navigate living as embodied, biological, phenomenal, and socialized beings. Critically, the ecology of mind framework suggests that the mind, as consciousness, is situated in the ecological niche, neither inside nor outside the organism or environment (see Figure 2.1). Of course, consciousness is never really "situated" as it is not a "thing" to be located in space. Less metaphoric and more accurate would be to refer to consciousness as a *situation*, and in particular an *embodied situation*. So, we might say then that the ecological niche is the embodied situation of consciousness, while, reciprocally, consciousness is the embodied situation of the ecological niche of organisms.

The nature of this niche is as a "third space" – neither entirely inside nor outside the organism – with underlying structural features that ordinarily transpire outside of conscious awareness as non-conscious or unconscious processes, as when external stimuli are translated into sensed experiences, for example. Yet, we live in the illusion, conditioned by consciousness itself, of a definitive break or difference between inside (our body-mind) and outside (the environment). This conveys the experience of some things being "inside," such as thoughts and sensations in the body, and others being "outside" in the phenomenal world. To experience or recognize awareness as a niche, as neither entirely inner nor outer, requires a decentred, non-dual meta-awareness cultivated through combining critical (e.g., analytical) and phenomenological (e.g., mindful) awareness. As "non-dual awareness," such a perspective is cultivated through mindfulness and direct insight into the stream of consciousness (Vyner, 2019).

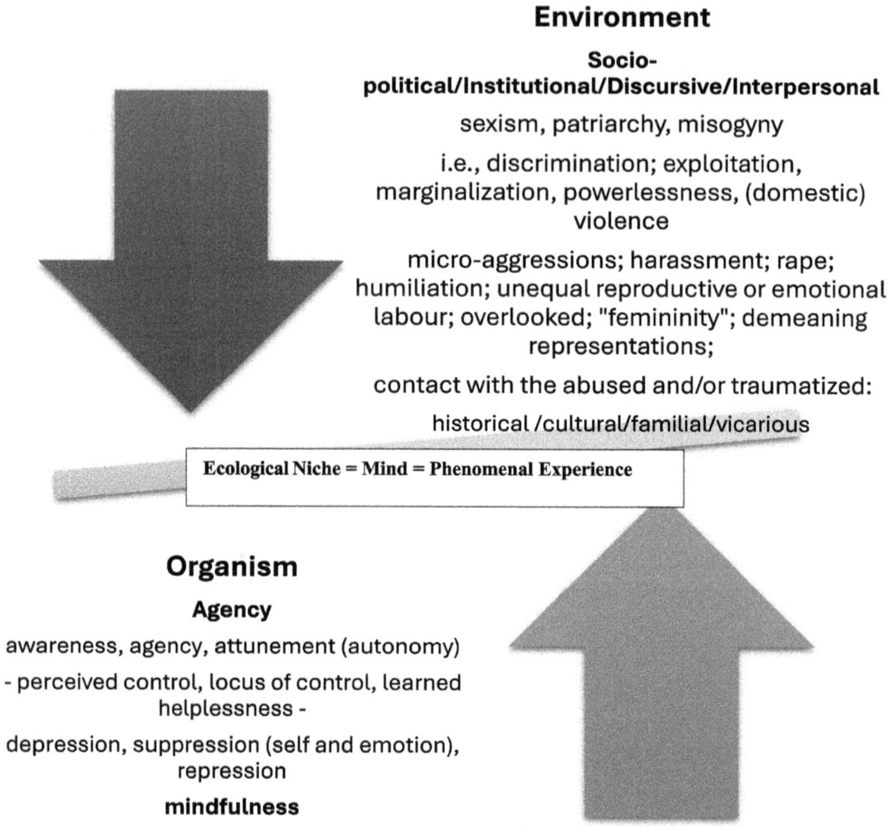


*Figure 2.1* An Ecological Model of (Gender-Based) Oppression.

*The Seven Attributes (7-As) of Consciousness*

The ecology of mind framework implies specific attributes of mind or consciousness that are affected by oppression. These seven attributes (discussed in detail in Chapter 5) are as follows: attention/awareness, affect, attunement, anticipation, agency, autonomy, and affiliation. These are not only psychological but *biological* conditions common to sentient human life. Once internalized, oppression negatively impacts all seven of these core functions of (human) consciousness: attention is diminished, diverted, or hacked; awareness suppressed, repressed, or resisted (i.e., avoided); affect used to instil biases against the self; attunement diminished or replaced with disassociation disconnecting the self from the environment; anticipation distorted with fear or false hope; agency muted or restrained through inhibition, self-silence, self-coldness, and depression; autonomy subverted by externally controlled or dysregulated states; and, finally, affiliation eclipsed by a sense of isolation. The net effect is a diminished consciousness with negative implications for adaptation and wellbeing.

### *Oppression as a Problem of Adaptation and Wellbeing*

This leads to the third implication, which is that, as an ecological condition, oppression affects adaptation and wellbeing. This suggests that oppression is an adaptation problem arising from hostile social environments that obstruct the capacity of an organism to recognize and self-regulate towards a state of flourishing or wellbeing. At the same time, these responses are reasonable coping and avoidance strategies to resist oppressive conditions as sustained environmental threats, which can be hostile or even violent. In some cases, the violence is implied rather than explicit, or inherited across generations as an implicit threat of violence conveyed in the family or community, as is the case of Indigenous people in the Americas or African-American descendants of slaves. From this perspective, the psychological responses to oppression can be a survival strategy within a hostile social environment, though not the most effective for fostering wellbeing.

### *Autonomous Self-Regulation*

Autonomous self-regulation describes how the embodied mind sustains wellbeing and the capacity to flourish across constantly changing and complex situations (i.e., environments). Self-regulation requires continuous monitoring (awareness), engagement (agency), and action (attunement) across internal states and external environments to realize goals and sustain projects and interests in the world. Autonomy, not to be confused with independence, can be thought of as a sustained state of *integrity* amid the ongoing *interactivity* with the world. Autonomous self-regulation is not to be confused with control. Self-control, as Ryan and Deci (2000) argue in the context of self-determination theory, is an external regulation strategy in which internal states are suppressed, repressed, or controlled to satisfy extrinsic motivators and environmental demands. In contrast, autonomous self-regulation involves the constant deployment of awareness, agency, and attunement or re-attunement across inner (states, desires, and goals) and outer (environments, demands) conditions. Its opposite is *external* regulation, often associated with oppression, wherein one is regulated by others and subjected to their demands and interests. Studies indicate that autonomous self-regulation is associated with higher self-reported levels of wellbeing than external regulation forms (Ryan & Deci, 2000, 2020).

## Aligning Epistemologies and Methodologies

How might an ecology of mind theory translate into a meaningful research method and praxis? Such a framework requires three domains be represented: the social and discursive (critical analytic), the biological (realism or the realistic), and the experiential (autoethnographic). Pre-existing scholarship in the study of oppression has identified eco-compatible epistemologies and methodologies by combining critical theory with an adapted form of empiricism, referred to as *critical realism*. By aligning *critical autoethnography* with such critical realism, I propose a combined epistemology and method rather awkwardly called *critical (realism) autoethnography*.

### *Critical Realism*

Critical realism is a method and epistemology based on distinguishing the *real* from the *observable* world. Realism is similar to empiricism in grounding and valuing knowledge derived from the observations of the world; however, it differs from empiricism insofar as it recognizes reality as a state beyond the capacity of a human observer to directly know. Critical realism embeds the assumption that we only ever know approximations of the real world filtered and constructed through the limitations of human sensory, cognitive, and conceptual frames of reference. This implicit critique of all knowledge presented as (objective) is missing in empiricism.

So, critical realism begins with the understanding that human beings have imperfect and limited access to the real world *out there*; instead, we can only study and represent the world as it appears to us as human observers. This observable world is nonetheless important to recognize, assert, and research as the place in which our living, suffering, and possibilities transpire. By differentiating the real from the observable world in this way, critical realism maintains the truth value of knowledge while shifting attention at the same time to its fallibility, limits, sources, and functions. Critical (realism), in turn, allows us to consider empirical findings but parenthetically, in a way that prevents their being misused as claims about an inaccessible reality or about "facts" in which underlying problematic social discourses remain obscured.

As a critical method, critical realism is also constructivist. The critical component considers the impacts of discourse on human experience, while the (realism) component places limits on what is interpreted as discursive, recognizing the (real) suffering and injustices in the world. Critical (realism) balks at constructivist extremes, however, that might minimize or dismiss the embodied facticity of the experience of suffering or its relief, as if it were merely an abstract or relative "truth." For these and other reasons, critical realism has been recognized and advocated as an appropriate method for the study of oppression (O'Mahoney et al., 2018); ecological thinking and action (Brunson et al., 2023); and mindfulness (Hamill et al., 2023).

### *Critical Autoethnography*

Feminist scholarship offers a long tradition of combining phenomenological and life writing with social critique, certainly beginning with de Beauvoir (1940/2011) but perhaps even earlier with, for example, Virginia Woolf's (1929/2021) essay, "A Room of One's Own," or even her fiction (Najafi, 2014). As in feminism, critical phenomenology and critical autoethnography recognize oppression as the effect of discriminatory social discourses, which critique has the power to dismantle, both in society and in the minds of the oppressed. Oksala (2021) explained of critical phenomenology:

> How are we going to investigate experience philosophically when our reflective experiences themselves are formed within normative practices of power? ... By de-naturalizing phenomena that are essentially social and political, critical phenomenology can open up new kinds of political spaces for resistance and situated freedom. ... The word "critical" embedded in the notion of critical phenomenology should not be understood to refer only to a critical investigation directed outward to surrounding society but must also refer to a form of self-critique: Critical phenomenology is phenomenology that is critical of its own methods, concepts, and limitations.
>
> (p. 140, 143, 146)

Chapman (2004) described a comparable method she referred to as "critical personal narrative (CPN)" to describe ways to represent experiences and stories to counter dominant political narratives:

> It is critical in that [CPN] works with issues of power and knowledge in practice. It is personal because it is about the author, often embarrassingly and deliberately so, even though the very intimate nature of personal writing and the visceral reactions it elicits can be both a strength and a weakness. But CPN is not just personal journaling, writing up the day's events; instead, by focusing on one event or a series of incidents or relationships and writing about them, it seeks to make this personal experience useful politically.
>
> (p. 98)

Critical autoethnography is related to both critical phenomenology and critical personal narratives in using life writing as a strategy to research and investigate social and cultural systems of oppression. Deriving from the ethnographic tradition of anthropology, it understands that the aspects of culture can be opaque and lost to an external observer, however diligent in skills of critical reflection. Therefore, the role of *key informants* as cultural insiders able to represent the insider perspective to the researcher, presumed to be an outsider, has long been acknowledged as central to the effectiveness of the qualitative fieldwork of ethnography. In *auto*ethnography, the researcher positions herself as an insider and key informant, with the added challenge of having sufficient analytical and reflective awareness to recognize interpretive biases.

The inclusion of the personal, however, doesn't preclude having the power to describe the features of the broader culture that may be obscured to insiders or outsiders alike. Like ethnography itself, Kempny (2022) points out that autoethnography attempts to generalize to the population despite focusing on personal intrapsychic experiences:

> [A]nalytical ethnographers concentrate on their experiences as insiders to a given culture, and they draw on their experiences to relate these to experiences of people under study. Seen from this angle, an analytical auto-ethnography provides very rich ethnographic material. While it does reflect the ethnographer's inner feelings/emotions, it also sketches the broader context in which the ethnographer finds him or herself.

Auto-ethnography is researching and writing about culture through the lens of the direct experiences of the narrator and researcher rather than moving away to second- and third-hand accounts. As a way to represent and assert women's experiences against dominant social narratives that might otherwise suppress or distort them, critical auto-ethnography offers a strategy to reduce interpretive frames that are subject to patriarchal or sexist biases. There is power in representing women's experiences directly against these frames, free of biased interpretation.

### *Critical (Realism) Autoethnography*

I opt to combine these two critical approaches – critical realism and critical autoethnography – to form what I call *critical (realism) autoethnography*. This is not done to collapse one into the other but rather to invite the design of research methods and texts that triangulate how oppression is represented across these three very different points of view: the critical analytic, the realist-realistic, and the autoethnographic. This aligns with Ussher's (2011) feminist "material-discursive-intrapsychic" approach. She argued that women's oppression (or her "madness") calls for a method that is at once material (i.e., realist), discursive (i.e., critical), and intrapsychic (i.e., phenomenological). She, too, referenced *critical realism* as a means to link constructivist critique to positivistic materialist orientations found in medicine and healthcare. She disagreed, however, with the tendencies of critical realism to omit phenomenological perspectives as overly individualistic. Instead, she proposed this adapted, tripartite, and wholistic way to correct and triangulate social, psychic, and somatic (bodily) accounts of women's oppression.

## Face(t)s of Internalized Oppression

Simone Weil (1909–1943) compared the lack of volition and consent in oppression to rape: "Rape is a terrible caricature of love from which consent is absent. After rape, oppression is the second horror of human existence. It is a terrible caricature of obedience" (quoted in Young, 1990, p. 39). No one consents to being oppressed, just as no one consents to being raped; indeed, they are both defined by the absence of consent. Oppression is a response to coercive power and force, whereby the memory or potential spectre of violence lingers. Oppression doesn't arise from an active intention or choice in how to respond to violence or its veiled threat; it develops unconsciously, often traumatically, through chronic exposure to direct or vicarious discriminative social contexts, discourses, and interactions.

Internalized oppression weakens consciousness itself. In the process, it limits the capacity of the oppressed to engage in autonomous self-regulation that might help them to resist or refuse complicity in systems that undermine their natural self-interest and embodied right to wellbeing. Wellbeing is, after all, a natural self-interest arising from the desire to flourish and fulfill potential, as all living organisms are motivated to do. According to self-determination theory, we pursue this self-interest most directly through the intrinsic motivation for autonomy, competence, and relatedness. The mindfulness-to-meaning theory also posits wellbeing as an end that is impacted by regulating attention via mindfulness. As the downstream effect of such mindful self-regulation, wellbeing is operationalized as the capacity to savour and derive meaning from experiences. When our capacities to self-regulate attention and to be intrinscially motivated are impaired through oppression and its negative impacts on the 7As, then we become susceptible to pathologies that share clinical features with depression, suppression, and repression, each explored in more depth, below.

*Depression* involves the loss of *perceived control*, a transdiagnostic category for symptoms across anxiety disorders, including depression (Rubenstein et al., 2016). The reduction in perceived control in major depression is associated with *anhedonia*, a muted affective tone with reduced motivation. Anhedonia includes a diminished capacity to experience pleasure, which Ly et al. (2019) connect neurologically to reduced reward sensitivity. Perceived control is implicated in autonomy and *learned helplessness*, the perception that one's actions and choices don't affect outcomes (Morgan, 2020). These are impacted, in turn, by *locus of control*, the predisposition to perceive outcomes as within or outside of one's control (Ryan & Deci, 2000). All of these psychological constructs constellate around the idea of personal control, efficacy, and agency over both self and environments, both in healthy ways to establish and conserve wellbeing or in restrictive ways as oppression. Carr et al. (2014) demonstrated the link between oppression and depression, finding that 42% of the variance in depressive symptoms experienced by low-income African-American women in their study was explained by experiences of sexual objectification, racism, and gendered racism, with internalization (attributing responsibility to the self) mediating effects for sexual objectification and racism.

*Suppression* is a regulatory coping strategy in which negative or unwanted emotions, thoughts, memories, or experiences are removed from attention so as to avoid them. As a feature of the internalization of oppression, suppression involves diverting attention and awareness from unwanted emotion, desire, or even authenticity and related aspects of identity (Munjee & MacPherson, 2023).

Srinivasan (2018) raised concerns about social pressures for the oppressed to suppress anger in particular, which she calls a form of "affective injustice" in which "victims of oppression must choose between getting angry and acting prudentially" (p. 127).

Archer and Mills (2019) expanded the critique of affective injustice in the context of four dominant approaches to emotion regulation (situation management, attentional deployment, cognitive reappraisal, and response modulation), each of which were found to embed harmful effects on the capacity of the oppressed to challenge their oppressor or the conditions of their oppression. The suppression of the experience (e.g., emotional blunting) and of the expression of emotions (e.g., as self-silencing, self-coldness) involved the fourth regulatory type: response modulation. The authors concluded that the evidence is clear that suppression does *not* do a good job at reducing negative emotions and has added negative effects on a range of wellbeing factors like mental and cardiovascular health.

This was reiterated in Aldao et al.'s (2010) review of 114 studies of six dispositional emotion regulation strategies and their relationship to various psychopathologies (anxiety, depression, eating, and substance-use disorders). They found that suppression, problem-solving, and avoidance had a medium-to-large effect size in their association with these psychopathologies, meaning that a significant number of people with these disorders relied on these regulatory strategies. Rumination, leaving the mind to ruminate on emotions, had an even larger effect. Even cognitive reappraisal and acceptance, associated with cognitive behavioural therapy, had a small effect in seeming to contribute to these disorders. Mindfulness wasn't included, but in a recent review that did focus on mindfulness, Raugh et al. (2025) found it to be effective in regulating emotions, especially when linking awareness with cognitive change.

Finally, *repression* is an internal cognitive response to unwanted experiences or emotions considered threatening. In repression, the threatening material is either forgotten or driven underground into the unconscious. This is in marked contrast to suppression, where they are left unexamined or unconsidered but still available to consciousness. Habibi et al., (2016) found "self-repression" in women mediated the relationship between depression symptoms and their marital maladjustment. Self-repression involved both expressive repression – for example, self-silencing – and emotional repression – for example, self-coldness.

The effects of depression, suppression, and repression are associated with the slow and incremental erosion and loss of autonomy over time. Autonomy is about discerning and making choices, and the curtailment of this capacity to exercise choices through agency may well be the most serious symptoms of oppression. As bell hooks (1984/2015) described it, "Being oppressed means the *absence of choices*. It is the primary point of contact between the oppressed and oppressor" (p. 5). Furthermore, it is not only that choices are externally restricted through abuses of power but also that the oppressed themselves learn *not* to see or exercise choices that are available. So, oppression involves both the loss of choices through their external withdrawal *and* the suppression of the internal capacity to recognize and make choices.

What distinguishes oppression from depression, suppression, and repression is the central role of identity and its indirect effects on wellbeing. Oppression harms both identity and the sense of self, which together can and often do lead to toxic effects on mental health. For example, oppression is associated with increased negative rumination and, hence, with psychopathologies (Aldao et al., 2010), self-coldness (Watson-Singleton et al., 2022), lack of autonomy (Stoljar, 2022), inauthenticity (Weatherby, 2025), and identifications with dominant oppressing groups (Munjee & MacPherson, 2023). Yet, when oppressed families or communities form cohesive ideologies about oppression, young people benefit when exposed to that ideology as they grow up. In their study of Black American youth, Banales et al. (2021) found that families with a race ideology socialized children to have more racial awareness and empathy, which directly led to their experiencing more positive social relations with others. This research demonstrates the value of social critique and social action in oppressed communities for both individual and collective recovery.

## Snapshot of an Emerging Awareness of Oppression

> But what singularity defines the situation of woman is that being, like all humans, an autonomous freedom, she discovers and chooses herself in a world where men force her to assume herself as Other: an attempt is made to freeze her as an object and doom her to immanence, since her transcendence will be forever transcended by another essential and sovereign consciousness. ... How, in the feminine condition, can a human being accomplish herself? What paths are open to her? Which ones lead to dead ends? What circumstances limit women's freedom and can she overcome them?
>
> (de Beauvoir, 2011, p. 17)

As a teen-ager, I didn't have the (conscious) sense that I was oppressed or at-risk of becoming so; instead, my life seemed at times painfully normal. I was a member of a gang of "girls" who moved through school and later university together. We met and began hanging out in junior high, but it was during the summer between grades 7 and 8 that we became a "girl gang," after being invited to form a cheerleader team for a community all-star (male) baseball team. The boys were the "all-stars" and we were there to adore – and adorn – them as they travelled throughout the province to compete. We became popular with active social lives and networks that spanned across several high schools. Our fathers were white collar professionals, and our siblings were much like us. I did well academically but opted to skip school frequently, to the consternation of teachers and even some friends.

Yet there were signs foreboding that all was not necessarily well. First, there was my mother's unhappiness and the vague awareness of discontent among my friends' mothers, too, none of whom had an enviable life. Another foreboding came from the fact that, though I self-identified as a feminist, it didn't quite fit with the subculture I found myself in. No one in my family or circle of friends talked about feminism, and I'm unsure now where my emerging feminist sensibilities even came from. My single aunts distanced themselves from the term, one correcting me sharply when I used "Ms." rather than "Miss" in a letter to her. Then, around the time of my 17th birthday in 1975, I had a dream that seemed to speak to why I might label myself as a feminist:

I was living in a girls' boarding school, a gothic compound with old stone buildings enclosed by a wall and beyond that a river. One afternoon, I passed some school administrators in the stairwell of the residence, where I overheard them describing a plan to give all the girls "pills, to put them under our control." Running to the classroom block, I found a close friend in the corridor: "We have to get out of here, Jackie!" I urged, telling her what I'd overheard. As she listened, I noticed her eyes glazing over, and I realized she had already taken the pill.

Alarmed, I turned back and left the classroom block to return to the residence. At the entryway, I was stopped by a man in a white lab coat who directed me to follow him to the basement of the residence. Once there, he led me into a room where the pills were being dispensed. A woman appeared and instructed me to take the pill. I took it, placing it in my mouth but secretly tucking it under my tongue. Feigning the glassy gaze, I opened my mouth so the man in the lab coat could check to confirm that I'd swallowed it. They let me go, believing I was now pacified and under their control. Climbing the stairs, I slipped out through the front door and spit the pill out.

As I looked up, the sun was setting, bathing the grounds in an orange glow that was fast dimming into dusk. I walked over to the stone wall and pulled myself up. Standing on the wall, I looked down at the river with its gentle, dark blue waves edged with white moonlight. Readying to dive, I turned back to gaze at the school I was leaving behind. The grounds were empty, and the old buildings seemed frozen in time and haunting, if not haunted. I realized I was abandoning my friends, and this thought brought great sadness. Yet I also felt I had a mission and meaning in my life that filled me with determination. I vowed I would get help and return one day to save them. I turned and dove into the water. A strong swimmer in life, the water felt invigorating as I swam confidently through its cold waves in the dream. I didn't know where I was going, but I felt confident that I would find help, eventually. And so I swam.

The following year after this dream, I changed high schools. It was the beginning of grade 12. My mother had separated from my father and decided that we needed to move to mark the beginning of this new chapter in our family's life. The school drew covered some wealthy subdivisions, which may explain why it was academically more challenging than my previous school. I felt isolated and marginalized, but the social isolation allowed me to dedicate more time than I might have to studies. I received high grades at Christmas as a result. After the holiday, I had a new boyfriend and began to skip more classes than I attended. I heard from another student that our male history teacher had told the class that I got the highest grade in the school for the grade-12 history exam. The school had about 2,000 students. Then, to my horror, she told me that he said: "Imagine, looks like *that* and brains, too." I was appalled that a teacher would comment on my appearance and imply that I was sexy. Then, soon afterwards, other male history teachers began to stop to talk to me in the hallways, teachers I didn't even know. It made me want to skip even more classes, which I did.

Soon, a French teacher and self-described feminist began treating me rudely. I later realized that the male teachers must have talked about me in the staffroom. The fact is she didn't even know me because I missed so much school. Later that winter, at the end of a class, she asked me what I hoped to do after graduating. I said I wanted to go to university. She replied: "Why? To get your MRS?" I didn't know what she was talking about at first and thought it might refer to some graduate degree. When I realized what she was insinuating, I was hurt and rather bemused. Rather ironically, I was one of the few if only student(s) at that school to self-identify as a feminist (unbeknownst to her).

At the end of the year, that same French teacher "accidentally" omitted ten marks from my final grade for the class, which I had correct the next autumn. Then, in her grade 13 French literature class, despite giving me an A+ (91%), she accused me of plagiarizing an essay I wrote on the play *Antigone* by Jean Anouilh. In the paper, I argued that both Antigone and Creon were right (the assigned topic) insofar as society needed both conformists and creatives to flourish -- conformists to offer stability and continuity through obedience and conformity to family and the state and creatives to edge humanity forward by risking their own personal safety and even lives to stand up for what is right.

Taken aback by her accusation, I said I would *never* plagiarize and, anyway, weren't my frequent errors in French evidence that I hadn't? She said it was about the ideas not the French. I said, "Well, I didn't plagiarize. I have straight As in your classes and others?" She then said, "Well, it's just that you sometimes seem like such a dumb blonde." Appalled, I said: "So you think I should appear more intellectual and distance myself even more from all of these people?" She didn't respond. Even after I graduated and began university, she occasionally turned up at the store where I worked to harass me, asking rhetorically on one occasion why I was studying Journalism and then answering before I could speak: "So daddy can get you a job?" with a sneer. My father, a former editor of the local newspaper, had recently almost died from alcohol-related cirrhosis of the liver. He no longer lived with us.

During this same period, I was constantly harassed by men as well—in the streets, at school, at work, and even at home, where I received ongoing prank phone calls. One came late on a Saturday night from someone who claimed to be a police officer. He said that there was a serious accident, and my phone number was in the wallet of the person who died. He said he was under a highway overpass, where he needed me to come to identify the body. I called the police immediately, and they said it wasn't true. Another time someone called to say that he was going to commit suicide, and when I tried to comfort him, he made it clear that he was masturbating. Even at my high school graduation, the commencement speaker, a local Journalism professor, told me he wanted to sleep with me even as my father was approaching us in the hallway.

During this final year of high school, I researched and wrote an extended paper on the topic of creativity and education. As a case study, I used my younger sister, who was quite creative and had started to meditate (using Transcendental Meditation or TM) the previous year. I concluded that meditation seemed to offer the best promise for cultivating creativity through education. In the paper, I summarized early controlled scientific studies on the topic, leaving me so convinced of my own argument that I resolved to learn to meditate myself. So, after my first year of university, I decided to pay the significant (for me) $80 fee to learn how to do it. After a short ceremony in front of a shrine, the initiator, a woman, left me alone in the room. Soon I stopped saying the mantra. The window next to where I sat was left open. A gentle breeze brushed the side of my cheek, and then a bird began to sing. The song was captivating and sounded nothing like a bird had ever sounded to me in the past. In a very real sense, I was hearing a bird for the first time.

I wondered how it could be that in all my schooling, I had never learned to hear a bird sing in this way. What was it about my life that had closed my senses, never mind my thoughts and mind? Savouring the sound of the bird was enough for me to carry on, to cultivate the capacity to know the world in this intimate, direct way, to attune my senses, and to be present to the world.

Through university, I became increasingly disillusioned and felt progressively less motivated and supported over time. This discontent coalesced as confusion over what to choose as an academic major. I first applied to, and was accepted, in English, but then I switched over to the School of Journalism before the year started. Early in my second year, I dropped out of the journalism programme and shopped around until eventually settling on economics in my third and final year. It wasn't out of interest but rather out of the conviction that if I couldn't discern what I wanted to do, then perhaps I should just try to get rich! I thought I'd do an MBA afterwards. Except that economics didn't work either. The catalyst came early in the first term when, in a micro-economics class on marginal utility, the professor introduced us to the *assumption of the rational consumer*. He explained that all micro-economic modelling was built on this assumption. With only a cursory consideration of my own conduct, I knew the assumption wasn't true, so the entire model seemed to come crashing down, graphs and formulae and all. I knew I wasn't a rational consumer, so that meant that at least some others weren't as well. My evidence was that I had purchased an expensive sweater a month earlier, which I subsequently never wore and never would wear, despite not having enough money to eat. It was, in short, irrational. This led me to conclude that there was a certain deception in micro-economics theory, a fact later corroborated by Daniel Kahneman's research on slow and fast thinking, which won him a Nobel Prize in Economics.

Despite being disillusioned, I resolved to finish the degree. Then, early in the winter of 1980, to help me stay engaged, I decided to audit an anthropology class recommended by a friend. The course was on the topic of consciousness and culture, and the professor was a cognitive anthropologist and Buddhist meditator. I soon realized that what I was learning in that seminar was what I wanted to know. Recommitting to my TM meditation practice in February, I decided to drop my university classes with only a few months remaining for the year.

When I approached the anthropologist for advice, he offered for me to move in with him and a friend – a social worker and wife of his grad student, who was away at Oxford at the time. I heartily agreed. The professor lived a rather stoic existence, which I loved. We woke at 6:00 am each morning to meditate and do yoga. We drank good coffee and ate delicious bread with organic peanut butter and jam. We listened to music – Van Morrison and Maria Muldaur. I was happy. So happy, in fact, that after a few weeks, when he asked me to be his lover, I eagerly agreed. We lived together for only a few months before he left on sabbatical. I then arranged with friends – other students from the university who were learning to meditate as well – to rent an old duplex together and to invite a (Canadian) Buddhist monk to live at the house to teach us, and he agreed.

One of these students, Alex, was a psychology graduate and research assistant in a sleep and dream lab at the university. He asked me to volunteer as a subject in a sleep and dream experiment, and I agreed. On the second of three required overnight stays in the sleep lab's anechoic chamber, he began kissing me and trying to make out. I relented, and we were soon involved. I suggested that he consider moving into the meditation house. The monk agreed, so long as Alex stopped having sex with me. I had considered breaking it off with him anyway, but somehow this abrupt ending created a lot of conflict between us. Then another housemate made overtures to start a relationship, too, just as the professor started to write to me from Africa to urge me to marry him. Around this time, I had the following dream:

> I am on campus, where I see my close friend, Diana, in a child's playground next to monkey bars and a sandbox. "What are you doing?" I ask. She looks up, clearly preoccupied: "I'm writing an essay on the modern plight of women, and I'm late." Looking upwards, she says in

> a panicked voice: "Oh dear, here comes my teacher now!" I gaze up and see Mary Poppins descending from the sky, her umbrella opened as a parachute with a carpet bag in her right hand. "Hurry! Get out of here." Diana insists, "Haven't you heard? The Prostitution Hour is coming." Diana resumes writing frantically as I walk towards the bus loop. Looking up towards the uppermost floor of an old building, I see dangling from each window the limp bodies of stuffed female mannikins, with faces painted like Pierrot. The light is muted, and dusk is descending. I'm afraid and start running towards the bus loop, but by the time I get there, the sun has set and it's dark.
>
> I join a lineup for a bus, but as I do so, a young woman near me begins to remove her coat. A spotlight moves across the crowd and lands on her, illuminating her as she stands in a sequined silver bathing suit with high heels and a multicoloured feather headdress. Another spotlight appears on another woman who is similarly attired. Meanwhile, the disembodied voice of an auctioneer invites bids for each of them as I wonder how I will escape.

In the meditation house that autumn, we meditated each day at 6:30 am and ate meals together, alternating cooking and cleaning duties. We did therapy with the monk, art therapy classes with another teacher, and had week-end classes with visiting teachers. One day, perhaps noticing my struggles with male attentions, the monk gave me a book to read, Shulamith Firestone's (1970) *The Dialectic of Sex*. I devoured its radical message. Firestone argued that Marx was mistaken: It wasn't class but rather sex that was the template for all other inequalities. Because the oppression of women derived in part from biology and unequal reproductive burdens, women's liberation was more pervasive and difficult than other types of liberation but also more revolutionary in the scope of its impacts on social change. The key institution of oppression for Firestone was the nuclear family, which socialized both women and children into conditions of subjugation:

> The heart of a woman's oppression is her childbearing and child-rearing role. And in turn children are defined in relation to this role and are psychologically formed by it; what they become as adults and the sorts of relationships they are able to form determine the society they will ultimately build.
>
> (p. 65)

## Conclusion: The Location of Women's *Liberation*

When women navigate oppressive social conditions with oppressive social scripts, they face a disturbing dilemma in having to choose between authenticity and belonging (Seers & Hogg, 2023). To reconcile this dilemma, we triage the "embodied situation" of oppression by prioritizing basic needs, weighing the expense of authenticity and agency against social acceptance and belonging. While choosing belonging may seem cowardly, it may be necessary for survival, variously defined. Notions of consent and consensual relationships break down in these embodied situations.

As Srinivasan (2021a) argues with respect to professor-student sexual relationships, the question is not really about consent. Students are there to learn and teachers to teach, but when sex derails the education, as it inevitably will, then it isn't so much about consent as about the professor's failure to teach, thereby depriving the student of the right to learn. Rather than constituting an issue of consent, Srinivasan argues, such relationships are an instance of sex discrimination. Alluding to a hypothetical case of a student in a consenting relationship with a professor who subsequently loses her ability to learn with him, she argued: "[W]as she not denied the benefits of education on the basis of sex?" (p. 143). Writing on the topic for *The New York Times*, Srinivasan (2021b) points to patriarchy as the root of the desire some women students feel for male professors. She cites Regina Barreca who, addressing female professors, asked: "At what point ... did the moment come for each of us when we wanted to be the teacher and not sleep with the teacher?"

> In the best case, the teacher-student relationship arouses in the student a strong desire, a sense of thrilled if inchoate infatuation. That desire is the lifeblood of the classroom, and it is the teacher's duty to nurture and direct it toward its proper object: learning. The teacher who allows his student's desire to settle on him as an object, or the teacher who actively *makes* himself the object of her desire, has failed in his role as a teacher.

Likewise, despite its legal role in distinguishing free agency from force, consent is an imperfect ethical tool to use as an indicator of agency in the oppressed. This is evidenced in some trauma-linked fawning responses in complex post-traumatic stress disorder (PTSD), whereby people subjected to severe threats from situations like childhood sexual abuse learn to protect themselves by pleasing and pacifying potential abusers (Walker, 2013). A better indicator of free choice would be autonomy, wherein at least three conditions need to be met: the presence of a viable and recognized alternative (a choice); awareness of one's own desires, self-interest, or preferences (self-awareness and intention); and no intimidation or undue suasion (uncoerced) in what is chosen. Otherwise, threats, even implicit threats to social acceptance and belonging, can trump authenticity, despite both being important for wellbeing.

Internalized oppression impairs autonomy, making choice difficult if not impossible, even when leaving intact the capacity to consent (or not). This condition of impaired autonomy can intensify and aggravate oppression, leading to associated symptoms of depression (perceived control), suppression (self-silencing or self-coldness), and repression (of desire and self-awareness), all of which can further mute or inhibit autonomy. In this way, internalized oppression becomes self-perpetuating. This process is reflected in de Beauvoir's (2011) accounts of how women become complicit in their own unfreedom (Knowles, 2019). She attributed this complicity to woman's *situation*, notably her economic dependencies in which "men and women almost form two castes" (p. 9) and her *embodied* location in a sexual and socialized body.

Most oppressed people are involuntary members of discriminated social groups; they are ascribed such membership based on aspects of an identity they share with other members of the discriminated group. Often they are born into the condition that ascribes them membership in the group. These identities may or may not be relevant to their sense of personal authenticity. The ensuing social scripts, imposed from outside on their group, can be internalized as self-destructive narratives by individual members (McConnell, 2016). Yet as Mackenzie (2023) points out, an oppressed group can use an oppositional "we-narrative" to help individual members to resist these incursions into their self-respect and self-regard (e.g., Banales et al., 2021). These "we-narratives" constitute a "we-agency" for collective action against discrimination. At the same time, she calls for critical narrative practices to recognize the ethical limits of belonging in such groups and the constraints they may pose to individual autonomy and group agency. She cautions how we-narratives are often emotionally laden and bring with them hostile and emotionally negative "they-narratives."

If we cast our minds back to the quote that opened the chapter ("If woman discovers herself to be inessential and never turns into the essential, it is because she does not bring about this transformation herself" [de Beauvoir, 1949/2011, p. 8]), we see the suggestion that liberation may be contingent on the agency of individual women. Yet, subsequently, de Beauvoir described women's liberation as a collective action: "This liberation can only be collective, and it demands above all that economic evolution of the feminine conditions be accomplished" (p. 664). In the language of existentialism, this necessarily involves transcendence and a definitive break or departure from the immanence that characterizes women's inherited position.

This seeming paradox of oppression, that it arises both from personal agency *and* collective action, is clarified within an ecology of mind framework. As depicted in Figure 2.1, so long as a woman is resigned to tolerate an oppressive *environment*, she navigates and accommodates it using her limited agency to resist or divert the most egregious of its harms. Yet, as de Beauvoir (2011) suggests: "[I]n woman this freedom … cannot authentically assume itself except in revolt" (p. 664). In other words, it is only through *dis*locating oneself from oppressing situations via *revolt* (refusing, removing oneself) to *reconstitute* (re-create, re-frame) the social environment that the ability to *recover* (autonomy, wellbeing, flourishing) becomes possible. In this sense, the location of liberation (as wellbeing) rests in what Mackenzie (2023) calls the combined autonomous agency and we-agency of the oppressed, who together engage in these 3Rs: revolt, reconstitution, and recovery. Therefore, as Beauvoir reminds us, woman/women "must refuse the limits of their situation and seek to open paths to the future; resignation is only surrender and an evasion; for woman there is no other way out than to work for her liberation" (p. 664).

## References


Aldao, A., Nolen-Hoeksema, S., & Schweizer, S. (2010). Emotion-regulation strategies across psychopathology: A meta-analytic review. *Clinical Psychology Review*, *30*(2), 217–237. https://doi.org/10.1016/j.cpr.2009.11.004

Archer, A., & Mills, G. (2019). Anger, affective injustice, and emotion regulation. *Philosophical Topics*, *47*(2), 75–94.

Banales, J., Lozada, F., Channey, J., & Jagers, R., (2021). Relating through oppression: Longitudinal relations between parental racial socialization, school racial climate, oppressed minority ideology, and empathy in Black male adolescents' prosocial development. *American Journal of Community Psychology*, *68*(1–2), 88–99. https://doi.org/10.1002/ajcp.12496

Banks, K., & Stephens, J. (2018). Reframing internalized racial oppression and charting a way forward. *Social Issues and Policy Review*, *12*(1), 91–111. https://doi.org/10.1111/sipr.12041

Bateson, G. (1972). *Steps to an ecology of mind*. University of Chicago Press.

Bhabha, H. (1994). *The location of culture*. Routledge.

Brown, L. (2008). Feminist therapy. In J. Lebow, *Twenty-first century psychotherapies: Contemporary approaches to theory and practice*, (pp. 277–306). John Wiley & Sons.

Brown, L. S. (1994). *Subversive dialogues: Theory in feminist therapy*. Basic Books.

Brunson, L., Lauzier-Jobin, F., Olson, B., & Cote, L. (2023). Seven keys insights from critical realism and their implications for ecological thinking and action in community psychology. *Journal of Community Psychology*, 1–21. https://doi.org/10.1002/jcop.23054

Burnette, C. (2015). Historical oppression and intimate partner violence experienced by Indigenous women in the United States: Understanding connections. *Social Service Review*, *89*(3), 531–563. https://doi.org/10.1086/683336

Carr, E., Szymanski, D., Taha, F., West, L, & Kaslow, N. (2014). Understanding the link between multiple oppressions and depression among African American women: The role of internalization. *Psychology of Women Quarterly*, *38*(2), 233–245. https://doi.org/10.1177/0361684313499900

Chapman, V. (2004). Using critical personal narratives: A post-structural perspective on practice. *New Directions for Adult and Continuing Education*, *102*, 95–103.

Collins, P., & Bilge, S. (2020). *Intersectionality*. 2nd edition. Polity.

Conlin, S. (2017). Feminist therapy: A brief integrative review of theory, empirical support, and call for new directions. *Women's Studies International Forum*, *62*.

de Beauvoir, S. (2011). *The second sex* (C. Borde & S. Malavany-Chevallier, Trans.). Vintage. (Originally published in 1949).

Fanon, F. (1961). *The wretched of the earth*. Francois Maspero.

Fanon, F. (1967). *Towards an African revolution* (H. Chevalier, Trans.). Monthly Review Press.

Firestone, S. (1970). *The dialectic of sex: The case for feminist revolution*. Farrar, Straus, and Giroux.

Foucault, M. (1990). The history of sexuality, *Vol. 1: An Introduction* (R. Hurley, Trans.) Vintage Books. (Originally published in 1978.)

Freire, P. (2000). *Pedagogy of the oppressed* (M. Ramos, Trans.). Bloomsbury. (Originally published in 1970).

Garland, E., Farb, N., Goldin, P., & Fredrickson, B. (2015). Mindfulness broadens awareness and builds eudaimonic meaning: A process model of mindful positive emotion regulation. *Psychological Inquiry*, *26*(4), 293–314. https://doi.org/10.1080/1047840X.2015.1064294

Gibson, N., & Beneduce, R. (2017). *Franz Fanon, psychiatry, and politics*. Rowman & Littlefield.

Habibi, M., Mokhtar, S., Ghanbart, N., Nooripour, R., & Motabi, E. (2016). Marital maladjustment and depression in women: Mediating role of self-repression. *Romanian Journal of Experimental Applied Psychology*, *7*(2). 18 pages.

Hamill, J., Nguyen, T., & Henderson, F. (2023). The impact of mindfulness interventions in higher education to enhance engagement. *Journal of Further and Higher Education*, *47*(5), 619–632. https://doi.org/10.1080/0309877X.2023.2175652

Hooks, B. (2015). *Feminist theory: From margin to center*. Routledge. (Originally published in 1984).

Kempny, M. (2022). Towards critical analytical auto-ethnography: Global pandemic and migrant women (im)mobilities in Northern Island. *Anthropological Journal of European Cultures*, *31*(1), 14 pages. https://doi.org/10.3167/ajec.2022.310105

Knowles, C. (2019). Beauvoir on women's complicity in their own unfreedom. *Hypatia*, *34*(2), 242–265. https://doi.org/10.1111/hypa.12469

Ly, V., Wang, K., Bhanji, J., & Delgado, M. (2019). A reward-based framework of perceived control. *Neuroscience*, *13*, https://doi.org/10.3389/fnins.2019.00065

Mackenzie, C. (2023). Autonomous agency, we-agency, and social oppression. *The Southern Journal of Philosophy*, *61*(2), 373–389. https://doi.org/10.1111/sjp.12521

Martela, F., & Sheldon, K. (2019). Clarifying the concept of well-being: Psychological need satisfaction as the common core connecting eudaimonic and subjective well-being. *Review of General Psychology*, *23*(4), 458–474. https://doi.org/10.1177/1089268019880886

Maturana, H., & Varela, F. (1980). *Autopoiesis and cognition: The realization of the living*. D. Reidel Publishing.

McConnell, D. (2016). Narrative self-constitution and vulnerability to co-authoring. *Theoretical Medicine and Bioethics*, *37*, 29–43. https://doi.org/10.1007/s11017-016-9356-x

McKinley, C., Boel-Studt, S., Renner, L., Figley, C., Billiot, S., & Theall, K. (2020). The Historical Oppression Scale: Preliminary conceptualization and measurement of oppression among Indigenous peoples of the United States. *Transcultural Psychiatry*, *57*(2), 288–303. https://doi.org/10.1177/1363461520909605

Moi, T. (2005). *Sex, gender, and the body: The student edition of What is a woman?* Oxford University Press.

Morgan, T. (2020). Learned helplessness. *Encyclopedia of Behavioral Medicine*. Springer.

Munjee, R. & MacPherson, S. (2023). Mindfulness and compassion in response to to racism. *Diaspora, Indigenous, and Minority Education*, *19*(2), 91–107. https://doi.org/10.1080/15595692.2023.2254873

Najafi, S. (2014). A phenomenological reading of Virginia Woolf's fictions: The process of self-formation. *Proceedings of SOCIOINT14 – International Conference on Social Sciences and Humanities*. Accessed at: https://www.ocerints.org/Socioint14_e-publication/papers/53.pdf

O'Mahoney, J., Vincent, S., & Harley, B. (2018). Realist studies of oppression, emancipation and resistance. *Organization*, *25*(5), 575–584. https://doi.org/10.1177/1350508418789686

Oksala, J. (2021). The method of critical phenomenology: Simone de Beauvoir as a phenomenologist. *European Journal of Philosophy*, *31*(1), 137–150. https://doi.org/10.1111/ejop.12782

Prilleltensky, I., & Gonick, L. (1996). Polities change, oppression remains: On the psychology and politics of oppression. *Political Psychology*, *17*, 127–148. https://doi.org/10.2307/3791946

Proctor, C. & Tweed, R. (2016). Measuring eudaimonic well-being. In J. Vitterso (Ed.), *Handbook of eudaimonic well-being*, (pp. 277–294), Springer.
Raugh, I., Berglund, A., & Strauss, G. (2025). Implementation of mindfulness-based emotion regulation strategies: A systematic review and meta-analysis. *Affective Science*, *6*, 171–200. https://doi.org/10.1007/s42761-024-00281-x
Rubenstein, L. M., Alloy, L. B., & Abramson, L. Y. (2016). Perceived control and depression. *Perceived Control*, *50*, 229–252.
Ryan, R., & Deci, E. (2000). Self-determination theory and the facilitation of intrinsic motivation, social development, and well-being. *American Psychologist*, *55*(1), 68–78. https://doi.org/10.1037/0003-066X.55.1.68
Ryan, R., & Deci, E. (2020). Intrinsic and extrinsic motivation from a self-determination theory perspective: Definitions, theory, practices, and future directions. *Contemporary Educational Psychology*, *61*. 101860. https://doi.org/10.1016/j.cedpsych.2020.101860
Ryff, C., Boylan, J., & Kirsch, J. (2021). Eudaimonic and hedonic well-being: An integrative perspective with linkages to sociodemographic factors and health. In M. Lee, L. Kubzansky, & T. VanderWeele (Eds.), *Measuring well-being: Interdisciplinary perspectives from the social sciences and the humanities*, (pp. 92–135).
Said, E. (1978). *Orientalism*. Vintage Books.
Seers, K. & Hogg, R. (2023). "Fake it 'till you make it": Authenticity and wellbeing in late diagnosed autistic women. *Feminism & Psychology*, *33*(1), 23–41. https://doi.org/10.1177/09593535221101455
Srinivasan, A. (2018). The aptness of anger. *Journal of Political Philosophy*, *26*(2), 123–144. https://doi.org/10.1111/jopp.12130
Srinivasan, A. (2021a). *The right to sex: Feminism in the twenty-first century*. Picador.
Srinivasan, A. (2021b). What's wrong with sex between professors and students? It's not what you think. *The New York Times*, Sept. 03, 2021. Accessed at: https://www.nytimes.com/2021/09/03/opinion/metoo-teachers-students-consent.html
Stanford Encyclopedia of Philosophy. (2019). Franz Fanon. *Stanford Encyclopedia of Philosophy*. Accessed at: https://plato.stanford.edu/entries/frantz-fanon/#WretEart
Stoljar, N. (2022). Ineffective intentions: How oppressive scripts undermine autonomy. In B. Colburn (Ed.), *The Routledge Handbook of Autonomy*, Chapter 23 13 pages], https://doi.org/10.4324/9780429290411
Ussher, J. (2011). *The madness of women: Myth and experience*. Routledge.
Varela, F., Rosch, E., & Thompson, E. (1991/2016). *The embodied mind: Human experience and cognitive science*. Revised edition. The MIT Press.
Vyner, H. (2019). *The healthy mind: Mindfulness, true self, and the stream of consciousness*. Routledge.
Walker, P. (2013). *Complex PTSD: From surviving to thriving*. Azure Coyote Books.
Watson-Singleton, N. N., Womack, V. Y., Holder-Dixon, A. R., & Black, A. R. (2022). Racism's (un)worthiness trap: The mediating roles of self-compassion and self-coldness in the link between racism and distress in African Americans. *Cultural Diversity & Ethnic Minority Psychology*, *28*(4), 557–566. https://doi.org/10.1037/cdp0000398
Weatherby, B.(2025). *Obigatory inauthenticity: A grounded theory study*. Ph.D. dissertation completed at the University of Arizona. Proquest.
Wendell, S. (1990). Oppression and victimization; choice and responsibility. *Hypatia*, *5*(3), 15–46.
Woolf, V. (2021). *A room of one's own*. Capstone Press. (Originally published in 1929).
Young, I.M. (1990). *Justice and the politics of difference*. Princeton University Press.

# 3 Women Encounter Misogyny

Misogyny is a peculiar and misleading word. Hostile and oppressive, it evokes the personified image of a grumpy, nasty, unpleasant, even violent murky-coloured monster-man inclined to lash out at women who talk back. Yet how in the world does this disembodied demon of misogyny come to occupy the minds and actions of real human agents on the ground? One thing is certain: It has been with us for a very long time.

The Dalai Lama once said to me that the female exceptionalism of Vajrayana Buddhism was introduced to correct the misogyny of the time, when men (and patriarchy) dominated both monasteries and society. Yet, despite this exceptionalism, which included vows to never find fault with women and a higher rank accorded some female (vs. male) deity yoga practices, women continued to be excluded from the monastic education system and from positions of power in monastic and social hierarchies until very recently. Throughout history, there have been multiple attempts to purge misogyny from Buddhist mindfulness and higher meditative yoga practices, most of which proved quite ineffective in the end without radically reforming the social contexts in which these practices were taught and applied. Even now, misogyny rears its ugly face in Vajrayana Buddhism, evident in the many incidents of teacher abuses, even rapes, of female students and nuns (Agsar, 2022; Langenberg, 2021; Varvaloucas, 2017). These events regrettably support Manne's (2018) theory that misogyny need not involve the hatred of women, that it can manifest systemically in the ordinary business of institutions and social situations. No doubt some of these Tibetan teachers and their followers believe they acted secretly out of compassion and in deference to female exceptionalism, that it was an honour for the women to be chosen by them.

## Misogyny Across Cultures and Time

The demon/apparition Mara (lit. *causing death; killing*) is an early personification of misogyny in Buddhist mythology and lore. He appears as a kind of mental projection or narrative foil voicing afflictions in accounts of people struggling for freedom through meditation. In the story of the Buddha's own awakening, for example, Mara tempts the soon-to-be awakened Buddha with apparitions

DOI: 10.4324/9781003449355-3

of desire followed by thoughts of self-doubt. He argued that he, not the Buddha, had the right to claim awakening, and he had his army serve as his witnesses. He then challenged the Buddha, asking who would bear witness to the Buddha's right to awaken. At the time, the Buddha was meditating alone without a community. In response, the Buddha touched his right hand to the earth and declared (as I was taught in oral teachings:) "May the earth bear witness to my right to be, unmoved by desire or fear." In response, the earth shook in a small tremor, there by attesting to his implicit and abiding right to liberation. At dawn, his awakening came to fruition.

Early Buddhist women are depicted similarly facing down Mara (as misogyny) to claim their equal right to live free of oppressive fears and desires (their own or others') (Analayo, 2021, 2022). The *Therigatha* is a collection of the earliest poems and auto/biographical accounts of Buddhist women, both lay and ordained, providing a rare glimpse into their experiences from the time of the Buddha, 2,500 years ago, or at least by circa 100 BCE when the oral accounts were first recorded (Schelling & Waldman, 2020). In the following account, Mara challenges Uppalavanna, who responds bravely, unmoved by his taunts:

> My daughter / and I / married the same man! O horror / It's unnatural / My hair stands on end. Sensual desire is / a thick / and thorny jungle.
>
> **Mara**
>
> Such beauty is / vulnerable in / this fragrant grove. / Foolish girl – aren't you afraid of being raped?
>
> **Uppalavanna**
>
> Were there / a thousand rapists / no hair of mine / would stiffen or tremble.
> What can you do to me? I've got the same magic you do, Mara. / I can disappear
> I can slip into your entrails / Look! / I'm standing between your eyebrows you can't even see me.
>
> (pp. 57–58)

Analayo (2021) recounts another story of Mara discouraging a nun from practising mindfulness by questioning her ability to achieve the wisdom required of a sage (or teacher). The *bhikkhuni* rebukes Mara, asking "how womanhood could possibly be relevant once the mind is concentrated and endowed with knowledge. Mara would do better to go and challenge those who still identify with being a woman or man" (p. 29). Analayo concludes that this story illustrates how women were viewed as equals in early Buddhism, despite losing status in how they were depicted in later representations in more ascetic Theravadin texts and traditions. In the earlier *Therigatha* accounts, women seek freedom from afflictive desires as do men, whether from coveting sex themselves or being coveted for their bodies by men; however, when women were described as becoming liberated through practice and became teachers, they were often marginalized and ignored – at least by men. In one account of Sukka, meaning "bright" (as in *bright mind*): "What has happened to these men of Rajagaha? / They sit like they are drunk; they do not sit near Sukka / as she teaches what the Buddha taught" (Hallisey, 2015, p. 18). Like Mara before them, it is the men who are drunk and misguided for not seeing Sukha as a teacher. Taken together, these accounts convey both the ever-present nature of misogyny and also how women practitioners persisted and used mindfulness to transcend misogyny. Rather than reinforcing the inferiority of women, as Analayo reminds us, these stories emphasize the power of women to awaken despite misogyny.

A millennium later, Yeshe Tsogyal (circa 757 or 777–817 CE) helped to establish Buddhism in Tibet and co-founded the Nyingma (Old) school of Vajrayana Buddhism. Her biography recounts how she was raped by her first suitor, after which she was given to the King. The King, in turn, "gave" her as a gift to Padmasambhava, the Indian Buddhist lama who took her as his consort. She is depicted as resisting and railing against her oppressive situation as an object possessed by men to be passed along in power exchanges. Through her relations with Padmasambhava and the various meditations and teachings he shared with her, she was able to become independent and free. Yet, even after becoming enlightened and leaving Padmasambhava, Yeshe was reportedly raped by a gang of seven highwaymen, which she described in a song attributed to her (Dowman, 1996):

> Immediately you set eyes upon my body-mandala,
> Your mind was possessed by a lustful disposition,
> And your confidence won you the Vase Initiation.
> Apprehend the very essence of lust,
> Identify it as your creative vision of the deity,
> And that is nothing but the Yidam deity himself.
> Meditate upon lustful mind as Divine Being.
> (p. 118)

Through this (probably apocryphal) account, Yeshe is demonstrating her awakened status as a Bodhisattva by reappraising an oppressive encounter with misogyny, in the form of a gang rape, as an opportunity to practise compassion and teaching her rapists. This passage is from a *terma*, a found text or "treasure" she is attributed with authoring and then burying in the mind stream only to be rediscovered and revealed by someone later in time – inevitably a male yogi. This suggests that the author and audience are predominantly male. The account is inconsistent as well with the vows of Varjrayana Buddhism, which were violated by her rapists. Therefore, the text can read as a rationalism to understate the severity and harms of misogyny vis-a-vis male lust and rape while enhancing her status as an awakened woman. Suffice to say these accounts show how women practitioners' struggles with misogyny date back millennia, as do the use of meditation to navigate, if not correct, them.

## Where Oppression and Misogyny Intersect

Analayo (2021), a Buddhist scholar and ordained monk, argued that Buddhism's most serious and abiding *conceit* is its belief in the superiority of males and monks over females and nuns. He attributed this conceit to Buddhism's androcentrism and misogyny – which align more with "patriarchy" and "sexism" according to Manne (2018). *Patriarchy* is the power men hold over decision-making and resources so as to actively exclude women from sharing in that power. Analayo documented a range of such patriarchal challenges in early Buddhism, which began with the Buddha first excluding and then placing increased controls over female monastic communities, ultimately placing them under the male celibate monastic community. Even today, monks still oversee the individual ordination of nuns and are given superior places when they meet in common. *Sexism*, the theories used to rationalize and justify this inequity, appear both in textual references – for example, accounts of the Buddha stating that including women would shorten the life of his teaching – and in cultural ideas about the purported threat women posed to male celibacy.

Misogyny, on the other hand, is the sanctioning of women who threaten patriarchy (Manne, 2018). Analayo (2021) used a contemporary account to illustrate misogyny in the context of Buddhist monasticism. A Buddhist nun organized and hosted her teacher and a group of monks for a retreat at the centre she managed. During meals, the Buddhist monastic rules of hierarchy required that, as a nun, she stand at the back of the line to receive food after the monks. The meals included a range of curry dishes and white rice, and the monks were in the habit of ensuring other monks down the line had at least some of the curries. Yet when it came time for her to eat, the last monks took all the remaining curry dishes and left her with only plain rice. Analayo reports her as saying that in the end, "I only had my tears to go along with the plain rice" (p. 7).

Manne (2018) argues that *misogyny* is not really about the hatred of women by individual men as the "naive" use of the term might suggest. Instead, it transpires in the activities and passive aggressions of ordinary life, in situation and institutions in which people have plausible deniability that negative emotions played a part in their conduct. Also, it is seldom about *all* women and more likely about *certain* women who challenge or threaten patriarchy or hold positions of power that might allow them to do so. In this respect, sanctioning is enacted not only through explicit acts of violence, injustice, or rape but also through humiliations and micro-aggressions that force women to endure tears in hunger, silence, and isolation through the implicit and veiled threats of exclusion.

Most of the issues Analayo (2021) describes of Buddhist androcentrism and misogyny are more accurately described as sexism in that they propose theories about women's inferiority rather than describing how women are sanctioned on the ground for violating patriarchal norms. These historical texts that he draws on recount the many faults of women, including that they "never have enough of sex and giving birth" and "are envious, greedy, and without wisdom." Others describe women as subject to five dangers, including the tendency to betray friends and to be "dirty, smelly, frightening, and dangerous" (p. 26). Like other scholars, Analayo, himself a monk, concludes that these disparaging representations and sexist conventions reflect a fear of women arising from the predicament of male monastic celibacy and the potential threat women posed to undermining that celibacy because of men's own inability to discipline or renounce desires and impulses.

In the ecology of mind model depicted in Figure 2.1 in Chapter 2, these patriarchy-sexism-misogyny dynamics are located on the side of the environment and impose a hostile context and oppressive situations for women; yet, they don't in and of themselves constitute oppression if not internalized. For example, I am one among many women who have navigated Buddhist contexts sufficiently to find both freedom and wellbeing through mindfulness and other meditations, supportive communities, and good teachers. I use Buddhism as a case to examine misogyny not because it is extreme but rather because it has been a traditional site of education and refuge for women seeking access to mindfulness as an anti-oppressive tool for 2,500 years.

## Misogyny

In *Down Girl: The Logic of Misogyny*, Manne (2018) systematically unpacks misogyny not so much as the hatred of women but rather as sanctions directed at women who challenge male dominance: "Misogynists can love their mothers – not to mention their sisters, daughters, wives, girlfriends, and secretaries. They need not hate women universally, or even very generally. They tend to hate women who are outspoken, among other things" (p. 52). Misogyny uses tactics like scapegoating, punishing, policing, controlling, excluding, and exiling "bad" women who challenge male dominance. By singling out, isolating, and making examples of women who step outside gender conforming norms, misogyny sanctions in ways that deter other women from challenging patriarchy. At the same time, misogyny rewards "good" women who self-subjugate in support of male dominance (i.e., patriarchy) and in the service of others (e.g., children, elderly, community).

According to Manne (2018), misogyny complements patriarchy and sexism but with distinctive features. *Patriarchy* refers to the inherited power and privilege accorded men in specific contexts and situations, which is wielded so as to exclude or deter women from accessing them. *Sexism*, on the other hand, refers to the ideas, ideologies, or doctrines used to rationalize patriarchy based on weak or unfounded claims about sex differences and/or women's inferiority or superiority. *Misogyny,* in contrast, refers to the many ways women are controlled, punished, or threatened for challenging male dominance and patriarchy. These three – patriarchy, sexism, and misogyny – interact to create oppressive environments and hostile social "climates" for women. Most destructive among the three, according to Manne, is misogyny.

As Manne (2018) emphasizes, women may be agents of misogyny, and men may not be. Agents of misogyny are determined less by their sex and more by their attitude and unwillingness to question the unequal power yielded by men. Women who acquiesce and conform to sexist norms, women who are *nice*, servile, self-abnegating, self-silencing, and/or demure, are praised and viewed as praiseworthy by misogynists; they are also very likely to contribute to the misogynistic treatment of other women who aren't as accommodating of patriarchy.

Misogyny can wear women down incrementally by exposing them to incessant micro-aggressions, harassments, insults, and humiliations, which accumulate over time and across incidents to produce a toxic "climate." Perpetrators, if challenged, may gaslight victims, in turn, by explaining away or dismissing these micro-aggressions, making the victim feel overly sensitive or deluded. As Manne (2018) suggests: "[O]ne of the subsequent possibilities that I am trying to highlight here is that of a social system or environment that has a particular atmosphere or 'climate' for certain people, which needs to be described in broadly attitudinal terms" (p. 74). These attitudes include contempt, disdain, irritation, hostility, and aversion, even disgust, to be sure, but also indifference or even pleasure in bystanders who stand by and do nothing. Or perhaps there is fear in bystanders that they might be subjected to the same treatment if they do stand up, making them an easy a target. Manne's (2018) extensive list of examples of misogynistic acts or conduct is worth reviewing:

> Misogynist hostility encompasses myriad "down girl" moves...: adults are insultingly likened to children, people to animals or even to objects. As well as infantilizing and belittling, there's ridiculing, humiliating, mocking, slurring, vilifying, demonizing, shaming, blaming, patronizing, condescending, and other forms of treatment that are dismissive and disparaging in specific social contexts. Then there is violence and threatening behaviour – including "punching down" – that is, deferred or displaced aggression.
>
> (p. 68)

## Misogyny: A Spectrum of Harm

In empirical research on misogyny, most items on Manne's list would be classified as "sexist microaggressions." Cherry and Wilcox (2021) claim that such microaggressions "encapsulate contemporary manifestations of sexism" (p. 107). Yet it is a mistake to view misogyny as principally about microaggressions without recognizing their connection to overt aggression and violence against women, including intimate partner violence (IPV), includingas non-state torture, and femicide (Manne, 2018; Sarson & MacDonald, 2022). The threats that misogyny poses to the wellbeing of women, children, and society need to be considered on a spectrum from serious violence with mass casualties through to micro-aggressions and hostile climates. Even in less overt manifestations, misogyny embeds these more serious threats of extreme violence, contributing to the implicit threat and corresponding fear it can induce in victims and bystanders. So, we will begin there.

## Violence Against Women

Most violence against women is perpetrated by men and derives from misogyny (Manne, 2018; Fitz-Gibbon et al., 2023). Of course, internalized misogyny need not lead to its more violence extremes. When it does manifest as violence, misogyny is more associated with men who subscribe to a toxic or "traditional" form of masculinity (Braganza & Cardone, 2022; Mass Casualty Commission, 2022b). Added to this is a sense of male entitlement, including the entitlement to sex (Manne, 2020; Srinivasan, 2021), and a tendency for coercive and controlling behaviours in intimate relationships used "to hurt, humiliate, intimidate, exploit, isolate, and dominate their victims" (Stark, 2007, p. 5).

Although men can be victims of IPV, more women are victims with more serious harms and fatalities. In Canada, for example, over 80% of IPVs are reported by women, with 50–69 women a year dying from IPVs in Canada between 2017 and 2020. These are a lot of deaths considering that Canada had one of the lowest global rates (i.e., 3%) of reported IPV incidents in the previous 12 months in a 2018 World Health Organization report (WHO, 2018). The average rates for countries globally was 13% in the previous 12 months, while 27% of "ever-married/partnered women" between 15 and 49 years of age reported a lifetime experience of IPV. In developed countries, the rates of IPV reported were significantly lower for the previous 12 months (3–9%) and somewhat lower for lifetime incidents (16–25%); however, they were significantly *higher* for lifetime *non-partner* sexual violence rates compared to less developed countries, especially in Australia/New Zealand (19%) and North America (15%) when compared to a 6% global rate. This difference, however, could be related to differences in the willingness of unmarried women to report such violence (e.g., rape, etc.).

Misogyny distorts how IPV-related deaths are classified and reported. Represented as "domestic" violence, they suggest that these deaths less serous than other forms of homicide, as if they are partially justified or restricted to effects on the small social unit of a "domestic situation." Yet research tells quite a different story. IPVs are significantly associated with more extreme forms of violence, including serial or mass murders (i.e., mass casualty events). Below I present a recent Canadian mass casualty event as a case to demonstrate how misogyny fuels IPV, and how IPV, in turn, expands into other forms of violence.

On April 20, 2020, in the small Nova Scotia town of Portapique, a man went from house-to-house on a 12-hour rampage killing 22 people and setting 16 fires before he was himself killed at a gas station by Royal Canadian Mounted Police (RCMP) officers (Mass Casualty Commission, 2022a). Among the 22 victims were 13 women, including an RCMP officer and an unborn child. The first *non-fatal* victim of this rampage was his common-law partner, Lisa Banfield, who escaped into the woods after being subjected to hours of "non-state torture" at his hands. "Non-state torture" is the term Sarson and MacDonald (2022) use in lieu of "abuse" to better convey the severity of this and other instances of IPV.

A joint federal-provincial inquiry into the mass casualty event found that the perpetrator was himself a victim of multigenerational family violence – perpetrated by men and directed against both himself, as a child, and his mother (Mass Casualty Commission, 2022b). He had had multiple complaints lodged against him over years at his denturist practice by women staff and vulnerable women patients, many Black (Davenport & Ryan, 2022). As early as 2003, he was seen beating Lisa Banfield in a public location in the middle of the night, after which she left him only to return soon after for another 17 years. In 2013, he was reported to the RCMP by a neighbour and former military couple for terrorizing and assaulting his wife (Forbes, 2022; Mass Casualty Commission, 2022b) and for storing an arsenal of weapons at his home, some illegally. The perpetrator began to stalk and harass these neighbours, in particular the wife, when she tried to encourage Lisa Banfield to leave him. The couple was so concerned with his behaviour that they decided to move away, suffering a $100,000 loss on the sale of their home. Despite these complaints to the RCMP and to his profession, little to nothing was done.

The Mass Casualty Commission (2022a) prepared a summary of the inquiry in a seven-volume report. The main conclusions of Volume 2 concerned the incident itself, stating that officials and others who were in a position to act ignored the many red flags raised over the years, including the IPV reports, in part because of misogyny. These red flags were itemized (Mass Casualty Commission, 2022b, p. 4):

- Over many years, the perpetrator's pattern of violent and intimidating behaviours and illegal acquisition of firearms gave rise to numerous red flags and missed opportunities for prevention and intervention.
- In the six weeks before the mass casualty, the perpetrator further isolated his common-law spouse from her family as his behaviour became erratic and increasingly concerning to her.
- The mass casualty began with the perpetrator's violent assault of his common-law spouse, Lisa Banfield.
- The RCMP did not treat Lisa Banfield as a surviving victim of the mass casualty; that is, as an important witness who required careful debriefing and who would need support services.

The Mass Casualty Commission (2022b) concluded that it is false to draw lines of distinction between private or personal violence and public violence. In fact, many instances of private violence *are* witnessed by others, including strangers or the public – at least twice in this case: "Canadian society and our justice system have a history of responding to private violence in ways distinct from forms of violence that are considered more public, including violence between strangers" (p. 11). Furthermore, the report draws connections between private and public violence like mass casualty events: "For far too long, we have misperceived mass violence as our greatest threat without considering its relationship to other more pervasive forms of violence. We do so at the expense of public safety and community well-being" (p. 5). Relying on the expert testimonies of McCulloch and Maher (2022), the report identified four ways in which mass casualty events stemmed from gender-based violence (p. 247):

1 Perpetrators frequently target a specific woman at the outset of a mass casualty incident. Often, this is the perpetrator's current or former intimate partner, a woman with whom the perpetrator wanted to have an intimate relationship, or their family member.
2 Many perpetrators have a history of gender-based violence, including IPV, coercive control, sexual assault, stalking, and harassment.
3 Some mass casualties have been overtly motivated by hatred of women in general or by a belief that women don't deserve respect, security, or equality.
4 Some mass casualties are motivated by misogyny intersecting with other forms of extremism.

The report concluded "that the division between public and private violence is illusory and problematic" and that "violence is a gendered phenomenon, in that it is mainly perpetrated by men, and it has a disproportionate impact on women" (p. 12). Worth pointing out is that "women" here included girls, 2SLGBTQI+ people, and intersectional groups of women such as racialized or Indigenous women.

Also significantly, the report concluded that violence against women involves coercive forms of control that escalate into overt violence (surveillance, financial control, control through fear, and threats to victims and others).

The report identified 40 mass casualties that occurred in Canada between 1975 and 2021 (Mass Casualty Commission, 2022b, pp. 175–177). Approximately a third (29%) of these mass casualty events were directly attributed to misogyny, either as a case of IPV (9) or as anti-feminist backlash (5). Interestingly, in the first two decades (1975–1996) covered by the report, the proportion of IPV-to-anti-feminist motivated mass casualty events was 4:1 (the "1" being the Ecole Polytechnique 1989 Montreal massacre in which 14 female engineering students were killed). This proportion, however, flipped in the final decade (2014–2021) covered in the report, in which the ratio of IPV: anti-feminist motivated mass casualty events flipped to 1:4. In fact, it is more like 1:5 if we include a recent 2023 anti-feminist (anti-trans) attack at the University of Waterloo. This shift from IPV- to anti-feminist motivated misogyny as the catalyst for mass casualty events constitute the emergence of a form of terrorism, motivated by the intention to instil terror in women and gender non-conforming people.

Indeed, the rates of misogyny-related mass casualty events are themselves under-represented in this report table (Mass Casualty Commission, 2022b, pp. 175–177). I happen to have had personal knowledge of one of the first mass casualty incidents on the list, which happened in Ottawa in 1975. In the table, it is mislabelled as a "school grievance" when it was, in fact, catalysed by misogyny and violence against women. The incident culminated at a Catholic High School, St. Pius X, where the 18-year-old student-perpetrator killed himself and another (student) and injured five other students; however, the school shootings and suicide happened after he had raped and killed Kim Rabot, a 17-year-old neighbour, earlier that morning. Previously, the perpetrator had asked Rabot out on a date, and she had declined. It later came out from his journal entries that he was seriously addicted to pornography and sex toys and that he wanted to have sex before committing suicide. He never wrote of any intention to go to the school to harm his classmates. Experts believed the school shootings were merely an afterthought or postlude to the earlier rape and murder, which were fuelled by a fixation on the objectification of women and, by implication, misogyny, and toxic masculinity. The title of a book about the event written at the time by local journalists, Cobb and Avery (1977) hints at the role of misogyny on the perpetrator and his victims: *Rape of a Normal Mind.*

I was 17 years old at the time, the same age as Kim Rabot. We had lived only a few blocks from that high school until that summer, when we moved. My friends and I attended the nearby public (non-Catholic) high school, but we had close relations with the boys in that grade 13 classroom. My own boyfriend's best friend was shot that day, narrowly escaping death when a pellet punctured the outer casing of his heart.

I went to visit this victim in the hospital and, thereafter, began to have panic attacks every night for months. These panic attacks happened as I lay down and closed my eyes to go to sleep. The panic rose in my chest followed by images of my brother entering my room to kill me. This brother had beaten and bullied me through childhood, but he didn't pose the kinds of risks I imagined. I was quite aware that my thoughts were irrational and some sort of trauma response, but I couldn't control them. My fears transferred to my older brother because his was the closest face of misogyny that I could imagine at the time. After a few months of this torture, one night I decided to meditate on an image of the Sacred Heart of Jesus next to my bed. I imagined his image radiating light on the crown of my head After some time, the image dissolved and passed through the crown of my head and into my heart. The terror eased and disappeared immediately. I would later learn to do this same meditation, using other forms than Jesus, as part of Tibetan Vajrayana deity yoga practices.

In the Mass Casualty Commission (2022b) inquiry, Dr. McCulloch testified that misogyny hides under the radar in our midst, leading to it often being overlooked as a motive for violent crime:

> I think misogyny is so prevalent that it hides almost in open space. It's hidden, but once our eyes are opened to it it's very clear. And it's clear in the way incidents are reported, in the way incidents are researched, that people are investigated, even by police and security services, that they're looking for motivations, like sometimes racism or Islamic terrorism, but they're not looking in the same way for misogyny, so that gets really played down because of the cultural scripts, the cultural lens that tends to take the subjugation and violence against women for granted in some ways, so much so that it's not the same at all.
>
> (p. 254)

## Microaggressions

As misogyny-related mass casualty events, these macroaggressions involving harassment, sexual assault, and overt violence are noteworthy. Yet even more prevalent are misogynist microaggressions that take the form of passive aggressive acts of abuse, harassment, and undermining. As women moved more fulsomely into non-traditional professions, workplaces, and positions of power, misogyny has increasingly taken the form of micro-aggressions channelled to thwart, harass, and isolate women at work or in politics or organizations. As organizations increasingly instate formal equity policies against discrimination, those unwilling to give up power invested in them through patriarchy – male or female – suppress direct expression of their resentments, yet still express, indirectly, negative emotions like jealousy and the desire to subjugate. These indirect expressions involve everyday discriminations and microaggressions with plausible deniability to avoid the risk of legal or disciplinary actions.

Pierce (1970), an African-American Harvard-trained psychiatrist, coined the term "microaggressions" to describe the spectrum of racist aggression in the 1960s, contrasting macro-aggressions like lynching to everyday discriminations that were slowly eroding the mental health and wellbeing of those impacted:

> [T]hese assaults to black dignity and black hope are incessant and cumulative. Any single one may not be gross. In fact, the major vehicle for racism in this country is offenses done to blacks by whites in this sort of gratuitous, never-ending way. These offenses are micro-aggressions. Almost all black-white racial interactions are characterized by white put-downs, done in an automatic, preconscious, or unconscious fashion. These mini-disasters accumulate.
>
> (p. 513)

Pierce (1970) described microaggressions as "offensive mechanisms," similar to Freud's "defensive mechanisms," to imply that they were often unconscious. He attributed these microaggressions to an attitude of superiority and dominance in Whites, which pervaded their interactions with Blacks. These same racist attitudes were internalized and reproduced in some African-Americans as well. He used the construct of "microaggressions" to explain how these attitudes were perpetuated and impacted blacks

> The chief vehicle for proracist behaviors are microaggressions. These are subtle, stunning, often automatic, and non-verbal exchanges which are 'put downs· of blacks by offenders. The offensive mechanisms used against blacks often are innocuous. The cumulative weight of their never-ending burden is the major ingredient in black-white interactions.
> (Pierce et al., 1978, p. 66)

Parallels in women's experiences with misogyny led to "micro-aggressions" being used to describe forms of discrimination experienced by women. Sue et al. (2007) recognized microaggressions as pervasive across race, gender, and sexual orientation discrimination and defined them as "brief and commonplace daily verbal, behavioral, or environmental indignities, whether intentional or unintentional, that communicate hostile, derogatory, or negative racial slights and insults" (p. 271). The degree of intention has been a persistent issue since Pierce (1970, 1974). For Sue et al. (2007), microaggressions can be either intentional or unintentional, which makes sense as they are associated with both workplace bullying (intentional) and implicit bias (unintentional) (Ahmed, 2021; Ghosh & Wang, 2023). Torres et al. (2019) sidestep the issue of intentionality by defining them as "indirect expressions of prejudice that contribute to the maintenance of existing power structures and may limit the hiring, promotion, and retention of women and underrepresented minorities" (p. 868). They categorize microaggressions as micro-assaults, micro-insults, micro-invalidations, and environmental micro-aggressions.

Williams (2020) defended microaggression research against a range of related critiques implied in the following set of claims (p. 4):

- Microaggressions are operationalized with sufficient clarity and consensus.
- Microaggressions are interpreted negatively by most or all minority group members.
- Microaggressions reflect implicitly prejudicial and implicitly aggressive motives.
- Microaggressions can be validly assessed using self-report data.
- Microaggressions are linked to mental health outcomes, which include suicidality. Also, some studies established causality (beyond mere correlation).

The harm arising from microaggressions is often cumulative yet can reach a tipping point as an instance of "death by a thousand cuts." Cherry and Wilcox

(2021) investigated the effects of prolonged exposure to sexist micro-aggressions for women and found higher frequencies of micro-aggressions were related to higher trauma symptoms in women ($N = 370$ cisgender). This led the researchers to conclude that sexist microaggressions were a source of oppression-based trauma mediated by low self-compassion. This view was consistent with theories of the internalization of oppression as a cumulative trauma leading to negative views of the self that further increase trauma symptoms. In their study of the impact of mother-daughter experiences of microaggressions and internalized sexism on mental health, Feigt et al. (2021) found increased exposure to microaggressions increased mental distress rates in both the youths and middle-aged women. Furthermore, the mother-daughter scores were correlated for microaggressions, internalized sexism, depression, and anxiety.

Gender discrimination (GD) is a form of continuous trauma with ongoing and stable negative mental health effects (Kira, Omidy, et al., 2015). Reviewing 84 studies, de la Torre-Perez et al. (2022) found female gender and a younger age to be two key factors in GD, while poorer mental health was the most common effect. Two features they found critical to defining and measuring GD were undervaluation (different recognition, opportunities, evaluation standards, and expectations) and different treatment (verbal abuse and behaviour). In a study of Polish women, Kucharska (2018) found both GD and cumulative trauma led to increased symptoms of internalizing disorders, externalizing/substance abuse disorders, and psychoticism, which were mediated by reduced self-esteem and emotion suppression. Polanco-Roman et al. (2019) found that traumas differentially impacted women, especially ethnically diverse young women who were more prone to suicidal ideation arising from race-based trauma than their male counterparts. Kira et al. (2014, Kira, Hanaa, and Bujold-Bugeaud, 2015, Kira, Omidy, et al., 2015) found that GD predicted higher rates of PTSD, cumulative trauma disorders, general anxiety, annihilation anxiety, and decreased self-esteem and general functioning in vulnerable populations, specifically American Indians, Palestinians, clients of mental health clinics in Egypt, and torture survivors in the USA. Also, systemic institutional (vs. personal) GD encounters produced more negative outcomes.

## Gaslighting

Gaslighting is the final manifestation of misogyny's methods I will discuss. The three manifestations of violence, micro-aggressions, and gaslighting align on a spectrum from physical abuse to emotional abuse to psychological abuse. This spectrum situates misogyny on a range from more direct concrete to more symbolic abstract effects rather than on a range of severity. In fact, each form of control can have profound impacts on victims' wellbeing.

Graves and Spencer (2022) defined gaslighting as "a dysfunctional communication dynamic in which one interlocutor attempts to destabilize another's sense of reality" (p. 48), which closely aligns with Sweet's (2019) definition of "psychological abuse aimed at making victims seem or feel *crazy*" (p. 851). Extrapolating from this, the key features of gaslighting are: (i) the attempt to dominate and subjugate another; (ii) through interpersonal communication; (iii) aimed at manipulating and undermining the confidence, affect, and autonomy of an interlocuter; and (iv) regarding their sanity, experience, emotions, self-conception, and epistemic and/or moral integrity.

Stark (2019) identifies two forms of gaslighting: epistemic and manipulative. Epistemic gaslighting undermines an agent's status as a knower by casting doubts on her testimonies regarding harms perpetrated against her. Manipulative gaslighting, on the other hand, aims "to get another to see her own plausible perceptions, beliefs, or memories as groundless," which makes it "a form of emotional abuse" (p. 221). Such abusive manipulative gaslighting can occur in therapeutic contexts. Manne (2023) adds to these features the sense that gaslighting attacks a target's *morality*, not just their rationality. She argues that gaslighting is often a mask for misogyny, while misogyny is used to reinforce gaslighting by bringing into question the reliability of women's testimony on the basis of their conformity to gender norms.

Manne (2023) distils gaslighting down to convincing an agent that they are "*defective* – mad, bad, or similar – for harbouring a mental state to which they are entitled," in such a way as to be gaslit out of "not only beliefs, but also desires, intentions, feelings, emotions, reactive attitudes, and so on" (p. 142). Gaslighting is used to sidestep or avert confrontation or direct conflict by making another *feel* defective, and this feeling is associated with the emotion of shame. In this, Manne argues, gaslighting is not restricted to interpersonal communication but can be structural and conveyed through politics, media, and education, whereby misogyny and oppression become incrementally internalized against the self:

> Gaslighting can thus make us witnesses against ourselves. It makes us buy the stories of our abusers and feel good and reasonable for so doing. It makes us not just unreliable, but treacherous, as narrators. And it can operate on a large scale, even purely structurally, in some cases.
>
> (p. 142)

## Misogyny in Workplace Bullying

As a woman invested in university and academic work for over three decades, I am left with the disappointing realization that misogyny continues in this environment unabated. It is less overt than it once was, but that only makes it trickier to call out. In casual conversations in staff rooms, cafes, or hallways, we hear references to the latest casualties now on short- or long-term disability leaves alongside whispers of how they became unhinged before exiting. I notice as well the seeming institutional – and interpersonal – indifference to these accounts, as if those of us remaining are surviving as the fittest in our capacity to accommodate misogyny as microaggressions and more. As women in academe, we struggle in the aftermath of these experiences and the stories, whether testifying to abuses obsessively in pursuit of justice; avoiding peers trying to do so; or silently enduring the haunting internalized ruminations that inevitably follow. This process can leave us feeling isolated as these experiences accumulate over time, often making it difficult to continue to be effective in our work and relationships. My personal realization of the impact of misogyny in academia led to this book, and so I am dedicating this section to understanding it.

## Misogyny as Bullying

Misogyny gravitates to some situations, workplaces, or institutions more than others. The family is one such situation (Stark, 2007); politics another; the military or police; medicine (Torres et al., 2019); and academe (Ahmed, 2021). The key variables appear to be power and the extent to which women in these situations occupy roles that challenge patriarchy and gender norms. So, for example, early childhood educators have lower social power, receiving low wages despite increasing demands for credentials and skills. Also, they don't directly challenge patriarchy or gendered norms because they are working in more traditional care-giving capacities with children. These two conditions – low power and low threat – make them less prone to overt misogyny at work, despite facing covert misogyny (systemically) in their compensation and status. In contrast, as lawyers or professors, for example, women receive more harassment from colleagues and students or clients with greater negative consequences to careers, job satisfaction, job performance, and attrition rates than men (Becker et al., 2022; Lampman et al., 2016).

### *Bullying*

Notelaers and Van der Heijden (2019) undertook to validate the construct of workplace bullying by reviewing studies that used related and intersecting terms. First, they operationally defined bullying as the "systematic and long-term exposure to unwanted social behaviours that are primarily of a psychological nature" (p. 4). Then, they extrapolated a standard pattern to such bullying and concluded that it was an incremental process that began with acts of micro-aggression and continued below the radar for a prolonged duration before rapidly and catastrophically escalating. Harassment was more overt and public, typically involving belittling and low-grade humiliations, like micro-aggressions, that steadily escalated. Oppression resulted from systemic discrimination and depended on negative social discourses being appropriated and internalized by the oppressed, in ways that contaminated their identity and sense of possibility, including self-confidence, personal rights, and professional aspirations.

Notelaers and Van der Heijden (2019) review confirmed Einarsen's (2005) theory of workplace bullying transpiring in four stages, developing from aggressive behaviour to bullying, from bullying to stigmatization, and culminating in severe trauma. The authors represented this standard bullying trajectory in a graph format showing a slow then rapid increase in negative symptoms and behaviours with increased bullying, culminating in catastrophic (severe) trauma and anxiety in the fourth and final stage in which, if left unable to defend themselves, most workers leave altogether (p. 9). The key factor in determining a victim leaving or staying in the workplace was whether or not they were able to defend themselves against the bullying.

### *Misogyny in Academic Bullying*

The differential viciousness and impacts of academic bullying on women versus men are suggestive of misogyny's invisible hand (Lampman et al., 2016). Ahmed's (2021) research in the UK found evidence of systemic and persistent misogyny in higher education, including pervasive institutional avoidance, passive aggression, and gaslighting when women tried to report harassment, often despite strong official EDI policies. Many women found themselves marginalized or so exhausted, diminished, and isolated from the process that they opted to leave academia altogether. This was not true of their mostly male harassers, who were often protected by colleagues and administrators. The men viewed themselves as entitled to such protections while the women were perceived as somehow deserving of their rebuff. To avoid the internalization of these beliefs, many feminist critics concur that it is critical to help victims appreciate the systemic nature of misogyny-related oppression (Ellis & Bermudez, 2021; Stalter et al., 2019).

The trajectory of bullying described by Ahmed (2021) concurs with Notelaers and Van der Heijden (2019) in reinforcing how identity and wellbeing are negotiated socially in embodied situations that underpin a sense of connection, safety, belonging, and wellbeing or, alternatively, social isolation, exclusion, threat, unease, dis-ease, and trauma. Universities are at once specific places and networks of common places. In this, they are both a workplace and an idea(l) community. Belonging to such a community carries very specific implications about our place in defining humanity and our future. As women, we are entering universities as faculty members and researchers in increasing numbers, only to face new and emerging forms of harassment, bullying, incivility, and discrimination. Lampman et al. (2016), for example, found that women faculty faced significantly more psychological harassment from students' challenging, refusing, and disruptive and/or disrespectful behaviours. Women were also at higher risk of negative consequences from academic bullying, while perpetrators were more likely to be identified as male (63%) versus female (26.2%). Prevost and Hunt (2018) found perpetrators occupied a range of power relations: 28.4% superior rank; 22.6% same rank, and 21.4% junior level, with 13.6% administrators, suggesting the problem to be misogyny rather than power itself.

The theory of misogyny helps to explain women's ongoing and disproportionate experiences of harassment in academia. Here it is worthwhile revisiting Manne's (2018) distinctions between sexism, patriarchy, and misogyny. Universities have largely relegated theories of women's inferiority to the margins, where it belongs, given the lack of evidence and its associated harms. On the other hand, patriarchy, that is, the privileged power men enjoy in universities and the surrounding society persists. That said, women have entered academe in large numbers, giving them a situation to exercise power both within the institution and in the broader society through their research, teaching, and service. This sets up a condition rife for misogyny, which is evident in the increased acts of intimidation, threat, and violence, including micro- and passive aggressions and inequalities perpetrated disproportionately against women in that environment. Misogyny also impacts which women are selected for advancement to occupy power positions within academic patriarchies, where women who are gender-conforming (vs. challenging) find much easier pathways to enter and succeed in administration.

This all-too common outcome is well documented in Ahmed's (2021) book *Complaint!* Relying on testimonials from hundreds of women who reported harassment at universities in the UK, including many intersecting racialized or sexual minority women students and faculty, she found many ultimately decided to leave the institution or were forced out. Commonly, their mostly male perpetrators carried on after being protected by their colleagues, administration, and the system. In fact, this was true of Ahmed herself, who, despite a strong scholarly record and reputation, decided to leave a position at the University of London after encountering institutional indifference and obfuscation when she supported a collective student complaint of harassment. "What I learned about institutions led me to leave; at the time it did not feel like a choice but like what I had to do" (p. 7).

A critic might argue that if misogyny was, in fact, "a thing," then we would expect poor representation of women in the intellectual and artistic life of societies and cultures over time. That is changing, but it was the case for millennia. It also suggests that we may now be in a critical tipping period in which a lot is at stake for the future capacity of women, girls, and sexual minorities to flourish. The high stakes may help explain the proliferation of passive micro-expressions of misogyny today and the indifference of so many bystanders who witness it. Only a century ago, Virginia Woolf (2021/1929) wrote *A Room of One's Own* to draw attention to the then exclusion and marginalization of women in higher education at Cambridge University, where she was a visiting scholar. She described being denied access to the library and restricted from using walkways except a narrow path reserved for women. In this essay, she outlined the history of women's exclusion from the intellectual and literary life of England, which she attributed to misogyny, which was at once social and internalized (remembering that she, too, committed suicide):

> [A]ny woman born with a great gift in the sixteenth century would certainly have gone crazed, shot herself, or ended her days in some lonely cottage outside the village, half witch, half wizard, feared and mocked at. For it needs little skill in psychology to be sure that a highly gifted girl who had tried to use her gift for poetry would have been so thwarted and hindered by other people, so tortured and pulled asunder by her own contrary instincts, that she must have lost her health and sanity.
>
> (p. 72)

### "Down Girl" Experiences

The title of Kate Manne's (2018) book *Down Girl: The Logic of Misogyny* likens misogyny to dogs being forced to submit. In training dogs, the command *down* is very different from the command *sit*. A request to *sit* is given to receive a reward in the form of a treat, whereas *down* is an order to lie down and submit to human dominance. *Sit* can be said with a rising tone as a request, but *down* is said with a falling intonation as an order or command. With my dogs, I use *down* rarely, occasionally during meals when and if they start to beg, for example. I have a body signal I use with it: I raise my right arm up in the air and snap my fingers, drawing my fingers down in front of them. My (late) senior and dominant dog, Tashi (RIP), would invariably snap his teeth when I did this – chomping down with a few small barks and growls to voice his objections as he lowered himself down, resisting and threatening even as he acquiesced. (He never did bite a person or dog during his 12 years of life with us.)

There is in the experience of misogyny this same loss of control, agency, dignity, and autonomy for women who challenge patriarchy. In my own encounter with misogyny in the university context over the years, and when facing bullying in particular, I noticed how some people, both women and men, felt it was their place to humiliate me. They seemed to feel it was justified to teach strong women to submit in ways not expected of male colleagues. The women who seemed less subject to such treatment were those who didn't speak up or rock the (patriarchal) boat too much.

I can isolate four explicit take-aways about misogyny from my experiences of bullying in academe. The first take-away is that misogyny lurks in the shadows, behind closed doors, yet is nonetheless social, invovling the complicity of social agents. In this respect, misogyny is a *social pact*. The second take-away concerns bystanders and their culpability in passively yet knowingly observing misogyny while choosing to do nothing. In my case, this included women who purported to be feminists yet still disengaged and remained aloof. The third take-away concerned the university bureaucracy itself, where policies and procedures intended to deal with bullying were disabled, used, abused, or ignored to allow the abuse of power, male entitlement, misogyny, and patriarchy to continue unchallenged. This hypocrisy is well documented in Ahmed's (2021) extensive study of universities in the UK. The fourth and final take-away, and the most disappointing, is the critical role women themselves often play in misogyny-related ambushes and harms. In my case, four (non-academic staff and admin) women and two (union and academic) men were involved, all pushing against bureaucratic limits to "down" me. The women seemed to be of a similar type as well: feminine and attractive, quiet, appearing non-threatening yet wielding power in a threatening way.

Manne (2018) clarifies how women can collude in misogyny. Some women acquiesce and cater and serve patriarchy as active agents of misogyny and are far less likely to suffer from its sanctions. Invariably, they convince themselves that they are doing what is *right* or just *doing their job*. They believe the system endorses their conduct, even when they break the rules, and they are usually right (Ahmed, 2021). In this, I am reminded of Hannah Arendt's "banality of evil" described of Eichmann, the WWII Nazi officer and war criminal. As White (2018) concluded:

> Arendt found Eichmann an ordinary, rather bland, bureaucrat, who in her words, was "neither perverted nor sadistic", but "terrifyingly normal". He acted without any motive other than to diligently advance his career in the Nazi bureaucracy. ... Eichmann "never realised what he was doing" due to an "inability... to think from the standpoint of somebody else".

## Mindfulness and Misogyny

As a recent scientific study makes clear, mindfulness helps manage and reduce anxiety as effectively as pharmaceutical or (CBT) therapy (JAMA – 2023); however, identifying the role it might play in opposing or even recovering from misogyny is more difficult to determine. When I reconsider my own recovery from encounters with misogyny in academe over the years, mindfulness and mindfulness-related practices empowered five components of my recovery – what I call the 5Rs: *recovering* from misogyny-related injury and trauma; *responding* to or *resisting* misogyny; *restoring* wellbeing; *resilience* in the face of ongoing contacts with misogyny; and *reforming* misogynistic "climates" or environments.

I am writing this book after having practices, researched, and taught mindfulness now for 45 years. I am convinced that many feminists and women in the past who struggled against, and suffered from, misogyny, whether or in isolation or in public, would have found some refuge and support through its practice. These include poets like Virginia Woolf and Sylvia Plath, who committed suicide; activists who ended up institutionalized, destitute, or marginalized, like Shulamith Firestone; as well as the many nameless women who died at their own hands in despair or at the hands of intimate partners when they couldn't find the resolution or means to leave. Mindfulness empowers and heals, and it is for our self-care that it matters most.

## References


Agsar, W.B. (2022). Karmapa case discontinued: In the same month, a new initiative started mapping accounts of alleged abuse by the Tibetan Buddhist leader. *Tricycle: The Buddhist Review*, Nov. 21. 2022. Accessed at: https://tricycle.org/article/karmapa-case-discontinued/

Ahmed, S. (2021). *A complaint!* Duke University Press.

Analayo, B. (2021). *Superiority conceit in Buddhist traditions: A historical perspective*. Wisdom Publications.

Analayo, B. (2022). *Daughters of the Buddha: Teachings by ancient Indian women*. Wisdom Publications.

Becker, P., Vlacancich, J., & Leigey, M. (2022). "Misogyny is rampant:" Harassment, bullying, and their impact on professional satisfaction among female legal practitioners in California. *Women and Criminal Justice*. https://doi.org/10.1080/08974454.2022.2071380

Braganza, B., & Cardone, N. (2022). *Conceptions of masculinity and violence towards a healthier evolution of men and boys*. Expert Report prepared for the Joint Federal/Provincial Commission into the April 2020 Nova Scotia Mass Casualty. Accessed July 2025 at https://static1.squarespace.com/static/5b7ea2794cde7a79e7c00582/t/64996ae62e54835a1318f900/1687775976192/conceptions-masculinity.pdf

Cherry, M. & Wilcox, M. (2021). Sexist microaggressions: Traumatic stressors mediated by self-compassion. *The Counseling Psychologist*, *49*(1), 106–137. https://doi.org/10.1177/0011000020954534

Cobb, C., & Avery, B. (1977). *The rape of a normal mind*. Paper Jacks.

Davenport, R, & Ryan, H. (2022). N.S. mass shooter had a history of intimidation, violent altercations. *CBC News, Nova Scotia*. Accessed July 2025 at: https://www.cbc.ca/news/canada/nova-scotia/n-s-mass-shooter-had-a-history-of-intimidation-violent-altercations-1.6517256

de la Torre-Perez, L., Oliver-Parra, A., Torres, X., & Bertran, M.J. (2022). How do we measure gender discrimination? Proposing a construct of gender discrimination through a systematic scoping review. *International Journal for Equity in Health*, *21*(1). https://doi.org/10.1186/s12939-021-01581-5

Dowman, K. (1996). *Sky dancer: The secret life and songs of Lady Yeshe Tsogyel*. Snow Lion.

Einarsen, S. (2005). The nature, causes and consequences of bullying at work: The Norwegian experience. *PISTES: Perspectives Interdisciplinaires sur le Travail et la Sante*. 7–3.

Ellis, E. & Bermudez, J., (2021). Funhouse mirror reflections: Resisting internalized sexism in family therapy and building a women-affirming practice. *Journal of Feminist Family Therapy*, *33*(3), 223–243. https://doi.org/10.1080/08952833.2020.1717903

Feigt, N., Rodriquez, M., & Vazquez, A. (2021). The impact of gender-based microaggression and internal sexism on mental health outcomes; A mother-daughter study. *Family Relations*, *71*(1), 201–219. https://doi.org/10.1111/fare.12622

Fitz-Gibbon, K., Walklate, S., McCulloch, J., & Maher, J. (2023). Intimate femicide/Intimate partner femicide. In M. Dawson, S. Mobayed Vega (Eds.), *The Routledge international handbook on femicide and feminicide*, Ch. 27 (p. 10). Routledge. https://doi.org/10.4324/9781003202332

Forbes, B. (2022). *Neighbours tried to warn police about Portapique gunman's abuse, weapons*. CBC News. May 13, 2022. Accessed at: https://www.cbc.ca/news/canada/nova-scotia/neighbours-tried-warn-police-portapique-gunmans-abuse-weapons-1.6413460

Ghosh, C., & Wang, H. (2023). Implicit bias, microaggression, and bullying. *PS: Political Science & Politics*, *56*(2), 285–290.

Graves, C. & Spencer, L. (2022). Rethinking the rhetorical epistemics of gaslighting. *Communications Theory*, *32*(1), 48–67. https://doi.org/10.1093/ct/qtab013

Hallisey, C. (2015). *Therigatha: Poems of the first Buddhist women*. Harvard University Press.

Kira, I., Hanaa, S., & Bujold-Bugeaud, M. (2015). Gender discrimination (GD): A conceptual trauma-based framework for GD and the development gender discriminatory inventory. *Psychology*, 6(16), 2041–2070. https://doi.org/10.4236/psych.2015.616201

Kira, I., Omidy, A., & Ashby, J. (2014). Cumulative trauma, appraisal, and coping in Palestinian and American Indian adults: Two cross-cultural studies. *Traumatology: An International Journal*, *20*(2), 119–133. https://doi.org/10.1037/h0099397

Kira, I., Omidy, A., Fawzi, M., Rice, K., Fawzi, M., Lewandowski, L., & Bujold-Bugeaud, M. (2015). Are the negative mental health effects of gender discrimination (GD) salient across cultures? Does self-esteem mediate these effects: GD as a continuous traumatic stress and the pathways to its negative dynamics? *Psychology*, 6, 93–116. http://dx.doi.org/10.4236/psych.2015.61009

Kucharska, J. (2018). Cumulative trauma, gender discrimination and mental health in women: mediating role of self-esteem. *Journal of Mental Health*, *27*(5), 416–423. https://doi.org/10.1080/09638237.2017.1417548

Lampman, C., Crew, E., Lowery, S., & Tompkins, K. (2016). Women faculty distressed: Descriptions and consequences of academic contrapower harassment. *Journal About Women in Higher Education*, 9(2), 169–189. https://doi.org/10.1080/19407882.2016.1199385

Langenberg, A.P. (2021). The Buddha didn't teach consent: But can early Buddhism help us develop a better sexual ethics anyway? *Tricycle: The Buddhist Review*, Feb. 23, 2021. Accessed at: https://tricycle.org/article/buddhist-sexual-ethics/

Manne, K. (2018). *Down girl: The logic of misogyny*. Oxford University Press.

Manne, K. (2020). *Entitled: How male privilege hurts women*. Crown Publishing.

Manne, K. (2023). Gaslighting. *Aristotelian Society Supplementary*, *97*(1), 122–145. https://doi.org/10.1093/arisup/akad006

Mass Casualty Commission. (2022a). *Turning the tide together: Final report of the Mass Casualty Commission*, The Joint Federal/Provincial Commission into the April 2020 Nova Scotia mass Casualty. Accessed at: https://masscasualtycommission.ca/final-report/

Mass Casualty Commission. (2022b). *Turning the tide together: Final report of the Mass Casualty Commission, Vol. 3: Violence*. The Joint Federal/Provincial Commission into the April 2020 Nova Scotia Mass Casualty. Accessed at: https://masscasualtycommission.ca/final-report/

McCulloch, J., & Maher, J. (2022). *Understanding the links between gender-based violence and mass casualty attacks: 'Private' violence and misogyny as public risk*. Joint Federal/Provincial Commission into the April 2020 Nova Scotia Mass Casualty. https://masscasualtycommission.ca/files/commissioned-reports/COMM0053826.pdf?t=1715463922

Notelaers, G., & Van der Heijden, B. (2019). Construct validity in workplace bullying and harassment research. In P. D'Cruz, E. Noronha, G. Notelaers, & C. Rayner (Eds.), *Concepts, approaches, and methods: Handbooks of workplace bullying, emotional abuse and harassment I*. Springer Nature.

Pierce, C. (1970). Offensive mechanisms. In F. Barbour (Ed.), *The Black seventies* (pp. 265–282). Porter Sargent.

Pierce, C. (1974). Psychiatric problems of the Black minority. In S. Arieti (Ed.), *American handbook of psychiatry* (pp. 512–523). Basic Books.

Pierce, C., Carew, J., Pierce-Gonzalez, D., & Willis, D. (1978). An experiment in racism: TV commercials. In C. Pierce (Ed.), *Television and education* (pp. 62–88). Sage.

Polanco-Roman, L., Anglin, D., Miranda, R., & Jeglic, E. (2019). Racial/ethnic discrimination and suicidal ideation in emerging adults: The role of traumatic stress and depressive symptoms varies by gender not race/ethnicity. *Journal of Youth and Adolescence*, *48*, 2023–2037. https://doi.org/10.1007/s10964-019-01097-w

Prevost, C., & Hunt, E. (2018). Bullying and mobbing in academe: A literature review. *European Scientific Journal*, *14*(8), 14 pages.

Sarson, J., & MacDonald, L. (2022). Non-state torture of women; Reclaiming their human right. *Witness: The Canadian Journal of Critical Nursing Discourse*, *4*(1), 1–6. https://doi.org/10.25071/2291-5796.121

Schelling, A., & Waldman, A. (Trans.) (2020). *Songs of the sons and daughters of Buddha: Enlightenment poems from the Theragatha and Therigatha*. Shambhala Publications.

Srinivasan, A. (2021). *The right to sex: Feminism in the twenty-first century*. MacMillan Publishers

Stalter, A., Phillips, J., Wiggs, C., Brodhead, J., & Swanson, K. (2019). Systems perspective for incivility in academia: An integrative review. *Nursing Education Perspectives*, *40*(3), 144–150.

Stark, C. (2019). Gaslighting, misogyny, and psychological oppression. *The Monist*, *102*(2), 221–235. https://doi.org/10.1093/monist/onz007

Stark, E. (2007). *Coercive control: How men entrap women in personal life*. Oxford University Press.

Sue, D., Capodilupo, C., Torino, G., Bucceri, J., Holder, A., Nadal, K., & Esquilin, M. (2007). Racial microaggressions in everyday life: Implications for clinical practice. *American Psychologist*, *62*(4), 271–286. https://doi.org/10.1037/0003-066X.62.4.271

Sweet, P. (2019). The sociology of gaslighting. *American Sociology Review*, *84*(5), 851–875. https://doi.org/10.1177/0003122419874843

Torres, M., Salles, A., & Cochran, A. (2019). Recognizing and reacting to microaggressions in medicine and surgery. *JAMA Surgery*, *154*(9), 868–872.

Varvaloucas, E. (2017). What went wrong: An interview with Tibetan psychologist Lobsang Rapgay about student-teacher relationships that turn abusive. *Tricycle: The Buddhist Review*, Winter 2007. Accessed at: https://tricycle.org/magazine/what-went-wrong-tibetan-sex-abuse/

White, T. (2018). What did Hannah Arendt really mean by the banality of evil? *Aeon (in association with the American Philosophical Association)*. Accessed on Aug. 25, 2023 at: https://aeon.co/ideas/what-did-hannah-arendt-really-mean-by-the-banality-of-evil

WHO (World Health Organization). (2018). Violence against women: Key facts. Accessed at: https://www.who.int/news-room/fact-sheets/detail/violence-against-women

Williams, M. (2020). Microaggressions: Clarification, evidence, and impact. *Perspectives on Psychological Science*, *15*(1), 3–26. https://doi.org/10.1177/1745691619827499

Woolf, V. (2021/1929). *A room of one's own: The feminist classic*. Capstone Press.

# 4 Emotions in Oppression

Oppression conjures up images of poverty, deprivation, and the enduring scars of overt violence. This has led some to focus narrowly on poverty as a social indicator of oppression and overall health (e.g., McGibbon, 2021a). Yet neither poverty nor violence – nor domination itself – offers evidence of oppression, but only of risk factors for oppression. For women, oppression can and does live among the affluent and those living free of violence. As valuable as it may be to work towards greater material equity or to reduce violence, oppression is most effectively addressed where it endures, that is, *internalized* within the psyche. Internalization creates the key problems of oppression vis-a-vis its impacts on agency and wellbeing, and the key indicators and perpetuators of the internalization of oppression are emotions. Not only are collective emotions like shame and self-doubt a defining condition of internalized oppression, but their absence is an indicator of liberation, alongside emotions associated with wellbeing, like joy, self-possession, and compassion.

Until recently, scholarship on oppression has highlighted its economic and political dimensions, limiting its psychological manifestations to considerations of more abstract philosophical constructs like alienation and authenticity (de Beauvoir, 1949/2011; Fanon, 1961). This socio-political preoccupation stemmed from the early dominance of neo-Marxist accounts of oppression, when scholars were writing either within or narrowly against Marxist ideas of dialectical materialism and social inequality (e.g., Firestone, 1970; Freire, 1970). Emotions were rarely referenced in such accounts, perhaps because emotions were considered mere *contents* of consciousness arising as discrete, short-lived episodic states associated with individual temperaments, dispositions, and experiences.

In the 1990s, feminist scholars began thinking about emotions differently. They shifted focus from the socio-political to psychological dimensions of oppression. In Marxist terms, it was a shift of emphasis from oppression as a structural problem to oppression as a problem of agency. In her book on *Femininity and Domination: Studies in the Phenomenology of Oppression*, Bartky (1990) presented her study of the psychology of oppression through the lens of Fanon's idea of psychic alienation. In doing so, she explicitly argued that oppression, and women's oppression in particular, can be psychological rather than economic or political:

DOI: 10.4324/9781003449355-4

> It is possible to be oppressed in ways that need involve neither physical deprivation, legal inequality, nor economic exploitation; one can be oppressed psychologically – the "psychic alienation" of which Fanon speaks. To be psychologically oppressed is to be weighed down in your mind; it is to have a harsh dominion exercised over your self-esteem. The psychologically oppressed become their own oppressors; they come to exercise harsh dominion over their own self-esteem. Differently put, psychological oppression can be regarded as the "internalization of intimations of inferiority."
>
> (p. 22)

Bartky (1990) described the experiences of women oppressed by misogyny as dominated by the emotion of shame with its "pervasive affective attunement to the social environment." This perspective reinterprets emotions as long-lived patterns and processes rather than discrete mental events. This change was reflected in shifting approaches to researching emotions. To understand emotions as long-lived patterns, they were investigated best through narrative (e.g. auto/biographical) (Saenz-Benavides, 2019) and phenomenological (Garrau, 2024; Young, 1990), rather than objective empirical, accounts. In this way, these studies began to represent oppression as a *lived experience* rather than as social theory supported (or not) by data-backed generalizations.

As long-lived *relational* processes, emotions became attributed not merely to interpersonal relations but to broader social relations between groups and within social structures (Ahmed, 2004; Saenz-Benavides, 2019). Feminist scholars drew attention to the collective nature of some emotions beyond their individual aetiology and expression. Collective emotions are susceptible to political and cultural manipulation in ways that reinforce unjust social hierarchies, subordinating some and elevating other groups. Emotions like shame, for example, reinforce the subservience of women to patriarchal norms that can make some women complicit with misogynistic sanctions against other women who violate such norms. Traditional depictions of a "good woman" is one who is inhibited and concealed, the two key features of the emotion of shame (Deigh, 1983). The "blushing bride" reflects this norm and describes succinctly how femininity is traditionally performed. As artefacts of enduring social relations, emotions link lived experience to extant forms of structural discrimination. This is how and why oppression is at once social and psychological.

Mindfulness is an inductive process that favours direct perception over the habitual images and ideas we have about the world. Practitioners observe and describe lived experiences exhaustively before theorizing on the implications. The training focuses on recognizing the differences between direct perception, memory, habitual experience, and interpretation, leaning towards direct perception as more reliable; however, because it doesn't apply a consistent conceptual or theoretical lens, mindfulness can be weak in recognizing, naming, and regulating collective emotions associated with oppression. Consequently, for it to serve as an anti-oppressive process, mindfulness needs to support, but not impose, pathways to insights into shared collective emotional experience (MacPherson and Rockman, 2022; Munjee & MacPherson, 2023). It seems insufficient to merely name and attribute these emotions to the vagaries of one's own mind, circumstances, and immediate bodily or emotional experience. What is required is a sustained dialogue between direct, open, and reflexive awareness and critical interpretive analysis.

## My Own Story as a Case Study

Now semi-retired, I live relatively free of the oppressive circumstances and emotions that I navigated through much of my education and working life. Thus emancipated, I find myself choosing to participate more in science and activities related to mathematics and spatial skills. These include a science-oriented book club, snooker lessons and games, mahjong and bridge playing, and membership in the local Royal Astronomical Society, where I am learning to observe the sky, moon, and stars. These new arenas of interest and practice were absent both in my vocation and avocation before. Now I practise them as a true *amateur*, originally meaning *to love* in Latin. Freed of the need to establish expertise or belonging, participating out of interest or love alone allows me to experience being an imposter or outsider with more openness and light heartedness. Perhaps too, as a woman amateur, I pose less of a threat to men in these male-dominated communities than I might as an expert.

As a child, I tried unsuccessfully to pursue sciences and maths both in education and professionally. These efforts were undermined consistently and ultimately remained unfulfilled for a number of socio-cultural, institutional, dispositional, and internal reasons, many of which were linked to gender discrimination, implicit biases, and internalized oppression that left me feeling always the eager outsider and imposter. So, I pursued psychology, languages, and education instead.

Then, in 1986, during a silent retreat on Vancouver Island, we were invited by the teacher, Namgyal Rinpoche, to investigate strengths, weaknesses, and blocks using an adapted mindfulness-based inquiry method called the holistic clearing meditation. Now I realize that strengths, weaknesses, and blocks were related to feeling tones (positive, neutral, negative, respectively) that become calcified within the habitual ways that we view ourselves, our competencies, and the possibilities of our lives. To unearth these conditioned patterns, we were encouraged to bring to mind each category in relation to school subjects and then to identify an associated "texture" of the mind.

When it came to "weakness," I thought of science. A "block" would have been something I had no interest in whatsoever; however, I was aware of the persistent interest that kept leading me to choose, then abandon, science and mathematical studies repeatedly over the years. In the meditation, I narrowed my inquiry to "science" as I invited my mind to open to revisit experiences participating in science. The texture that first came to mind was of something hard, which soon became the image of a praying mantis with its hard, shell-like exoskeleton. The accompanying emotion was fear. It soon became clear to me that the image and associated texture alongside the emotion embodied my mental and emotional disposition towards science. Not lost on me at the time was noticing that "praying" was a homonym for "preying."

Then a memory arose in the wake of this image. In grade 3, I was academically ahead of other students, so I was placed in a grade 4 science class. One day, a boy came to class with a praying mantis in a glass jar, which the teacher proceeded to place in the class terrarium. The next day the boy returned with a monarch butterfly to feed the praying mantis. The teacher put the monarch butterfly in the glass terrarium and had students in the class line up to observe the praying mantis eat the butterfly. I refused, as did another (girl) student. The teacher insisted, and the other girl acquiesced. I resisted and continued to refuse, so the teacher told several boys in the class to accompany me forcibly me to the terrarium – one on each arm. When they approached, I said it wasn't necessary. I would go on my own. Yet, continuing to resist, with my back to the teacher, I shut my eyes as I passed by the scene.

I loved seeing monarch butterflies; they helped me to appreciate the beauty and uniqueness of nature. The science lesson, on the other hand, was teaching something else, that everything was "eating and being eaten." Yet I knew the classroom wasn't the wilderness and that this butterfly was not being captured by the mantis but by a human boy, who had placed it in a jar and brought it to class to win the approval of the (male) teacher. I knew I was appearing to be a typical "squeamish girl," which I found humiliating and a source of shame. Yet my love of butterflies mattered more to me than this teacher's view of science. My way of doing science was to appreciate the natural world, which isn't what I was encountering in that class. Thereafter, I learned to sublimate my affection and fear, performing both squeamishness and resistance in science.

During that retreat, as I resumed meditating, a sequence of later memories appeared in rapid succession: at 10 years of age, paralysed and pleading for my father to kill a bug approaching me in the bathroom; in grade 7, screaming in panic in a biology class as a flying beetle landed on my abdomen; in grade 10 physics class, poking and teasing my male lab partner to distract him and being reprimanded later by the teacher who refused me the A-grade I'd earned; and, in semi-retreat on the island of Crete 10 years later, desensitizing myself to wood lice who appeared each morning on the floor of my hut. I held the segmented, hard-shelled insects in my hand and watched them contract into balls, transforming into small marbles, before rolling them out of the room. As these impressions faded, so too did my fear and defensiveness. I was left feeling only appreciation for insects like the wood lice and the mantis and for science as a method to observe the natural world.

## Emotional Consciousness

LeDoux and Brown (2017) proposed that emotional states of consciousness are rooted in higher-order – not subcortical – cognitive processing. Although first-order non-conscious subcortical systems can provide inputs to consciousness, it

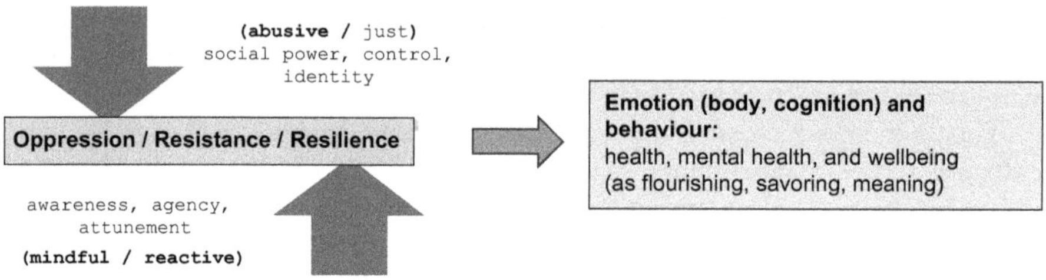


*Figure 4.1* Ecology of Mind Model of Oppression and Adaptive Resilience.

is only when they are reassembled in the higher-order experience of awareness that they become conscious and integrated within consciousness. Both perceptual and emotional consciousness are expressions of the higher cortical general networks of cognition (GNCs) of the lateral and medial cortex. The GNC involves capacities of attention, working memory, and meta-cognition, linking consciousness to "the self as a set of autobiographical memories about who you are and what has happened to you in your life, and how you think, act, and feel in particular situations" (p. E2020). In this way, self-consciousness, including the sense of self, is integral to emotional consciousness and vice versa, explaining why and how oppression is enacted through emotions and emotional states as a dysfunction in identity and the sense of self.

This process fits well with our ecology of mind theory, as depicted in Figure 4.1, in which oppression is conceived as an emergent property of the encounter between adverse social situations and the embodied psyche, irreducible to either environmental or organismic conditions on their own. This highlights how oppressive social conditions alone do not necessarily generate oppression and negative health impacts if the effects are minimized from enacting downstream effects on emotion, attention, and reactive *internal* cognitive or behavioural responses. With mindful resilience, adverse social conditions are more readily resisted. By engaging and practising awareness, agency, and attunement, mindfulness reduces stressors arising from oppression *and* resistance, thereby supporting adaptive resilience and mitigating the negative effects on emotions, health, and wellbeing.

## Emotions as Constructive or Destructive

In this ecological model, emotions are understood to be culturally inscribed *states of mind*. As states of mind, they may or may not be named well within any particular language. I will provide an example from my own experience teaching the refugee Tibetan [Buddhist] nuns of Dolma Ling in the Indian Himalayas in the early 1990s. We were doing an autobiographical unit to give them the language to talk about themselves to others. I introduced two concepts of emotions in English that I thought might be troubling them in exile, neither of which had a clear Tibetan language equivalent. The first emotion I identified was *loneliness*. However much I attempted to describe and define this emotion, it remained unfamiliar and incomprehensible. They explained to me that they were never alone, not as children nor now as adult nuns in a monastery. I then introduced *homesickness*. Despite not having an equivalent term in Tibetan, they reacted strongly, and positively, to this word, recognizing many of their current experiences in the term. Many said that they needed such a word in Tibetan as so many were now experiencing missing their families, homes, and communities back in Tibet.

This example points to two ways in which particular states of mind as emotions become culturally inscribed. First, they are inscribed by shared experiences that create conditions that favour particular emotional states, including how to interpret such states – as, for example, being "destructive" or "constructive." Second, these shared emotions and experiences are inscribed in language with varying degrees of descriptive nuance that may, or may not, reflect their interpretive frame. So, for example, some presumed "destructive" emotions may become pathologized as forms of mental distress or illness. Examples are *defiance* in boys or youth, *anger* in adults (with associated anger management training), and the lack of empathy or compassion as an indicator of sociopathy.

In working with emotions therapeutically or through self-regulation, the initial key step is naming the emotion, which points to the challenges associated with their cultural inscription, which may or may not support the naming of the associated emotion. In the final chapter, I will describe a practice to work with mindfulness of emotions that expands the capacity to name the emotion as a state of mind beyond its cultural inscription in language. In being first identified as a particular *texture*, the texture and associated object are used to find an adequate term or word that would describe it as an emotion. This allows some degree of freedom to name states of mind and emotions beyond a narrow cultural frame of reference. That said, it is helpful to consider some terminology used to classify emotions across both modern and Buddhist psychological contexts, and how they are classified as destructive or constructive.

Flanagan (2000) compared the Buddhist and modern framing of emotions with respect to anger. Anger is considered a basic emotion in the modern view, with iterations across the spectrum from destructive to constructive. He references a 1962 paper by Strawson titled "Freedom and Resentment," where the author suggested that there were a set of "reactive attitudes" like anger, which were both original, natural, and constructive when suitably expressed. Flanagan discusses these reactive emotions as "moral emotions, [the] … attitudes through which we express our common humanity, recognizing others as persons, and according them the positive and negative expressions that come from seeing and treating them as moral agents" (260). During a dialogue with the Dalai Lama on the topic of destructive emotions, what Tibetan Buddhism calls *afflictive emotions*, Wallace and Flanagan (2003) offered examples of emotions, as states of mind, considered more destructive and more constructive from a Western philosophical perspective (see Table 4.1).

*Table 4.1* Destructive and Constructive States of Mind (Wallace & Flanagan, 2003, p. 67)

| *Destructive "States of Mind"* | *Constructive "States of Mind"* | |
|---|---|---|
| Low self-esteem | Self-respect | Generosity |
| Overconfidence | Self-esteem (if deserved) | Benevolence |
| Harbouring negative emotions | Feelings of integrity | Love |
| Jealousy and envy | Compassion | Friendship |
| Lack of compassion | Seeing the true, the good, the right | |
| Inability to have close interpersonal relations | | |

*Table 4.2* Mental Afflictions in Buddhist Psychology (Wallace & Jinpa, 2003, p. 106)

| *Twenty Derivative Mental Afflictions* | | | |
|---|---|---|---|
| *Anger* | *Attachment* | *Ignorance* | *Ignorance and Attachment* |
| wrath | avarice | blind faith | pretention |
| resentment | inflated self-esteem | spiritual sloth | deception |
| spite | excitation | forgetfulness | shamelessness |
| envy/jealousy | concealment of one's own vices | lack of introspective attentiveness | inconsideration of others |
| cruelty | dullness | | unconscientiousness |
| | | | distraction |

In this dialogue, Wallace and Jinpa (2003) contrasted these with the six "mental afflictions" of Buddhist psychology: attachment or craving, anger, pridefulness, ignorance and delusion, afflictive doubt, and afflictive views, which were expanded as a set of 20 mental afflictions represented in Table 4.2. These 20 derive from the core three afflictions of anger, attachment, and ignorance. Distinctions between constructive and destructive emotions in Buddhist psychology are technically referred to as wholesome or unwholesome state of mind, respectively. I am unaware of a corresponding list of non-afflictive or wholesome emotions or states, though the seven factors of awakening identify four emotions or states associated with awakening: perseverance, joy, tranquillity, and equanimity (equal attention on objects of mind, whether of positive, negative, or neutral valence or feeling tone. Added to these four are three cognitive processes or states: mindful attention, investigation, and concentration.

The Buddhist perspective derives from a broader South Asian framing of emotions and states of mind. In *Words for the Heart*, Heim (2022) collated a glossary of classical terms for emotions in Pali, the language used by the historical Buddha and early texts attributed to his teaching; Sanskrit, used in later written texts; and Pankrit. These terms appear across classical South Asian texts and poetry, pointing to a distinctive cultural framing of emotions. Worth mentioning from Table 4.3 is the proliferation of, and distinctions

*Table 4.3* Classical Indian Terms for Emotions (the sample starting with "a") (Heim, 2022)

| ***abhaya*** *(Pali; Sk)* | *fearlessness* | ***abhijjha*** *(Pali)* | *covetousness* | ***abhilasha*** *(Sk)* | *longing* |
|---|---|---|---|---|---|
| *abhimana* (Sk) | conceit/sense of self | *adbhuta* (Sk) | wonder | *ahamkara* (Pali; Sk) | ego, "I" |
| *akkhanti/ ashanti* (Pali; Sk) | impatience | *amarsha* (Sk) | envy; resentment; vindictiveness | *amhas* (Sk) | torment of a tight place |
| *ananda* (Sk) | bliss | *anannatannas-samaitindriya* (Pali) | the "I-will-come-to-know-what-is-unknown" faculty | *anrishamsya* (Sk) | fellow feeling; compassion |
| *anukampa* (Pali; Sk) | compassion; trembling for others | *anukrosha* (Sk) | commiseration; crying out for another | *anumodana* (Pali; Sk) | applauding & rejoicing in others virtue |
| *anuraga* (Sk) | affection and attraction | *anushaya / anusaya* (Sk; Pk) | regret; remorse; underlying tendency | *anutapa* (Sk; Pali) | remorse; repentance |
| *appaccaya* (Pali) | petulance | *asava /ashrava* (Pali/Sk) | oozings *(discharging of emotions)* | *asha* (Sk) | hope, and often vain hope |
| *ahru* (Sk) | tears *(releasing/ expressing pent up sorrow)* | *asuya* (Sk) | indignation; envy | *atihasa* (Sk) | excess laughter or hilarity without reason |
| *atimana* (Pali; Sk) | the contempt of vainglory | *audarya* (Sk) | magnanimity | *autsukya* (Sk) | impatient yearning |
| *avajna* (Sk) | contempt | *avamana* (Sk) | disrespect; insult | *avega* (Sk) | panic; shock |

between, forms of compassion (fellow feeling, trembling for others, commiseration or crying out for others, rejoicing in others virtue, affection, and magnanimity.) And these were exclusively from those terms starting with the Sanskrit equivalent of "a". The process of emotion regulation begins with identifying and naming emotions, so this capacity to name the distinctive form of compassion implies more nuanced recognition and self-regulation of its corresponding state.

## Internalized Oppression

Despite these cultural differences, emotions have some degree of cross-cultural resonance given on our common experiences as human beings. In the case of oppression, it arises when discriminatory social relations become internalized and impact identity and self-perception. When these internalized discriminatory social relations become preconsciously integrated in psyches, they manifest predictably as implicit biases, collective emotions, and altered identities and identifications. Therefore, as a common experience of humanity, oppression is associated with clusters of common emotions. For the oppressed, these collective emotions affect their lived experience through negative and oppressive feelings. Such effects are common though not universal for members of marginalized communities and populations (e.g., people of colour, Indigenous, women, queer and transgender, immigrant, and religious or linguistic minorities) (David & Derthick, 2018). So too are sets of emotions common for those who oppress others.

## Oppression as a Sustained Threat

Once internalized, oppression can manifest as a mental disorder that the US government's National Institute of Mental Health (NIMH, n.d.) classifies as "a negative valence system" characterized by "sustained threat." Other sustained threat conditions associated with chronic negative affective disturbances are acute threat (fear), potential threat (anxiety), loss, and frustrative non-reward. The NIMH uses the following criteria to illustrate and define *sustained threat* as a negative valence system:

> An aversive emotional state caused by prolonged (i.e., weeks to months) exposure to internal and/or external condition(s), state(s), or stimuli that are adaptive to escape or avoid. The exposure may be actual or anticipated; the changes in affect, cognition, physiology, and behaviour caused by sustained threat persist in the absence of the threat and can be differentiated from those changes evoked by acute threat.

Sustained threat is presented by the NIMH as a construct used to organize research and represent a number of conditions like chronic stress, cumulative trauma, and oppression. Table 4.4 provides units of analysis identified by the NIMH (n.d.) to study the impacts of sustained threat. These units enable oppression and related conditions to be investigated more holistically as integrated embodied (and ecological) phenomena with distinctive yet interrelated impacts on molecules, cells, circuits, physiology, behaviours, and self-reported measures or indicators.

Investigating oppression as a sustained threat, Williams et al. (2023) administered the self-report Trauma Symptoms Discrimination Scale (TSDS) to a national sample ($n$ = 923) of diverse participants in the USA and found a direct relationship between marginalized identities and trauma-related stress. These findings confirmed that oppression constitutes a sustained threat associated with trauma that is reinforced through general discrimination, microaggressions, and race-based traumas. Furthermore, higher rates of lifetime trauma rather than acute (past year) trauma increased the degree of trauma symptoms. This finding suggests that oppression (as a sustained threat) arises from cumulative versus acute incident traumas that are associated with broader impacts, including increased rates of PTSD, traumatic cognitions, anxiety, and depression. Furthermore, the highest rates of cumulative trauma were experienced by participants with intersectional marginalized identities. Interestingly, although women experienced significantly higher rates of discrimination, there were no differences between men and women in their traumatic symptoms. One explanation may be that intersectional identity effects like those arising from race had a stronger negative effect on men. On the other hand, those facing marginalization from sexual orientation (LGBTQ status) faced increased discrimination *and* traumatic symptoms compared to heterosexuals.

## Three Mechanisms Reinforcing the Internalization of Oppression

Once internalized, oppression becomes infused across experience as a sustained threat with multiple impacts. As indicated, in Table 4.4, these potential impacts range from the biological to the behavioural, often extending across the lifespan and even across generations. Critically, these processes usually transpire below the threshold of consciousness, making oppression an automatic, habitual, and "fast" response, to use Kahneman's (2011) distinction between fast and slow thinking. In this sense, oppression is as an implicit bias against the self and one's identity group. This is how the oppressed can become active oppressors of their own group. The internalization of oppression involves the shift to a negative valence system dominated by collective emotions like shame and anger, which are reinforced and sustained through such mechanisms as impostorism, the stereotype threat, and microaggressions (Nadal et al., 2021), each of which are discussed below.

*Table 4.4* Units of Analysis in Interpreting Oppression as Sustained Threat (NIMH, n.d.)

| *Units of Analysis* | *Sites of Effects* |
|---|---|
| **Molecules** | ACTH, CRH, HPA-axis hormones |
| **Cells** | Hippocampal, Microgalia, prefrontal |
| **Circuits (neural)** | Attention network, Dysregulation of amygdala reactivity, dysregulation of cingulate reactivity, Habit systems (Striatum/caudate/accumbens), Hypothalamic nuclei, PVT, Vigilance network |
| **Physiology** | Dysregulated HPA axis, Error-related negativity |
| **Behaviour** | Anhedonia/decreased appetitive behaviour, Anxious arousal, Attentional bias to threat, Avoidance, Decreased libido, Helplessness behaviour, Increased conflict detection, Increased perseverative behaviour, Memory retrieval deficits, Punishment sensitivity |
| **Self-report** | Measures of childhood trauma, risky families, youth life stress, and trauma systems are examples. |

### *The Impostor Syndrome*

As an effect of internalized oppression, impostorism involves persistent and unfounded feelings of inauthenticity and not belonging despite being fully competent and qualified to belong (Nadal et al., 2021). Parkman (2016) characterized impostorism as "feelings of fraudulence" that make a person unable to "attribute their success to their own abilities despite many achievements and accolades" (p. 52). When discriminatory social views become internalized, so do implicit biases against oneself and one's capacities, competence, and ability to serve in certain roles from which one's identity group were traditionally excluded. When internalized, such biases can begin to surface and intrude in consciousness, leading to self-doubt and the sense of being a fraud, regardless of evidence to the contrary.

The impostor syndrome is associated with a range of cognitive, affective, and behavioural effects that can make it a self-fulfilling prophesy. Clarke et al. (2025) identified perfectionism, anxiety, and depression as key aspects of impostorism reduced through mindfulness in psychologists in training ($N$ = 231), for whom mindfulness overall was negatively associated with impostorism. Of the five known facets of mindfulness (observing, describing, applying, non-judging, and non-reacting), the increase in non-judging and nonreactivity with mindfulness was most associated with reduced imposterism. Lausch (2021) reported reduced impostorism in female STEM graduate students who engaged in mindfulness, while Pastan et al. (2022) reported a comparable reduction in impostor feelings in dental students. Orbe-Austin and Orbe-Austin (2024) propose meditation more broadly as an intervention for historically marginalized people experiencing the impostor phenomenon, as does Caldwell (2020) for Whites to mitigate White fragility associated with oppressing.

### *The Stereotype Threat*

The stereotype threat occurs when known negative social stereotypes about one's identity group interfere with performance. Interestingly, the stereotype threat can exist even without such stereotypes being internalized (Nadal et al., 2021; Steele, 1997). Meta-analytical synthesizing studies provide evidence that discrimination and social stereotypes (from media and non-media sources) result in significant obstacles to achievement and mental health for women and other marginalized groups (Appel & Weber, 2021; Emmer et al., 2024).

### *Microaggressions*

Before discussing microaggressions, it is worthwhile remembering that oppression – and the internalization of oppression – often arise through explicit macro-aggressions like domestic violence, rape, or colonial occupation. Such explicit forms of violence become the bases of power differences that drive and enable the implicit threats of symbolic violence used to perpetuate oppression as a sustained threat. Symbolic threat was a construct used by the French sociologist Pierre Bourdieu to describe how media and culture in the aftermath of forced occupation, for example, exacts ongoing domination in the seeming absence of explicit force. In this respect, the potency of internalized oppression is always backed by real or imagined threats to one's biological and psychological integrity and wellbeing.

Therefore, microaggressions are the aftermath of concrete historical threats and abuses to marginalized groups like women. Often, microaggressions appear when explicit macroaggressions are restricted or inhibited by norms, rules, or laws, resurfacing as a kind of *return of the repressed*, to use a Freudian term. Microaggressions are subtle insults and slights within commonplace daily situations that persistently undermine and erode the confidence of targeted members of marginalized populations, including women (Nadal et al., 2021). Sue (2010) describes such microaggressions as "the everyday verbal, nonverbal, and environmental slights, snubs, or insults, whether intentional or unintentional, that communicate hostile, derogatory, or negative messages to target persons based solely on their marginalized group membership" (p. 3). In the last few decades, gender microaggressions against women have been extensively researched, operationalized, and measured in many public and workplace environments (Gartner et al., 2020). This research has shown significant negative effects from microaggression to psychological wellbeing, physical health, and job outcomes (Costa et al., 2022).

It is important to reiterate that an oppressed person may themselves become an oppressor. In fact, it has long been documented in research and scholarship how internalizing oppression can lead certain members of marginalized or oppressed groups to identify with their oppressors as an avoidance strategy (Freire, 1970; Manne, 2017; Nadal et al., 2021). Emotions may well have a role to play in this switch given the strong negative valence of the sustained threat of oppression in contrast to the emotions of oppressing, which may seem less threatening.

## The Emotional Aftermath of Internalized Oppression

Sustained threat conditions like oppression develop through internalized, not just external, threats. Internalized oppression develops by preconsciously overgeneralizing and habituating to negative valence systems through prolonged "exposure to internal and/or external condition(s), state(s), or stimuli that are adaptive to escape or avoid" (NIMH, n.d.). Negative, neutral, or positive does not refer to the value of the emotion itself but rather to its associated affective tone. The preconscious pairing of sensory experiences with negative, neutral, or positive affective tones condition consciousness to engage in automatic responses on the basis of habitual affective tones rather than adaptation or reason.

Once internalized, oppression enacts harms on consciousness itself, beyond particular states or behaviours. Most of these effects happen preconsciously, with emotions serving as the more conscious and visible tip of the iceberg that is consciousness writ large. In so doing, emotions provide feedback to awareness of preconscious oppressive processes, serving as a kind of early warning system. These emotions are not merely an effect of oppression but also a cause of its continuing threats to wellbeing (Ahmed, 2004; Saenz-Benavides, 2019). The emotional impacts of internalized oppression enact the ongoing "pressing," that is, inhibiting, restricting, and suppressing in the absence of immediate causes.

The negative, neutral, or positive valences underlying habitual responses lead us to avoid, ignore, or move towards phenomena, respectively. Emotion appears as a second-order "felt" experience of mind rather than a first-order preconscious process (Barrett et al., 2005). In sustained threat conditions like oppression, overgeneralizing and habituating to a negative valence system occur largely unconsciously, giving rise to the characteristic negative emotions of oppression; however, oppression impacts other emotions that are neutral or positive as well. What these emotional constellations in oppression appear to have in common is that they reinforce experiential avoidance, a known transdiagnostic category across a range of anxiety and depressive disorders (Akbari et al., 2022).

The discriminatory sociopolitical conditions that give rise to oppression tend to persist across the lifespan and across generations. These systemic reinforcers and associated stressors further fuel negative emotions, which function to reinforce oppression by dampening agency, attunement, and affiliation. This makes oppression a key social determinant of health (McGibbon, 2021a). For women, these systemic forces include increased exposure to family violence, which disproportionately impacts women and children, and higher rates of depression from unequal material resources and PTSD associated with childhood sexual abuse and adult sexual violence. These lead to unequal psychiatric diagnoses, often in the face of reduced access to psychiatric services, especially for racialized women (McGibbon, 2021b, Ussher, 2011). McGibbon (2021b) refers to this process as the "psychiatrization of oppression," whereby oppression, rooted in systemic social problems, "is re-framed as individual psychiatric disorders" that "heavily rely on psycho-pharmaceuticals" despite the fact that "chronic stress and anxiety related to oppressive living conditions cannot be ameliorated with pills" (p. 148).

Although its secular-scientific variant has been highly medicalized, mindfulness is rooted in practices and training aimed at enhancing and cultivating consciousness itself – for example, by empowering agency, attunement, and affiliation. Key to this role is the capacity of mindfulness to enhance self-regulation and autonomy (e.g., choice not control) in our emotional life with impacts on agency, wellbeing, and the capacity to enact the life we choose. Accordingly, in Buddhist psychology, mindfulness is represented as a path to wellbeing as freedom, not just as health. This freedom is not fundamentally

*Table 4.5* Sample/Salient Emotions on the Oppression Spectrum

| | *Negative* | *Neutral* | *Positive* | *Regulation Style (Roth et al., 2019)* |
|---|---|---|---|---|
| **Oppressed** | **shame**<br>**fear**<br>**self-doubt**<br>**suppression**<br>**anger** (frustrated) | **indifference** (dissociation)<br>**ignorance** (dullness/ delusion) | **empathy**<br>**hope** (w/ certainty) | **amotivated** (dysregulated)<br>**controlled** (suppressed) |
| **Oppressors** | **anger** (unmet expectations)<br>**anger** (afflicted pride)<br>**contempt**<br>**disgust** | **indifference** (nonempathic)<br>**ignorance** (delusion) | **entitlement**<br>**expectancy**<br>*himpathy* | **amotivated** (dysregulated)<br>**controlled** (suppressed) |
| **Liberating** | **anger** (indignation) | **perseverance**<br>**equanimity** | **joy**<br>**hope** (w/ uncertainty)<br>**self-possession**<br>**self-confidence** (pride)<br>**compassion** | **integrated** (autonomous self-regulation) |

freedom from sociopolitical conditions that may lie outside our control; instead, it is freedom from afflictive emotions that perpetuate captivity to the ongoing legacy of oppression.

## The Emotions of Oppression

Oppression is associated with a set of predictable collective emotions that help define and sustain the condition and its threats to wellbeing. Bartky (1990) refers to these pervasive effects as a condition of "affective attunement." Affective attunement involves a state of hyper-awareness, sensitivity, and vigilance to the environment and the affective tones it engenders. Feeling tones valence experience negatively, positively, or neutrally, leading to tendencies to avoid, want, or ignore, respectively, all of which can be problematic. The most significant problem is posed to freedom, autonomy, and choice from conditioned habitual behaviour arising from these feeling tones. When left unexamined and automatic, these feeling tones manifest in consciousness as the emotions of oppression. Table 4.5 outlines some of these predominant oppression-related emotions, including those associated with freeing oneself from oppression. Some of these emotions are heavily researched and some are evident from observing personal or collective experiences. They are distinctive in being collective emotions that reinforce oppression as a sustained threat or as liberating emotions that empower the oppressed to resist oppression as they continue to encounter it in their social environments.

## The "Negative" Emotions of Oppression

As a sustained threat, oppression is perpetuated through a negativity bias reinforced through negative emotions. The key negative emotion identified by researchers associated with oppression is shame, alongside the related emotions of self-doubt, suppression, and anger (as frustration).

### *Shame*

For the oppressed, the dominant negative emotion of oppression is shame. Shame is dominated by impulses to inhibit and conceal that lead to self-silencing (Deigh, 1983; Bartky, 1990; Manne, 2021). Deigh (1983) critiques early distinctions between shame and guilt that characterized shame as an emotion associated with failure and guilt with transgression, associated with the idea that "shame is felt over shortcomings, guilt over wrongdoings" (p. 225). Instead, Deigh concluded that shame was a self-protective emotion with two key characteristics or impulses: to inhibit and to conceal. In particular, shame is a response to the social threat of *humiliation*. As a defence against humiliation, shame protects the self by inhibiting and concealing the self to avoid social exposure with its associated threats of ridicule or sanctions. This same emotion of shame is responsible for internalizing oppression in the face of threatening social norms or biases against one's identity group. While guilt *may* function positively to safeguard morals, goals, and norms, the same is not true of shame. Shame is a disabling emotion, harming both consciousness and agency by concealing feelings of inferiority and inhibiting action in the world. As a result, oppression-related shame is something to be *unlearned* and overcome for wellbeing.

Bartky (1990) described the shame arising from oppression as "a pervasive sense of personal inadequacy that, like the shame of embodiment, is profoundly disempowering" leading to "a pervasive affective [negative] attunement to the social environment" (p. 85). Oppression-related shame is a habitual *flight* response from perceived (social) environmental threats, with the body shrinking to reduce itself in a gesture of flight from the perceived source of threat: head down, shoulders and back curved as panic ensues with raised heart rates, adrenaline, and other stress hormones that make it difficult to function effectively. In this respect, it is a chronic stress response to sustained threat. Furthermore, this flight response can switch to a fight response characterized by exaggerated defensiveness or defiance. Like the body, the mind so debilitated by shame is held back, too, and prevented from seeing the world accurately by a limited, habitual appraisal of circumstances as threatening that serves to reinforce a socially inscribed, harmful narrative about one's limitations and possibilities. In this respect, oppression is driven by fear and the sense of a looming and *sustained* threat. At the same time, this points to the importance of courage (as perseverance) and mindfulness (as "self-possession," the original term used to translate *sati*, and self-regulation) as an antidote to oppression-related fear.

### *Self-Doubt, Suppression, and Anger*

Three related negative-valence emotions of oppression are self-doubt, suppression, and anger. Once internalized, oppression functions like a virus of the self, eroding confidence and instilling self-doubt. The (social) environment can reinforce such self-doubt through ongoing interactions with both oppressors and the oppressed. Together, shame and self-doubt enhance susceptibility to expressive suppression that can inhibit the recognition and expression of other emotions. Such suppression can lead to frustration erupting in unregulated anger, a kind of "leaking" in response to suppressive controls. Such dysregulated anger arising from frustration is quite different from anger channelled as righteous indignation as one moves out of oppression (see discussion of anger in the emotions of liberation). This kind of frustrated anger may manifest as irritation.

## The "Neutral" Emotions of Oppression

Emotions with neutral valence reinforce impulses to avoid sustained threats by ignoring, downplaying, or not noticing information, people, and experiences within oppressive environments. In oppression, the dominant neutral emotions are indifference (as dissociation) and ignorance (as dullness or delusion), both of which can lead to either a freezing or fawning response.

### *Indifference (from Dissociation)*

With oppression, there can be a numbing of emotions and a curtailing of the capacity to respond, not unlike the dissociation associated with post-traumatic stress responses. This points to a challenge of oppression, whereby the combination of shame, as inhibition and concealment, combined with such numbing or dissociation, can make it difficult to discern the signs and indicators of oppression needed to motivate one to move out of the condition. This dissociative indifference can lead the oppressed further down the rabbit hole of habituating to oppressive states and conditions.

### *Ignorance (from Dullness and Delusion)*

Ignorance as dullness involves contracting or losing attention so as to miss information available in present experience. Ultimately, it involves the weakening of self-awareness, whereby critical information concerning oneself or the environment is overlooked. The broadening of awareness associated with mindfulness, as outlined in the mindfulness-to-meaning theory or MMT, suggests that as mindfulness expands awareness it leads to downstream effects on enhanced meaning and the capacity to savour experiences(Garland et al., 2015). In this respect, using reverse logic, the constriction of awareness associated with ignorance as dullness leads to a reduction of the capacity to savour experience and to derive meaning, with implications for wellbeing.

Ignorance as delusion, on the other hand, refers to the tendency of the oppressed to form a "false consciousness" to overlook or misconstrue how they interpret oppression in their social environments. Arguably more of a cognitive habit than an emotion, this kind of ignorance involves the active deployment of false appraisals to divert attention away from the difficult knowledge of oppression. In oppression, both forms of ignorance function as avoidance strategies to distract attention from the awareness of oppression. It is worth mentioning that in Buddhist psychology, the critical afflictive emotion is ignorance as it is considered to ultimately obstruct liberation.

## The "Positive" Emotions of Oppression

Apparent positive emotions can also contribute to sustaining the threat of oppression. Two examples described below are empathy and hope.

### *Empathy*

Empathy imagines others' suffering and generates similar affective responses in oneself through identification. It is a vicarious experience, aimed at understanding others without direct communication. Harris (2014) emphasized empathy as a way to foster pro-social behaviours like cooperation and coordination between in-group members, thereby cultivating solidarity and social action within oppressed communities. Yet exposure to other in-group members who suffer from oppression, whether in the family or in the community, may also involve secondary traumatic stressors and vicarious or intergenerational traumas that can magnify and reinforce personal oppression-related traumas (Leung et al., 2023). Indeed, recent research in affective neuroscience has raised question about the link between empathy and pro-social behaviour given that it can lead to increasing personal distress rather than empathic concern. Stevens and Taber (2021) advocate combining empathy with compassion, a more action-oriented response, as way to cultivate enhanced pro-social effects, a topic covered in more detail later in the chapter. Furthermore, as Manne's (2021) critique of *himpathy* demonstrates well, empathy can be misdirected towards oppressors in ways that legitimate and reinforce their abuses and aggression, thereby fuelling oppression.

### *Hope (with Certainty)*

Hope is another emotion with a seemingly positive valence that can reinforce threat-avoidance in a counter-productive way. Hope has a long history in being presented as an emotion associated with optimism for the oppressed (e.g., Stockdale, 2021; Solnit, 2016); however, it is important to recognize that as much as it may provide relief and refuge, hope can be an avoidance strategy to shift attention from the present struggle against oppression to the fantasy of relief in an imagined future. Stolnit distinguishes these two kinds of hope by their certainty versus uncertainty. As certainty, hope is a fantasy of the inevitability of a future release from suffering that serves to distract from and avoid its present tangibility. This harkens back to Marx's "religion is the opiate of the people," which seems to equate religious hope in future redemption with drug-induced delusions. The full quote, however, clarifies that he seems to refer to the false hope it engenders: "Religion is the opium of the people. It is the sigh of the oppressed creature, the heart of a heartless world, and the soul of our soulless conditions" (Papke, 2015). As harsh as this critique may seem, it is important to recognize the truth it sheds on oppression. Religion can serve as a source of solidarity and support for anti-oppressive action or as a way to divert and avoid it.

I learned the problem with hope from my mother, who was oppressed as a woman both in her marriage (which she acknowledged) and as a mother (which she didn't). Her unhappiness and lack of social support led to what she called her "conversion experience", which didn't fit well with her Anglican upbringing. Finding herself more and more isolated, she struggled against the rather subdued forms of Anglican devotion until deciding to convert to Catholicism. This decision only accentuated her status as a cultural outsider, distancing her further from her own family and community, while eliminating the one practical step she might have taken to escape her oppression: divorcing my father.

Instead, inspired by classical continental European literature, such as the works of Tolstoy, Dostoevsky, and Hugo, she became preoccupied with the suffering of prisoners, with whom she identified, spending considerable money and time buying, packaging, and sending these books to inmates in penitentiaries, who for a time became her imagined community. Her religion was coloured by a fanatical, miraculous hope for a future after death, a future with the promise of eternal relief from suffering, which she believed she would earn as redemption for her perseverance. That her children's wellbeing was sacrificed in the process *did* concern her, but she deflected such worries by including us in her hopes for heaven. In this way, hope became a path of learned helplessness for her and our entire family. Despite the deepening strains it placed on her relations with her children, husband, extended family, and friendship, she persisted in her ecstatic devotion to an afterlife free of suffering, leaving the problems of the present unaddressed. As she aged and eventually did divorce, she repeated her wish to die and join Jesus in heaven rather than to address the challenges of the present here on Earth.

As a child, I saw her cry often in distress. I couldn't understand why she was so unhappy when my unmarried, childless paternal aunts seemed so content. I presumed marriage and children made people happier, so I was left quite confused. As this bind became clearer to me with time, I worried that I might not marry, on the one hand, or that I might marry, on the other, and end up unhappy like she was. So, at just 4 years of age, I constantly sought advice from her about who I might marry. She would laugh, dismissing my concerns as childish: "Don't worry. When that time comes, you'll find someone." Later she would add: "Just because I have a bad marriage, doesn't mean you will." This was her habitual response based on an uncritical hope in an imagined future generated against all evidence. In the end, I gave a boy on the street a dime for a chocolate bar if he promised to marry me. He accepted but then, dime in hand, reneged on his promise and ran away, laughing. Bulgarian writer Maria Popova called for a balancing of critical thinking and hope: "Critical thinking without hope is cynicism, but hope without critical thinking is naivete" (in Solnit, 2016). As Solnit herself argues in *Hope in the Dark*, when hope is held alongside the uncertainty of all imagined futures, only then does it become a resource against oppression.

## The Emotions of Oppressors

Oppressors can themselves be oppressed and belong to the same identity community as those they are oppressing, including in the family; however, more often, they are the members of dominant out-groups. Although subject to different emotions, oppressors also experience emotions that diminish their wellbeing (see Table 4.2).

## The "Negative" Emotions of Oppressors

Entitlement (a positive valence emotion) gives rise to the negative emotions of oppressors, all connected to anger arising in the face of perceived threats to entitlement.

### *Anger (from Unmet Expectations)*

Anger is a complex and ambiguous emotion in oppression, appearing in its generation, perpetuation, and removal. As an approach emotion (i.e., forward moving and confronting), anger is associated with both positive (reparative) and negative (aggressive) social behaviours. Usually, it arises when we don't get what we want and the perceived obstacle is an agent or person. When misfortune arises from bad luck, the emotion might naturally be a subdued kind of disappointment. Yet, in contrast to this kind of disappointment, Zitek and Jordan (2021) described increased anger and perceptions of unfairness in those with higher degrees of psychological entitlement when facing personal experiences of bad luck. This anger led the more entitled to blame out-group members as scapegoats for their bad luck and for the perceived unfairness of their circumstances. This tendency may explain the intense anger, bordering on disgust, that typifies right wing political rhetoric opposing diversity, equity, and inclusion and their unwarranted claims that they undermine merit. In fact, many DEI policies are intended to protect merit as a standard in the face of known implicit biases that unfairly discriminate against qualified members of marginalized groups.

### *Anger (as Afflicted Pride)*

Nussbaum (2015) argues that "the idea of anger as a central threat to decent human interactions runs through the Western philosophical tradition" (p. 41). This is based on interpreting anger as the desire for retribution for significant injuries or for wrongful acts affecting status – what Aristotle refers to as "down-ranking." He defined anger, accordingly, as "a desire accompanied by pain for an imagined retribution on account of an imagined slighting inflicted by people who have no legitimate reason to slight oneself or one's own" (1378131–3) (p. 42). Five components characterize this form of anger: "[an imagined] slighting or down-ranking; of the self or people close to the self; wrongful or inappropriately done; accompanied by pain; and linked to a desire for [an imagined] retribution" (p. 42).

As Nussbaum's (2015) opening quotation by Aristotle makes clear, this view of anger is a response to offences to status that arise from afflicted pride, when a victim is down-ranked according to their own "imagined" status and sense of entitlement. Entitlements are not rights but rather unrealistic expectations for goods one perceives as owed to oneself. Therefore, the sense of entitlement behind such anger suggests that it is a form of anger experienced by oppressors rather than the oppressed. To not be "wrongful," the correct or apt behaviour of the oppressed is explicitly described as being humble and silent (associated with the shame of oppression). Aristotle uses as evidence oppressors of "imagined status" who feel calm when the oppressed "acknowledge that they are our inferiors" by demonstrating obedience, humility, and silence:

> We feel calm toward those who humble themselves before us and do not talk back. For they seem to acknowledge that they are our inferiors. ... That our anger ceases toward those who humble themselves before us is shown even by dogs, who do not bite people when they sit down. – Aristotle, Rhetoric, 1380a21–25.
>
> (in Nussbaum, 2015, p. 41)

Two aspects of such anger distinguish it from anger as righteous indignation, an emotion of liberation. First, Aristotle defines such afflicted anger as emanating from a pain generated by an *imagined* (vs. actual) slighting and involving an *imagined* retribution for a personal, rather than collective, slight injury. Yet, in the case of anger arising through the process of liberating oneself from states of oppression, the emotion arises from pains associated with *actual* injuries requiring actual correction (vs. retribution) if the injuries are to be prevented from causing future harms to oneself or others.

### *Contempt*

Contempt is another collective social emotion associated with both anger and oppression. Fischer et al. (2022) present contempt as an extension of anger that foreshadows divisions and ruptures between people or groups. Contempt diminishes the other, paving the way for their maltreatment by casting them as inferior or incompetent. Karppinen et al. (2023) differentiate contempt, as appraising someone as being unworthy or incompetent, from disgust, which is related to contamination and purity. In their study, they found that it was disgust, more than contempt, that predicted aggressive behaviour and less reparative action in personal relations.

### *Disgust*

Karppinen et al. (2023) investigated the relation between anger, contempt, and disgust in personal relationships (romantic and friendship), finding that anger led to reparation but not to aggression. Their findings were consistent with the theory that anger serves the social function of attempting to change other people's behaviour. Furthermore, they found that disgust, more than contempt, involved less reparation and more aggression *in friendships*. In this respect, contempt and, even moreso, disgust may be the derivatives of anger that are most directly involved in oppressing others. Yet a critical limitation here is the question of how closely emotions involved in interpersonal romance and friendships mirror those in more socially distanced relations.

## The "Neutral" Emotions of Oppressors

Indifference and ignorance are two *neutral* emotions associated with oppressors, the same two identified in the oppressed but with significant differences. That the same general emotions are involved suggests that certain emotions shape oppression in perpetrators and victims alike. This reinforces the need to see oppression ultimately as a disorder of consciousness rather than as a set of behaviours or attitudes.

### *Indifference (Non-Empathic)*

Indifference, for oppressors, arises as a lack of empathy for the suffering of outgroup members. Such indifference is associated with "collective narcissism," an exaggerated sense of the greatness of one's group with a corresponding cognitive belief that the group is not adequately recognized (Golec de Zavala et al., 2022). Montoya et al. (2020) identified four factors in collective narcissism: entitlement/exploitativeness, dominance/arrogance, apathy, and admiration. Apathy and entitlement/exploitativeness were responsible for negative intergroup responses while dominance/arrogance was responsible for ingroup-enhancing responses. Accordingly, collective narcissism gives rise to oppression through group identification, ingroup loyalty, and outgroup hostility. Apathy describes the muted empathy felt towards outgroup members and reinforces the belief of the inferiority of outgroup members leading to their exclusion and ultimately feeding hostilities directed against the outgroup.

### *Ignorance (from Delusion)*

The other neutral emotion in oppressors is ignorance. Like that described in the oppressed, this form of ignorance involves delusions; however, for oppressors, the emotive aspect of ignorance stems from collective narcissism with its entitlement and arrogance, while the cognitive side stems from the committed belief in the greatness of the ingroup alongside the threatening belief that they are unrecognized or under-appreciated. These combined beliefs make collective narcissists prone to delusional conspiracy theories that can reinforce irrational motives to oppress out-group members through unfounded theories about the threats they pose (Golec de Zavala et al., 2022; Neville et al., 2024).

Collective narcissism based on nationalism and gender are related. Golec de Zavala and Keenan (2024) compared national and gender collective narcissism in Poland with respect to their impacts on views about gender equality. They found that gender collective narcissism among women predicted an overall egalitarian outlook and intentions to engage in collective action *for* gender equality, whereas for men, increased gender collective narcissism led them to reject gender equality altogether. Increased national collective narcissism, on the other hand, predicted negative attitudes towards gender equality and the refusal to support it in both men and women. In these ways, collective narcissism can be said to generate combined emotional and cognitive conditions in which oppressors are supported and legitimated in their discriminatory attitudes towards women and minorities conceived of as threats to their perceived entitlements. Taken together, we can conclude that collective narcissism gives rise to a form of ignorance that combines emotional afflictions (e.g., toxic pride and anger) with cognitive distortions (i.e., inflating the belief of the greatness of one's identity group and the relative inferiority of outgroup members).

## The "Positive" Emotions of Oppressors

### *Entitlement*

Entitlement is a dominant emotion in oppressors, and on superficial consideration, it would seem to be a positive valence emotion. I classify it as positive because it emboldens confidence, albeit unreasonably, without justification, and at the expense of others. Yet, as research suggests, because it is associated with downstream distress, thereby giving rise ultimately to a negative affective tone, entitlement's classification is ambiguous. Deriving from internalized norms and beliefs, entitlement can present as being more cognitive than emotional, as a set of ideas about oneself, one's identity group, and out-group; however, on closer examination, entitlement is also a collective emotion characterized by inflated arrogance and pride giving rise to false assumptions and beliefs about one's relative superiority. The emotion drives the implicit bias and belief rather than vice versa. Research links entitlement with deservingness, specialness, and exaggerated expectations that lead to discriminatory behaviours and acts that can further suppress or burden the oppressed (Deigh, 1983; Grubbs & Exline, 2016; Manne, 2021).

### *Expectancy*

Entitlement occupies a classification spectrum from being a collective emotion to a cognition to a personality trait to a mental disorder. As a collective emotion, it is associated with an exaggerated, presumptive pride with a distorted assumption of privilege and rights that can lead to unrealistic expectations. As mentioned, although seemingly positive in affective tone, entitlement is a potential source of vulnerability to psychological distress. Grubbs and Exline (2016) refer to this as the "dark or pathological side of entitlement," demonstrating how, as a personality trait, entitlement can lead to inflated, unreasonable expectations that make the entitled vulnerable to ongoing and escalating distress. As an initial inflated sense of deservedness gives rise to unmet expectations, it further fuels chronic disappointment, ego threat, and perceived injustice. These, in turn, lead to psychological distress indicators like anger, volatile emotions, and disappointment across multiple life domains. This is in contrast to healthy or adaptive forms entitlement based on reasonable expectations for basic rights that research suggests often predict enhanced self-esteem and adaptive self-confidence.

### *Himpathy*

Manne (2021) argues that entitlement fuels misogyny by reinforcing male privilege, patriarchy, and what she calls *himpathy*. *Himpathy* refers to an unjustified, sympathetic response by women and men towards men who are denied traditional masculine goods, such as "power, authority, and claims to knowledge," and sanctions women who attempt to claim them. Women, in turn, are expected to give traditionally female goods to men like "sex, caring, nurturing, and reproductive labour" (p. 11). Consequently, misogyny is not the hatred of women so much as the acceptance of collective entitlements that favour men, obligate women, and subject women to unfair sanctions for claiming comparable gendered social goods. The presumptions of entitlement, including *himpathy*, are emotional states that, when frustrated, give rise to anger manifesting as hatred and hostility towards women perceived to be obstacles to the expected privileges to which (some) men feel entitled. In this respect, this seemingly positive emotion of expectancy for positive outcomes or goods harbours a more sinister and distressing aspect (Grubbs & Exline, 2016)

## The Emotions of Liberation

Liberation is a broad concept associated with wide-ranging conditions from idealism to personal freedom to social upheaval to violent transformation through war and revolution. Here, I use it specifically to refer to an intrapsychic condition of liberation *from* oppression. The emotions of liberation are those associated with the process of liberation as well as the state of liberation itself. Therefore, they are most relevant to those who were either previously oppressed or susceptible to oppression but resisted or overcame it. As a state free of oppression, liberation implies a state of enhanced wellbeing. As wellbeing, liberation avails one of at least some of the emotions and conditions needed to flourish. These emotions derive from all three affective tones working together to foster agency and engagement and to reduce avoidance tendencies.

That said, although I label them as negative, neutral, or positive, the emotions of liberation don't adhere to a valence in the same way as emotions of oppression. Emotions of oppression maintain their valences throughout their implicit, habitual, and conditioned formation and expression. Emotions of liberation, on the other hand, arise through conscious and mindful encounters with experiences in the present. In this way, mindfulness cultivates a distinctive type of positive affective tone that is different from the habitual positive affective tone of conditioned, sensory-based experience, such as tasting food that we find delicious. For example, when bringing mindful attention to otherwise neutral or even negative experiences, rather than avoiding or ignoring it, you may notice that the affective tone shifts from negative or neutral to positive. This positive affect arises from the curiosity, interest, and engagement cultivated through mindfulness. This is reflected in Buddhist psychology's theory of the seven factors of enlightenment, where the emotion of *joy* or *bliss (piti)* is represented as arising from the first three (mindfulness, investigation, energy = a state of interest).

The wellbeing arising from mindfulness is not mere happiness. Closer to the Aristotelean concept of *eudaimonia*, often translated as *flourishing*, this form of wellbeing is at once both objective and subjective, personal and collective. Calling it "liberation" accentuates the critical role of struggle and resistance in anti-oppressive praxis, which may entail deferring present pleasures for broader long-term objectives. Ahmed (2010) critiques the problem with a narrow focus on "happiness" through cases of "feminist killjoys," "unhappy queers," and "melancholic migrants." She questions the idealism and naive hope of the desire to move beyond suffering, asserting instead the value of what is, in essence, mindfulness: that is, attending to "wanted and unwanted feelings":

> The desire to get over suffering is of course an understandable desire, one that might express a longing to do more than describe social relations of force and harm. … [Yet,] to recover can be to re-cover, to cover over the causes of pain and suffering. … We might need to attend to bad feelings not in order to overcome them but *to learn how we are affected by what comes near*, which means achieving a different relationship to all our wanted and unwanted feelings as an ethical resource.
>
> (p. 216)

How does the mere awareness of emotions through mindfulness transform them into an ethical resource for liberation? *Decentring* is a construct used to describe what seems to distinguish habitually reactive emotional states from mindful emotional states (Garland et al., 2015; Segal et al., 2019; Guo, 2024). Decentring shifts perspectives from a narrow, self-centred attention to a broadened and more open view. In mindfulness, decentring involves the shift from self-referential to momentary experiencing evident in MRI studies (Farb et al., 2007). Both Buddhism and science view decentring as a process of cognitive transformation, marked by the shift from affliction to psychological health or liberation; however, Buddhism describes it as stepping outside of self-centred frames of reference, whereas cognitive science understands it differently as "disidentification and non-reactivity to mental events" (Guo, 2024, p. 1875). These two interpretations differ in the emphasis placed on deconstructing the self and on the relative role of the self in consciousness (see the next chapter).

Investigating the relationships between mindfulness, decentring, and psychological problems, Guo (2024) conducted a meta-analysis of 57 studies with 110 effect sizes from 18,515 participants. This analysis found that mindfulness exerts a large positive direct effect on decentring and a small-to-medium negative effect on psychological problems. Decentring had a modest negative direct effect on psychological problems and a small but significant indirect effect on the relations between mindfulness and psychological problems. In this way, mindfulness appears to increase decentring, thereby decreasing psychological problems and improving wellbeing. In this respect, decentring may be the value-added component of mindfulness that enables a practitioner to move through oppression to arrive at a form of liberation on the other side.

## The "Negative" Emotions of Liberation

To be human is to experience *many* emotions. Liberation from oppression doesn't mean transcening emotions so much as enhancing the flexible expression of emotions in ways that promote flourishing. What liberation *does* remove though is the affliction associated with emotions and their capacity to prolong distress. Emotions – negative, neutral, or positive – are experienced as passing through consciousness much like sensations, in varied and impermanent manifestations responding to circumstances. They just don't habitually "stick" in the same way as they might have in the grasp of oppression, including "attunement to shame". Reducing or removing oppressing emotions naturally leave a state of free of disturbing emotions, replaced by the emotions of wellbeing. In Buddhist psychology, these are four of seven factors of awakening: perseverance, joy, calm, and equanimity. These factors of awakening or wellbeing develop from the effortful application of mindfulness, investigation, and energy (perseverance) – as *interest* and reinforced through concentration, the sixth factor; however, this is not to suggest that the emotions of liberation are necessarily *positive*. There are some negative and neutral valence emotions associated with liberation, especially when extricating oneself from oppression. I explore three of these negative or neutral emotions of liberation below: anger (from indignation), perseverance, and equanimity.

*Anger (as Righteous Indignation)*

Arising from a perceived harm, anger is a reactive gesture of the mind directed at protecting oneself (and kin or social group) by changing others. Alhough it can be directed at the self, anger tends to arise from personal, interpersonal, or social dissatisfaction and the desire for change oneself or, more commonly, others, which can lead to aggression but also to making amends or reparative action (Karppinen et al., 2023). Despite its association with personal and social transformation, anger is impugned in human history – by Aristotle, the Stoics, and Buddhists and by their modern re-interpreters (Nussbaum, 2015; Wallace & Jinpa, 2003). More recently, scholars and psychologists are highlighting and redeeming anger in the name of affective justice. Given that anger is an apt and reasonable response to the harms of discrimination and oppression, it is unjust to judge the oppressed for having or expressing such an emotion. Instead, as a form of righteous indignation seeking change, anger is considered to be a constructive emotion for those liberating themselves and others from oppression (Archer & Mills, 2019; Srinivasan, 2018).

Srinivasan (2018) and Archer and Mills (2019) argue that the social expectation to control anger puts unequal pressure on the oppressed to regulate an emotion that is apt to their unjust circumstances in a way that may compel them either to disregard their oppression or to regulate it through suppression in harmful ways. In this respect, normalizing anger as an expression of the desire for personal or collective change is a critical component of anti-oppressive praxis. In directing agency and attention externally to insist on change, this type of anger might be called *righteous indignation*. Such anger is a natural emotion to arise when becoming liberated from unjust situations and circumstances. Freed of the inhibitions and concealment associated with oppression-based shame, anger is a natural expression in the transition to greater freedom and liberation. Furthermore, it can channel energy for social action to deepen liberation from a merely personal to a broader collective significance. African-American poet and activist Audre Lorde (1984) expressed this in her essay on "The uses of anger":

> Every woman has a well-stocked arsenal of anger potentially useful against those oppressions, personal and institutional, which brought that anger into being. Focused with precision, it can become a powerful source of energy serving progress and change.
>
> (p. 127)

## The Neutral Emotions of Liberation

Although the following emotions associated with liberation are categorized as having a neutral valence, it doesn't mean that they are necessarily neutral in their effects or that they are experienced with indifference. They are "neutral" in that they expand the capacity to experience stimuli of all valences with increasing ease rather than engendering a distinctive mood.

### *Perseverance*

Perseverance, as a kind of patience, is not a classic emotion so much as a capacity to weather other emotions and distressing states. Perseverance, originally meaning "abiding + strictly," is not a wilful and directed mind so much as a strong, stable, and disciplined quality of attention. Given its capacity to endure in the face of unwanted and challenging experiences, I label it (imperfectly) as a neutral valence emotion that supports liberation. A pivotal "emotion" of mindfulness, perseverance functions to sustain attention on experiences without judgement, including unwanted or otherwise ignored experiences that might otherwise be avoided. Mindfulness works in part through supporting this capacity for perseverance, thereby interrupting approach/avoidance habits associated with distressful states, such as those associated with addiction or depression. The *intention* to heal combines with the regulation of *attention* to enable the self-regulatory capacities of consciousness to shift experience towards wellbeing.

Perseverance is closely related to *viriya* (energy), the third of seven factors of enlightenment in Buddhist psychology. Etymologically related to both *virile*, as power and potency, and *virtue*, as moral valour, viriya is often translated as *energy* but further suggests effort and discipline. Etymologically, the world effort, for its part, refers to a directed (*ex*, for "out") type of strength (*forte*, for "strong"), a kind of motivated forward movement of consciousness and action. While matter may move and interact without effort through natural forces, life forms move principally through the mediation of consciousness, with effort, even in such basic actions as waking up and getting out of bed in the morning. In this respect, viriya and perseverance are where intention and attention intersect. In the seven factors, energy (viriya) follows mindfulness (sati) and investigation (dhamma-vicaya) to generate a state of sustained interest, with the final four arising effortlessly in succession from such interest: joy, calm, concentration, and equanimity.

### *Equanimity*

*Equanimity* is the culminating emotion or mind state of the seven factors of enlightenment (or awakening). As the ultimate or end-state of mindfulness proposed in Buddhist psychology, it is the "emotion" or state in which liberation becomes possible. Equanimity refers to a state in which all experience is attended to with equal interest and attention, regardless of its affective tone (negative, neutral, positive). This gives it a quality of objectivity, though a kind of objectivity that includes joy, the fourth factor. In this respect, though equanimity may seem like the absence of emotions, that would be an incorrect conclusion. It is the absence of conditioned emotions that drive conditioned, habitual responses and attention. Also, the seven factors are not sequential so much as cumulative in that each factor contributes to the previous one(s) to generate a stronger and more resilient state of consciousness. Equanimity is not indifference nor is it classically "neutral" but highly "interested" and engaged while stable and balanced. This is reflected in the definition by the Buddhist scholar Buddhaghosa that depicts equanimity as "a balance of arousal without hyperexcitability or fatigue" (Vago & Silbersweig, 2012, p. 2).

Juneau et al. (2020) theorized mindfulness-based equanimity to have two factors, which they validated for use in a questionnaire: an even-minded state of mind (E-MSM) and hedonic independence (HI). Even-mindedness described a state of reduced emotional interference, greater emotional stability, and enhanced inner peace with reduced distress, a calm, stable, and non-reactive state in which decisions and behaviours are "the least contaminated by stress and arousal as possible." From other studies, they found evidence that mindfulness-based equanimity decoupled initial approach/avoidance craving reactions from their hedonic tone (e.g., positive affect), thereby decreasing the approach/avoidance reactions associated with addiction. On validating their questionnaire, they concluded that E-MSM was positively related to emotional stability, adaptive emotional regulation, and mindfulness-related abilities, and HI was correlated negatively with addiction-related tendencies. In lay terms, this suggests that mindfulness-based equanimity fosters enhanced emotional stability with benefits for decision-making and decreased approach/avoidance to experience pleasure freer from conditioned reactivity and habitual or addictive behaviours.

## The Positive Emotions of Liberation

Bearing in mind Ahmed's (2010) critique of the narrow pursuit of happiness in her book *The Promise of Happiness,* what defines liberation from oppression must surely be a state of enhanced wellbeing, including a felt, subjective sense of increased happiness and flourishing. Otherwise, liberation from oppression would just be an abstract theory speculating on the redistribution of social goods. It seems fair to assume a natural motivation for such liberation from oppression given the implications for consciousness and life quality. We might reference self-determination theory here and the natural motivation for autonomy as part of this motivation for liberation. Research in self-determination theory has demonstrated a strong relationship between autonomy, mindfulness, and wellbeing, leading the theorists to further corroborate their claim that autonomy, and the struggle to attain and sustain autonomy, is a natural intrinsic motivation associated with embodied consciousness in living systems (Ryan & Deci, 2000, 2020). Therefore, it is natural to expect certain emotions with a positive valence to be associated with liberation to be related to autonomy. I have narrowed these down to four: joy, hope (as uncertainty), self-possession, and compassion.

### *Joy*

As the fourth of the seven factors of enlightenment theory, *joy* is a key emotion demarcating the factors that require effort (mindfulness, investigation, energy) and together form a state we might describe as *interest* or *interest-taking* (Rigby et al., 2014). Note that this *joy* is not merely happiness but a kind of *bliss* (piti), connected to the body with physical, not just mental, qualities. Although now a trope from the past, Joseph Campbell's popular advice from *The Power of Myth* comes to mind: "follow your bliss." He was in fact advising people to follow their interest, which they might discern through the presence of joy. This corresponds to the later theory, MMT, which posited positive emotions like joy as a downstream effect of mindfulness, ultimately culminating in wellbeing through increased meaning and capacities to savour experience (Garland et al., 2015).

### *Hope (with Uncertainty)*

There is a less afflicted form of hope that people experience in the process of becoming liberated from oppression. Such hope develops from the optimism that nonetheless recognizes, realistically, the uncertainty of the future without erring to the side of elation (fantasy) or dread (cynicism). Our sense of the future is always imagined, predicted, or constructed, often to reduce anxiety and uncertainty, often to control perceived threats. To live at ease with uncertainty is hopeful because it highlights the probability of unexpected outcomes, thereby acknowledging the need to adapt to, rather than avoid, accommodate, or control, change. In my experience, the future is often surprisingly better than what we imagined, even in our best-case scenario, because it includes the unpredictable, unimaginable, and impossible. In this way, uncertainty opens our awareness to possibility, not just probability and expectancy.

Such radical hope makes possible the unbounded energy and agency required to help others to resist oppression. Too often we continue to live in the thrall of a deterministic, Newtonian universe in which we are captive to cause-effect structures in which agency is irrelevant. Yet we have known this view to be in error for decades now, via quantum insights that consciousness itself impacts the future, with the possibility of generating even highly improbable outcomes (Siegal, 2016). This is why this kind of uncertain hope is more realistic and not idealistic or naively optimistic. It is closer to the truth of things.

### *Self-Possession*

The original phrase used to translate *sati* into English was "mindful and self-possessed," employed by Rhys Davids in his 1899 translation of the *Digha Nikaya* to translate the repeated reference to *sato sampajano* (i.e., mindfulness with clear comprehension). In his later 1910 edition, he replaced this phrase with the single term "mindfulness," which became the accepted standard (Gethin, 2011). Yet I think there is something in this idea of "self-possession" worth retaining to describe liberation from oppression, especially given the connection with mindfulness.

According to the *OED*, "self-possession" evolved in use from the 17th century, when it referred to a kind of patience, to mean being confident, poised, calm, and having control over the body (describing ponies climbing stairs). The current definition is to be in command and control of feelings. In considering this term, Rhys Davids was no doubt trying to represent the self-regulatory effects of mindfulness. I use it here in the context of the psychology of oppression as a state of self-possession: that is, the experience of autonomy over one's body and mind. Furthermore, I am claiming that it is an emotion (positive valence) common to the experience of liberation, or becoming liberated, from oppression.

This emotion arose for me most clearly and distinctly in 2016, during an MBSR teacher training intensive. I had arrived in Toronto after a busy term, exhausted by the demands on my body, attention, and time from students, colleagues, staff, family, friends, dogs, and now travel. After doing a body scan together, we conducted an inquiry into the experience. I recounted how, by refocusing attention on my legs and other parts of my body, the practice had helped me to reclaim my bodily integrity and the autonomy it signified. With ithis sense of self-possession came an experience of exquisite pleasure. Several years later, during a silent retreat I was facilitating, I shared this experience with participants. At the end of the retreat, a mother of three young children came to say goodbye and expressed gratitude for the opportunity to experience this same emotional quality or state. She described her relief and pleasure at being freed for a time from the endless claims – poking, prodding, touching, hugging, etc. – made by her children over her bodily autonomy, which had eroded her patience and forbearance. Now, she said, she felt refuelled and eager to be with them again.

### *Self-Confidence (Non-afficted Pride)*

Self-confidence is a non-afflicted pride with positive affect. As a distinctive emotion of liberation distinguishable from the afflicted pride of some forms of anger, self-confidence derives from a realistic and reasonable recognition of rights possessed by the self rather an oppressor's sense of imagined privileges believed to be wrongfully withheld. The pride generating self-confidence reinforces agency and autonomy. Such self-confidence replaces the shame (inhibition; concealment) and self-doubt of oppression with the interest-taking, agency, and willingness to enact the self in the world, including taking risks. Such self-confidence relies on intrinsic motivators and loci of control and the autonomy associated with mindfulness and wellbeing (Ryan & Deci, 2000, 2020; Rigby et al., 2014; Roth et al., 2019).

### *Compassion*

A growing body of scholarship is linking mindfulness to compassion, and both to liberation from oppression, as a combined strategy for "metabolizing personal and collective trauma" (Owens, 2023). A positive valence emotion, compassion involves a deep concern with, and action-orientation towards, suffering, including oppression. As an action-oriented response to suffering oriented on mitigating it, compassion is distinct from, though related to, empathy. Meta-analytic studies suggest that mindfulness is associated with both compassion (Luberto et al., 2018) and self-compassion (Wasson et al., 2020). Also, compassion appears to be both a transitional emotion, motivating the oppressed to liberate themselves and others from oppression, and a culminating emotion characterizing the state of liberation.

Kolchraiber et al. (2025), for example, reported on a qualitative case study of a mixed meditative approach introduced in Brazil targeting people at-risk from diverse systems of oppression (93% women; 78% black). The meditation system, referred to as cognitively-based compassion training (CBCT) combined mindfulness (aka "resilience"), compassion training, and cognitive behaviour therapy. Results suggested that structural oppressions and individual autonomy were negative related and the value of "strengthening of care in the collective dimension." As one manager reported: "The team and the community began to understand that they have to work on their body and mind, an internal process from the inside (person and team) to the outside (community)." Another participant concluded: "The spontaneous process of caring for the community was important to recognize that one was capable of caring for oneself and caring for other people."

## Self-Regulating Emotions

The oppressed, oppressors, and those becoming liberated from oppression each show distinctive approaches to emotion regulation that impact their autonomy and wellbeing. Emotion regulation refers to the activities and strategies a person uses to experience, modulate, and express emotions. A useful framework for emotion regulation comes from Roth et al. (2019), who proposed an integrative emotion regulation (IER) model using self-determination theory. They focus on emotion regulation given its critical role in autonomy and self-determination, critical areas of attention for the oppressed, who can suffer from self-doubt and reduced self-efficacy. Emotion regulation is key to autonomous functioning at the internal boundary of the self, both helping to define the self and how it is expressed. The resulting autonomy brings positive impacts on motivation (e.g., intrinsic), emotions (e.g., self-confidence), and consciousness itself (autonomy being one of seven attributes of consciousness, with implications for agency – see Chapter 5). In this way, emotion regulation is a key component of self-efficacy and wellbeing, as the capacity to flourish and fulfil our intentions.

## Emotion Regulation Processes

Roth et al.'s (2019) used self-determination theory to propose three forms of emotion regulation: (i) integrated (IER), (ii) controlled, and (iii) amotivated emotion regulation styles. As Table 4.5 displays, amotivated and controlled emotion regulation are associated with oppression (and oppressing), while IER is associated with liberation as well as mindfulness and wellbeing (Ryan et al., 2021). MRI studies suggest that these distinctive regulation styles are also associated with different brain systems, principally involving the PFC and its modulation and inhibition or disinhibition of the emotion centres, such as the amygdala and other components of the limbic system.

### Emotion Regulation in Oppression: Controlled and Amotivated

Controlled or amotivated forms of emotion regulation are associated with oppression, both in the oppressed and the oppressors. Controlled emotion regulation involves suppressing unwanted emotions or feigning unfelt emotions, whereas amotivated forms involve a lack of regulation altogether, characterized by impulsivity and the unfiltered expression of emotion in ways that harm the self or others. The emotions that are regulated can be of negative, neutral, or positive valence. Controlling regulation can be externally controlled or introjected (self-controlled) and reduce wellbeing or flourishing (Ryan et al., 2021).

Although both the oppressed and oppressors show patterns of both amotivational and controlling forms of emotion regulation, the two populations engage in very distinctive regulatory processes. There is some evidence, for example, that oppressors actively inhibit empathy towards the victims of their oppressing conduct. Marin-Morales et al. (2021), for example, used MRI data to investigate patterns of emotion suppression and experience in men who committed IPV as compared to controls. They found significant differences in their experiences and responses to pictures of IPV in two areas. First, they showed little empathy with the victims, and, second, they showed maladaptive forms of emotion regulation. The authors concluded that treating such disorders required increasing empathy towards partners and teaching more adaptive forms of emotion regulation. For the oppressed, in contrast, emotion regulation tends to be controlling, leading them commonly to suppress emotions based on internalized social norms. This is consistent with the inhibitory and concealing aspects of shame.

### Mindfulness as Emotion Regulation

Roth et al., (2019) define their third and most functional form of emotion regulation as integrative or IER, the effect of openness and a non-judgemental "experience-validating stance," awareness of emotions, and an orientation of curiosity towards emotions. They identified three steps or characteristics of IER: (i) a non-judgemental, receptive attention to emotional experience "consistent with mindfulness" (p 946), (ii) an active step involving interest-taking (investigation), and (iii) an informed choice about how to respond, including withholding or flexibly expressing emotions. The authors conclude:

> In explicating IER, we note that it entails an open acceptance of emotions, and a capacity to take interest in them as carrying information value rather than as a source of pressure to act, feel, or think in a specific way, allowing a sense of choice with respect to subsequent actions. Research thus far suggests that such integrative processing is not only associated with higher wellbeing and high-quality relationships but also can help "immunize" the individual for subsequent emotional events.
> (p. 952)

Mindfulness trains the mind in attention, openness, and the acceptance of present experience without judgement, thereby encouraging intrinsic versus extrinsic loci of control. Given that it is strongly associated with both intrinsic motivation and integrative autonomy, but not with externally controlled or introjected (self-controlled) motivation (Ryan et al., 2021), mindfulness is well suited to serve as an IER approach. As such, it is well suited to support the oppressed in untangling themselves from external sources of discrimination and with the internalization of oppression. These combined conditions further associate mindfulness with enhanced wellbeing (Schultz & Ryan, 2015).

As-emotion regulation, mindfulness appears to be highly effective. Brockman et al. (2017) compared mindfulness to two other emotion regulation strategies, suppression and cognitive reappraisal. They found that mindfulness was associated with lower negative and higher positive affect, clear indicators of enhanced subjective wellbeing. The reverse was true for suppression, with increased negative affect using this strategy. For reappraisal, although daily positive affect was improved, daily negative affect remained unaffected. For half the sample, cognitive appraisal conferred no benefit to the regulation of negative affect. Furthermore, the effects were age-dependent in that, for adolescents, reappraisal was associated with *increased* negative affect, a negative effect that decreased with age.

In their meta-analysis, Raugh et al. (2025) determined that mindfulness functioned as an effective form of emotion regulation, alongside associated components of monitoring (increasing awareness) and equanimity (lowering reactivity). Also, notably, they found that strategies that focus exclusively on emotional awareness (i.e., monitoring alone) were less effective than those that included cognitive change (i.e., reappraisal). They found mindfulness particularly effective for those suffering from fear-based disorders (e.g., social anxiety, trauma). Although oppression is not itself a clinical disorder, it is a sustained threat condition associated with prolonged exposure to fear posed by discriminatory social environments. The dominant emotion of oppression, furthermore, is shame, which is associated with the fear-associated "flight or freeze" responses of inhibition and concealment.

Mindfulness may itself involve different regulatory strategies depending on amount of practice and expertise. Chiesa et al. (2013) reviewed a range of MRI studies to ascertain if mindfulness fostered "top-down" (cognitive reappraisal via PFC modulating emotions in limbic regions) or "bottom-up" (peripheral body and limbic area inputs modulating PFC-mediated responses) emotion regulation strategies. Overall, they found evidence of both; however, one line of research suggested that the amount of experience in mindfulness may alter the strategy. In particular, short-term (i.e., novice) practitioners tended to show more top-down (i.e., controlling or suppressive) patterns, whereas more experienced (i.e., expert) practitioners displayed more bottom-up (i.e., integrative) patterns. This suggests that, as an IER strategy, mindfulness may take time to learn and integrate.

## Affective Injustice and Emotion Regulation

There is a growing critique of the emphasis placed on emotion regulation in oppression given the danger of a disproportionate responsibility being placed on the oppressed to regulate emotions that ensue from unjust treatment. Srinivasan (2018) argues that while anger in the oppressed may not always be appropriate or prudent, it is often apt as it involves responding to a moral violation. She contrasts anger to disappointment, which does not involve moral violations but merely not getting what one wishes. For the oppressed, anger is apt when fuelled by a recognition of a moral violation. This is not the classical interpretation of anger as the desire for revenge (Nussbaum, 2015). Therefore, to pressure the oppressed to control or regulate such anger would be unjust and likely lead to harmful effects from suppression (Archer & Mills, 2019). Furthermore, such expectations, pressures, and suppression would only further fuel the experience of shame and its associated inhibition and concealment.

Villa (2024) extends this critique by arguing that the social norms placed on girls and women to regulate their emotions may deepen oppression in patriarchy. If and when norms deflect responsibility from perpetrators (oppressors) to girls and women, then a disproportionate responsibility for the emotional labour associated with regulating emotions in the aftermath of misogynistic aggression falls on the girls and women, the victims. This added burden only further privileges oppressors and oppresses girls and women struggling with misogyny. While suppression may lead to alienation from emotions that may be entirely apt, expression may lead to social ostracization, pathologizing, and marginalization that only further fuels oppression. To get around this double-bind, she calls for more moral accountability in the social assessment of the aptness or fittingness of emotions.

In a similar vein, Ahmed (2010) critiqued normative assumptions underlying expectations to be happy and the stigma associated with emotions perceived to be negative, destructive, or socially disruptive. Using the examples of "feminist killjoys," "unhappy queers," and "melancholic migrants," she argues that unhappiness is inevitable in the pursuit of ways of life or modes of being that are not yet widely accepted as social norms or pathways to a good life. The inflexibility or outright hostility of social systems and norms cast people engaged in change into situations in which their adverse emotional responses may be apt yet used to further marginalize them. Expectations for happiness then become forms of emotion suppression. She argues instead for "hap movements," concluding:

> The struggle against happiness as a necessity is also a struggle for happiness as a possibility. I now think of political movements as hap movements rather than happiness movements. It is not about the unhappy ones becoming the happy ones. Far from it. Revolutionary forms of consciousness involve heightening our awareness of *just how much* there is to be unhappy about. ... A politics of the hap might embrace what happens, but it also works towards a world in which things can happen in alternative ways. To make hap is to make a world.
>
> (pp. 222–223)

All of these critics recognize the importance of emotion regulation to subjective wellbeing and agency. The injustice comes from two directions: the normative assessment of emotions that classifies them as constructive or destructive and the strategy of emotion regulation and the burden or harms it may inflict on the psyche or person. The first issue involves the acceptance of a broader spectrum of emotions as apt to the condition of oppression, including recognizing anger or other negative valence emotions as being both healthy and constructive. The second issue can be addressed by recognizing a broader scope of regulatory processes, some negative or less functional to be unlearned, like amotivated forms of dysregulation or controlled forms of suppression, and others like mindfulness, a form of integrated emotion regulation, to be fostered based on openness and flexibility (Roth et al., 2019).

To conclude, what is critical to consider in measuring and responding to these debates are the rights of each and every person, as a living being, to pursue, realize, and sustain wellbeing as they know or discover it to be. This requires agency and autonomy on the part of that person, deploying self-regulation strategies to move towards the desired internal and external states or conditions they identify as wellbeing. To relinquish expectations for self-regulation is to relinquish expectations for wellbeing, and to relinquish expectations for wellbeing is to condemn the oppressed to a Promethean curse giving them responsibility for removing the social barriers oppressing them while enduring the debilitating effects of internalized oppression. In this, we might conclude that, ethically, in most cases, self-care trumps social change. Only when we know wellbeing ourselves, intimately, are we in any position to bring it to others.

As an emotion regulation strategy, mindfulness is based on monitoring and flexibly responding to internal felt experiences rather than externally sourced ideas stemming from social norms. In this, it is particularly well suited to serve the emancipatory needs of the oppressed by removing the need for a social mediator to cultivate awareness, to assess and regulate emotions, and, ultimately, to extricate themselves from, and resist, oppression. In this, I am reminded of the words of the historical Buddha who, guided by mindfulness over 2,500 years ago, was said to have liberated himself from suffering. Just prior to his liberation, sitting under a tree as the sun rose, he was purported to say (as I was taught): "May the Earth bear witness to my right to be, unmoved by desire or fear." And the Earth shook.

## References

Ahmed, S. (2004). *The cultural politics of emotion*. Edinburgh University Press.

Ahmed, S. (2010). *The promise of happiness*. Duke University Press. https://doi.org/10.1016/j.jcbs.2022.03.007

Akbari, M., Seydavi, M., Hosseini, Z., Krafft, J., & Levin, M. (2022). Experiential avoidance in depression, anxiety, obsessive-compulsive related, and posttraumatic stress disorders: A comprehensive systematic review and meta-analysis. *Journal of Contextual Behavioral Science*, *24*, 65–78.

Appel, M. & Weber, S. (2021). Do mass mediated stereotypes harm members of negatively stereotyped groups? A meta-analytical review on media-generated stereotype threat and stereotype lift. *Communication Research*, *48*(2), 151–179. https://doi.org/10.1177/0093650217715543

Archer, A., & Mills, G. (2019). Anger, affective injustice, and emotion regulation. *Philosophical Topics*, *47*(2). 75–94.

Barrett, L., Niedenthal, P., & Winkielman, P. (Eds.) (2005). *Emotion and consciousness*. The Guilford Press.

Bartky, S. (1990). *Femininity and domination: Studies in the phenomenology of oppression*. Routledge.

Brockman, R., Ciarrochi, J., Parker, P., & Kashdan, T. (2017). Emotion regulation strategies in daily life: Mindfulness, cognitive reappraisal and emotion suppression. *Cognitive Behavior Therapy*, *46*(2), 91–113. https://doi.org/10.1080/16506073.2016.1218926

Caldwell, V. (2020). *Softening resistance towards diversity initiatives: The role of mindfulness in mitigating emotional White fragility*. A dissertation prepared for Seattle Pacific University.

Chiesa, A., Serretti, A., & Jakobsen, J. (2013). Mindfulness: Top–down or bottom–up emotion regulation strategy?. *Clinical psychology review*, *33*(1), 82–96. https://doi.org/10.1016/j.cpr.2012.10.006

Clarke, O., Pickard, J., Gonsalvez, C., Deane, F., & Martin, J. (2025). Mindfulness predicts impostorism in trainee psychologists in professional programs. *Clinical Psychologist*, *29*(1), 82–92. https://doi.org/10.1080/13284207.2024.2447426

Costa, P., McDuffie, J, Brown, S., He, Y., Ikner, B., Sabat, I., & Miner, K. (2022). Microaggression:Mega problems or micro issues? A meta-analysis. *Journal of Community Psychology*, *51*(1), 137–153. https://doi.org/10.1002/jcop.22885

David, E., & Derthick, A. (2018). *The psychology of oppression*. Springer.

de Beauvoir, S. (1949/2011). *The second sex* (C. Borde & S. Malavany-Chevallier, Trans.). Vintage. (Originally published in 1949).

Deigh, J. (1983). Shame and self-esteem: A critique. *Ethics*, *93*, 225–245.

Emmer, C., Dorn, J., & Mata, J. (2024). The immediate effect of discrimination on mental health: A meta-analytic review of the causal evidence. *Psychological Bulletin*, *150*(3), 215–252.

Fanon, F. (1961). *The wretched of the earth*. Francois Maspero.

Farb, N., Segal, Z., Mayberg, H., Bean, J., McKeon, D., Fatima, Z., & Anderson, A. (2007). Attending to the present: Mindfulness meditation reveals distinct neural modes of self-reference. *Social, cognitive, and affective neuroscience*, 2(4), 313–322. https://doi.org/10.1093/scan/nsm030

Firestone, S. (1970). *The dialectic of sex: The case for feminist revolution*. Farrar, Straus, Giroux.

Fischer, A., Roseman, I., & Giner-Sorolla, R. (2022). Contempt: The emotional rejection of those who are beneath our standards. In M.H. Jacobsen (Ed.), *Emotions in culture and everyday life*, Ch. 10. https://doi.org/10.4324/9781003208556

Flanagan, O. (2000). Destructive emotions. *Consciousness and Emotion*, *1*(2), 259–281. https://doi.org/10.1075/ce.1.2.05fla

Freire, P. (1970). *Pedagogy of the oppressed*. [Trans. M.B. Ramos]. Herder & Herder.

Garland, E., Farb, N., Goldin, P., & Fredrickson, B. (2015). Mindfulness broadens awareness and builds eudaimonic meaning: A process model of mindful positive emotion regulation. *Psychological Inquiry*, *26*(4), 293. https://doi.org/10.1080/1047840X.2015.1064294

Garrau, M. (2024). Between gender and subjectivity: Iris Marion Young on the phenomenology of lived experience. *Recognition Theory and Contemporary Moral and Political Philosophy*. Manchester University Press. https://doi.org/10.7765/9781526183781.00016

Gartner, R., Sterzing, P., Fisher, C., Woodford, M., Kinney, M.K., & Victor, B. (2020). A scoping review of measures assessing gender microaggressions against women. *Psychology of Women Quarterly*, *44*(3), 283–306. https://doi.org/10.1177/0361684320920834

Gethin, R. (2011). On some definitions of mindfulness. *Contemporary Buddhism*, *12*(1), 263–279. https://doi.org/10.1080/14639947.2011.564843

Golec de Zavala, A., Bierwiaczonek, K., & Ciesielski, P. (2022). An interpretation of meta-analytical evidence for the link between collective narcissism and conspiracy theories. *Current Opinion in Psychology*, *47*, https://doi.org/10.1016/j.copsyc.2022.101360

Golec de Zavala, A., & Keenan, O. (2024). Gender and national collective narcissism: Gender asymmetries and obstacles to gender equality. *Sex Roles*, *90*, 565–586. https://doi.org/10.1007/s11199-024-01443-8

Grubbs, J., & Exline, J., (2016). Trait entitlement: A cognitive-personality source of vulnerability to psychological distress. *Psychological Bulletin*, *142*(11), 1204–1226. https://doi.org/10.1037/bul0000063

Guo, L. (2024). The correlation between mindfulness, decentering, and psychological problems: A structural equation modeling meta-analysis. *Mindfulness*, *15*, 1873–1895. https://doi.org/10.1007/s12671-024-02395-6

Harris, A. (2014). The psychological mechanisms of oppression: Empathy, disgust, and the perception of group membership. *Oregon Undergraduate Research Journal, 7.1*. Scholar's Bank. Accessed July 2025 at: https://scholarsbank.uoregon.edu/items/4d3f0805-6bf4-44d4-8d86-98be0b6efdb2

Heim, M. (2022). *Words for the heart. A treasury of emotions from classical India*. Princeton University Press.

Juneau, C., Pellerin, N., Trives, E., Ricard, M., Shankland, R., & Dambrun, M. (2020). Reliability and validity of an equanimity questionnaire: The two-factor equanimity scale (EQUA-S). *PeerJ*, *8*:e9405. https://doi.org/10.7717/peerj.9405

Kahneman, D. (2011). *Thinking fast and slow*. Farrar, Straus and Giroux.

Karppinen, H., King, O., & Russell, P.S., (2023). Hostile emotions and close relationships: Anger can be related to constructive responses. *Personality and Individual Differences*, *212*. https://doi.org/10.1016/j.paid.2023.112258

Kolchraiber, F., Tanaka, L., Negi, L., Nunes, R., deSouza, E., & deSouza, K. (2025). Vulnerability, compassion meditation and well-being: Community-based participatory research. *Physis*, *35*(01). https://doi.org/10.1590/S0103-73312025350114en

Lausch, S. (2021). *I will not stand in my way – Exploring the effects of mindfulness on impostor feelings through self-authorship in female STEM graduate students*. A dissertation prepared for Boise State University.

LeDoux, J., & Brown, R. (2017). A higher-order theory of emotional consciousness. *Proceedings of the National Academy of Sciences*, *114*(10), E2016–E2025. https://doi.org/10.1073/pnas.1619316114

Leung, T., Schmidt, F., & Mushquash, C. (2023). A personal history of trauma and experience of secondary traumatic stress, vicarious trauma, and burnout in mental health workers: A systematic literature review. *Psychological Trauma: Theory, Research, Practice, and Policy*, *15*(Suppl 2), S213–S221. https://doi.org/10.1037/tra0001277

Lorde, A. (1984). *Sister outsider: Essays and speeches*. Crossing Press.

Luberto, M., Shinday, N. Song, R., Philopotts, L., Park, E., Fricchione, G., & Yeh, G. (2018). Systematic review and meta-analysis of the effects of meditation on empathy, compassion, and prosocial behaviors. *Mindfulness*, *9*, 708–724. https://doi.org/10.1007/s12671-017-0841-8

MacPherson, S., & Rockman, P. (2022). *Mindfulness-based teaching and learning: Preparing mindfulness specialists in education and clinical care*. Routledge.

Manne, K. (2017). *Down girl: The logic of misogyny*. Oxford University Press.

Manne, K. (2021). *Entitled: How male privilege hurts women*. Crown Publishing.

Marin-Morales, A., Perez, M., Catena-Martinez, A., & Verdejo-Roman, J. (2021). Emotional regulation in male batterers when faced with pictures of intimate partner violence. Do they have a problem with suppressing or experiencing emotions? *Journal of Interpersonal Violence*, *37*(11–12). https://doi.org/10.1177/0886260520985484

McGibbon, E. (Ed.) (2021a). *Oppression: A social determinant of health. (2nd ed)*. Fernwood Publishing.

McGibbon, E. (2021b). The politics of mental health: Pathologizing the impacts of systemic oppression. In E. McGibbon (Ed.), *Oppression: A social determinant of health. (2nd ed)*, pp. 134–153 Fernwood Publishing.

Montoya, M., Pittinsky, T., & Rosenthal, S. (2020). A multidimensional model of collective narcissism. *Journal of Theoretical Social Psychology*, https://doi.org/10.1002/jts5.71

Munjee, R. & MacPherson, S. (2023). Mindfulness and compassion in response to to racism. *Diaspora, Indigenous, and Minority Education*, *19*(2), 91–107. https://doi.org/10.1080/15595692.2023.2254873

Nadal, K., King, R., Sissoka, D., Floyd, N., & Hines, D. (2021). The legacies of systemic and internalized oppression: Experiences of microaggressions, imposter phenomenon, and stereotype threat on historically marginalized groups. *New Ideas in Psychology*, *63*, https://doi.org/10.1016/j.newideapsych.2021.100895

National Institute of Mental Health (NIMH). (n.d.). Sustained Threat. Accessed on March 06, 2025 at: https://www.nimh.nih.gov/research/research-funded-by-nimh/rdoc/constructs/sustained-threat

Neville, L., Fisk, G., & Ens, K. (2024). Psychological entitlement and conspiracy beliefs: Evidence from the COVID-19 pandemic. *Journal of Social Psychology*, *165*(1), 65–87. https://doi.org/10.1080/00224545.2023.2292626

Nussbaum, M. (2015). Transitional anger. *Journal of the American Philosophical Association*, *1*(1), 41–56. https://doi.org/10.1017/apa.2014.19

Orbe-Austin, L. & Orbe-Austin, R. (2024). Critical issues of the impostor phenomenon and interventions for historically marginalized people. In K. Cokley (Ed.). *The impostor phenomenon: Psychological research, theory, and interventions* (pp. 269–284).

Parkman, A. (2016). The imposter phenomenon in higher education: Incidence and impact. *Journal of Higher Education Theory & Practice*, *16*(1).

Owens, L.R. (2023). Compassion practice, social justice, and collective liberation. In J. Loizzo, F. Brandon, E. Wolf, & M. Neale (Eds.), *Advances in Contemplative Psychotherapy*, 13 pages. Routledge, https://doi.org/10.4324/9781003243588

Pastan, C., McDonough, A., Finkelman, M., & Daniels, J. (2022). Evaluation of mindfulness practice in mitigating impostor feelings in dental students. *Journal of Dental Education*, *86*(11), 1513–1520. https://doi.org/10.1002/jdd.12965

Raugh, I., Berglund, A., & Strauss, G. (2025). Implementation of mindfulness-based emotion regulation strategies: A systematic review and meta-analysis. *Affective Science*, *6*, 171–200. https://doi.org/10.1007/s42761-024-00281-x

Rigby, C.S., Schultz, P., & Ryan, R. (2014). Mindfulness, interest-taking, and self-regulation: A Self-Determination Theory perspective on the role of awareness in optimal functioning. In A. Ie, C. Ngnoumen, & Ellen Langer (Eds.), *The Wiley Blackwell handbook of mindfulness*, (pp. 216–235), John Wiley & Sons. https://doi.org/10.1002/9781118294895.ch12

Roth, G., Vanstreenkiste, M., & Ryan, R. (2019). Integrative emotion regulation: Process and development from a self-determination theory perspective. *Development and Psychopathology*, *31*(3), 945–956. https://doi.org/10.1017/S0954579419000403

Ryan, R., & Deci, E. (2000). Self-determination theory and the facilitation of intrinsic motivation, social development, and well-being. *American Psychologist*, *55*(1), 68–78. https://doi.org/10.1037/0003-066X.55.1.68

Ryan, R., & Deci, E. (2020). Intrinsic and extrinsic motivation from a self-determination theory perspective: Definitions, theory, practices, and future directions. *Contemporary Educational Psychology*, *61*. 101860. https://doi.org/10.1016/j.cedpsych.2020.101860

Ryan, R., Donald, J., & Bradshaw, E. (2021). Mindfulness and motivation: A process view using self-determination theory. *Current Directions in Psychological Science*, *30*(4), 300–306. https://doi.org/10.1177/09637214211009511

Saenz-Benavides, M.L. (2019). *Instruments of power: How emotions contribute to oppression*. [Doctoral dissertation, Birkbeck College, University of London]. https://doi.org/10.18743/PUB.00040428

Schultz, P., & Ryan, R. (2015). The "why," "what," and "how" of healthy self-regulation: Mindfulness and well-being from a self-determination theory perspective. In B. Ostafin, M. Robinson, & B. Meir (Eds.), *Handbook of Mindfulness and self-regulation*, (pp. 81–94), Springer.

Segal, Z., Anderson, A., Gulamani, T, Dinh Williams, L., Desormeau, P., Ferguson, A., Walsh, K., & Farb, N. (2019). Practice of therapy acquired regulatory skills and depressive relapse/recurrence prophylaxis following cognitive therapy or mindfulness based therapy. *Journal of Consulting and Clinical Psychology*, *87*(2), 161–170. https://doi.org/10.1037/ccp0000351

Siegal, D. (2016). *Mind: A journey to the heart of being human*. W.W. Norton & Co.

Solnit, R. (2016). *Hope in the dark: Untold histories, wild possibilities*. Haymarket Books.

Srinivasan, A. (2018). The aptness of anger. *The Journal of Political Philosophy*, *26*(2), 123–144. https://doi.org/10.1111/jopp.12130

Steele, C. (1997). A threat in the air: How stereotypes shape intellectual identity and performance. *American Psychologist*, *52*(6), 613–629.

Stevens, F. & Taber, K. (2021). The neuroscience of empathy and compassion in pro-social behavior. *Neuropsychologia*, *159*(20). https://doi.org/10.1016/j.neuropsychologia.2021.107925
Stockdale, K. (2021). *Hope under oppression*. Oxford University Press.
Sue, D. (2010). *Microaggressions in everyday life: Race, gender, and sexual orientation*. Wiley.
Ussher, J. (2011). *The madness of women: Myth and experience*. Routledge.
Vago, D., Silbersweig, D. (2012). Self-awareness, self-regulation, and self-transcendence (S-ART): A framework for understanding the neurobiological mechanisms of mindfulness. *Frontiers in Human Neuroscience*, 6. https://doi.org/10.3389/fnhum.2012.00296
Villa, K. (2024). Affective injustice and responsibility for emotion regulation. Special Issue: Revolutionizing Responsibility. *Feminist Philosophy Quarterly*, *10*(1/2), 23 pages.
Wallace, A., & Flanagan, O. (2003). The Western perspective. In Goleman, D. (Ed.), *Destructive emotions: How can we overcome them? A scientific dialogue with the Dalai Lama*, (pp. 45–71), Bantam Books.
Wallace, A., & Jinpa, T. (2003). The anatomy of mental afflictions. In Goleman, D. (Ed.), *Destructive emotions: How can we overcome them? A scientific dialogue with the Dalai Lama*, (pp. 87–115), Bantam Books.
Wasson, R., Barratt, C. & O'Brien, W. (2020). Effects of mindfulness-based interventions on self-compassion in health care professionals: A meta-analysis. *Mindfulness*, *11*, 1914–1934. https://doi.org/10.1007/s12671-020-01342-5
Williams, M., Osman, M., & Hyon, C. (2023). Understanding the psychological impact of oppression using the Trauma Symptoms of Discrimination Scale. *Chronic Stress*, *7*, 1–12. https://doi.org/10.1177/24705470221149511
Young, I. (1990). *Justice and the politics of difference*. Princeton University Press. https://doi.org/10.2307/j.ctvcm4g4q
Zitek, E., & Jordan, A. (2021). Individuals with higher psychological entitlement respond to bad luck with anger. *Personality and Individual Differences*, *168*, https://doi.org/10.1016/j.paid.2020.110306

# 5 Consciousness, Oppression, and Mindfulness

This chapter is on the topic of consciousness and its role in both oppression and mindfulness. I present a perspective on consciousness that derives from two key sources: the "new science" of consciousness (Seth, 2021) and the Buddhist phenomenological science of mind (Wallace, 2011, 2018). These sources are sufficiently compatible to provide a fairly coherent view on the topic. Consciousness matters in the study of oppression for two reasons: First, the focus on consciousness itself – beyond its contents as identity, emotion, and thought – highlights the pervasive nature and scope of oppression. Second, this focus helps clarify the promise of mindfulness in countering oppression. During its 2,500-year development in Buddhism, mindfulness has been applied as a path to develop consciousness so as to reduce and remove suffering. The desired outcome is to realize the potential of the human consciousness to "awaken." Waking up suggests a change in consciousness, as when we wake up from sleep. We are more present to the world and able to exercise our agency to fulfill our intentions. Although oppression, *per se*, is a modern construct, it relates to subtle forms of suffering and delusion consistent with those described in Buddhism and to their removal through mindfulness.

Endeavouring to understand oppression through its impacts on consciousness is not new. In the mid-20th century, as it emerged within largely philosophical studies, the problem of oppression was framed as a problem of consciousness. Existential, feminist, and critical writing of the period presented oppression as a dysfunction of consciousness itself. In *The Ethics of Ambiguity* (1948), for example, Simone de Beauvoir described oppression as arising from two situations: (a) being reduced to the status of an object in the service of others and (b) being excluded from communities entrusted with making social meanings and establishing values. According to de Beauvoir, the principal harm of oppression was to diminish consciousness itself by reducing or impairing these twofold functions. To live in oppression was to be subjected to living in *bad faith*, a condition in which one abdicated – by choice or through threat of force – the responsibility and burden of meaning-making and freedom via consciousness. *Authenticity*, the alternative to *bad faith*, defined the state that ensued from engaging consistently in the meaning-making and freedom functions of consciousness.

DOI: 10.4324/9781003449355-5

Later, Franz Fanon (1961) and Paulo Freire (1970) theorized how internalized oppression gave rise to the inauthenticity and dissociation of the self that de Beauvoir described as *bad faith*. This split subject turned against itself, thereby diminishing the capacity to cultivate an integrated, autonomous self as the expression of a fully human consciousness. Concurrently, second-wave feminists like Shulamith Firestone (1970) popularized "consciousness-raising" as the key anti-oppressive method to correct internalized oppression through education and encounter groups. In this way, feminism and other liberation philosophies did not restrict their musings to arcane texts but popularized ideas within social movements. These movements grew out of the belief that freedom from oppression was best accomplished through changing the *consciousness* of the oppressed.

In the 1990s, "consciousness" came under increased scrutiny. Post-structural critiques claimed that the term was ill-defined and essentialized mind and identity in ways that misrepresented the importance of everyday acts of resistance in the struggle against oppression. These critiques were suspicious of the modernist roots of the term "consciousness" and its seeming endorsement of modernist subject-object dualisms. Concurrently, critiques of the *practice* of consciousness-raising claimed that it led to divisiveness and that it privileged entitled group members over more marginalized others. Consequently, the emphases in oppression studies shifted from a focus on agency to structural change and, ultimately, to the identification of structural violence as trauma enacted on the oppressed. Social action and individual therapy replaced consciousness raising methods, with a corresponding emphasis on removing oppressive environmental structures and addressing the cumulative traumas of oppression. What was lost was the fuller human and biological frame of reference afforded by the consideration of consciousness itself.

As philosophical interest waned, the scientific inquiry into consciousness increased during the 1990s. These distinctive disciplinary trajectories had intersected several decades earlier in Nagel's (1974) landmark philosophical paper, "What is it like to be a bat?" In that paper, he argued the non-reductive, non-objective nature of the "phenomenological features" of mind. Nagel popularized the notion that consciousness was best understood by what it *feels like* to be something, a feeling not fully knowable outside of that organism's biological condition and associate experience: "Our own experience provides the basic material for our imagination, whose range is therefore limited" (p. 439). He used the example of bats, whose webbed limbs and use of echolocation to navigate the world gave them a distinctive consciousness, which he described as the "feeling" of being a bat. Not only did a bat have consciousness, but that consciousness was not fully knowable by human beings: "So if extrapolation from our own case is involved in the idea of what it is like to be a bat, the extrapolation must be incompletable" (p. 439). This suggested that human observers were unreliable in assessing, imagining, or knowing the consciousness of other species and, arguably, even the experiences of other human beings inhabiting different biological conditions.

Griffin (1976) extended this argument in *The Question of Animal Intelligence* in framing the evolutionary argument for animal consciousness; however, he received considerable backlash from the scientific ethology community for being "anthropocentric." Like Nagal, Griffin's thesis also derived from studies of bats, whom he had observed for over 30 years. Griffin argued that consciousness could be validly inferred when an organism altered its behaviour using new and changing sensory information. He saw intelligence arising from consciousness as occupying a spectrum across species rather than as a distinctive human capacity. The resistance of many in the scientific community created such a backlash that even the idea that animals had "behaviour" at all was in question, with some claiming that behaviour was a distinctively human activity. Instead, according to this critique, animals displayed only instinctive reflexive and mechanistic actions. That said, whether as a characteristic of human beings or many living organisms, consciousness became scientifically operationalized in the process as behavioural responses, intentions, and the capacities to make choices and to learn.

Like a teeter-totter, as philosophical interest in consciousness waned in the 1990s, scientific studies of consciousness began to burgeon. Seth (2018) pinpoints this "rehabilitation of consciousness within neuroscience" to a paper published by Crick and Koch (1990), "Towards a neurobiological theory of consciousness." The authors proposed a theory of visual consciousness associated with gamma-band (~40 Hz) oscillations. This paper stimulated interest within cognitive neuroscience on how to define, characterize, and explain consciousness as a biological phenomenon without reducing it to biological materials (e.g., biochemistry); structures (e.g., the brain); or processes (e.g., neural activity). Instead, consciousness became defined variously as experience, phenomenology, and mind: that is, knowing what something *feels like*. As Seth (2021) concluded: "Wherever there is experience, there is phenomenology: and wherever there is phenomenology, there is consciousness" (p. 16).

In Buddhist psychology, the construct "mind" is used interchangeably with consciousness. The terms derive from three synonymous Pali terms *mano/mana* (holistic *mind*), *citta* (specific processes of *mind*), and viññāṇa (*consciousness*). The term *mano* is the first word of the first line of one of the oldest extant Buddhist texts, *The Dhammapada*, dating back to the 3rd century BCE: *Mano punnam gamma dhamma, mano seta, mano maya* – translated by Analayo (2018) as "The mind precedes phenomena; the mind is foremost" (p. 181). The translation I learned and memorized was slightly different (though same meaning): "Mind is the source of all things; great mind; creative mind.

Like feminist and philosophical investigations into consciousness, Buddhist psychology and the "new" sciences of consciousness struggled to locate consciousness as a process connected to, but greater than, both distal (e.g., biological, neurological, or "karmic") and proximal (e.g., experience as sensation, thoughts, emotions, imagery, memory) factors. Though this is debated by Buddhists, most scientists view consciousness as an emergent property of biological systems, whereby consciousness is located somewhere between its distal causes and proximate appearances. It functions to weave together disparate experience to create the semblance of an *a priori* world characterized by subject-object dualism and conditioned by sensory and environmental experiences. This ensuing world appears more independent, concrete, and fixed than it actually is. All three of these perspectives of consciousness - Buddhist, philosophical, scientific - focus on the role of the self, whether as a key to strengthening and integrating consciousness through self-awareness or in solidifying and bolstering self-centred delusions that narrow and restrict perception and conscious awareness.

There are other points of conflict between these perspectives beyond their view of the role of the self in consciousness. For example, scientific and Buddhist perspectives differ with respect to what is called "the hard problem of consciousness." This refers to the challenge to explain why consciousness exists distinct from physical phenomena in the first place. Advocates of the "new" science of consciousness like Seth (2021) hold to materialist views that consciousness is an emergent property that derives from biological systems and the brain, whereas Buddhist-scientific scholars like Wallace (2018) argue the ultimate separation of consciousness from matter, using scientific arguments like the conservation of mass to reason through that consciousness could not derive from matter when it has no mass or detectible energy. Neither side has sufficient evidence to settle the matter, but each has sufficient evidence to support and rationalize their own biased perspective, which they tend to subscribe to with ideological vigour.

I am more interested in what the "new" cognitive and old Buddhist sciences of consciousness have in common. These shared insights include that consciousness gives rise to our experience of the world; that consciousness constructs a naive impression that the world is real and *out there* and we are *in here* and separated from that world as observers; and that it is possible to observe consciousness constructing experience via a form of meta-awareness that by *decentring* deconstructs the illusion of integration and fixity generated by its habitual functioning. The latter is why mindfulness matters.

## Consciousness Re/Defined

To recover some of the promise of consciousness studies in the context of oppression, I have distilled a range of philosophical, cognitive scientific, and Buddhist insights about consciousness to offer an overview of what consciousness is, in order to then understand how it might function. To be conscious is to recognize what things *feel like*. Such an awareness is not to be found in rocks, water, or minerals, though new research suggests that plants have intelligence but it functions differently in the absence of a nervous system (Simard, 2021; Schlanger, 2024). The idea of consciousness as knowing what it *feel like* to be something harkens back to Nagel's (1974) paper on bats.

These decades since Nagel's paper was published, there is relative consensus that consciousness is entangled with, but irreducible to, the body and sensory-motor systems and environments. As the basis of *experience* itself, consciousness appears to us as what phenomena *feel like* rather than their objective thingness. This capacity of consciousness to recognize what phenomena *feel like* has come to dominate the way scientists and philosophers alike describe phenomenal consciousness in books like O'Regan's (2011) *Why Red Doesn't Feel Like a Bell* and Seth's (2021) *Being You*. Across these studies, consciousness is encapsulated by what it *feels like* to be or to experience something, whether that "something" is a particular life form, an organism that is a member of a species, a distinctive colour or sound, or a self who is developing and living within a particular situation. To this, we can add what it *feels like* to be a member of an oppressed class like women and what it *feels like to be a woman* free of oppression. This points to the value of framing oppression by its impacts on consciousness, where it has the capacity to literally define and redefine the limits, boundaries, and possibilities of our self, experience, and world.

Childhood memories are windows into consciousness and how the experience of what it *feels like to be me* develops. As refrains of memory, their mnemonic bars repeat and echo through time in ever-expanding and meaningful spirals to render that ambient, barely discernible yet familiar and intimate *feeling of being me*. These memories render consciousness rather like genes render physical bodies, replicating and developing over time, attenuating to accommodate new environments, to form *the experience* of a life. As a source code for consciousness itself, these memories define, refine, and replicate what it *feels like to be me* over time, persisting and evolving as tropes of the *experience*, rather than physical formations, of a life.

## The Phenomenology of Consciousness

The most vivid memories from my own childhood involve epiphanies arising from either suffering or self-reflection. I notice that memories of suffering correspond to experience with negative affect and a sense of chaos, while memories of self-reflection and meta-awareness are associated with positive affect and a sense of calm and optimism. Both types involve heightened self-awareness, where I am not merely a passive observer or bystander witnessing the world but an active and embodied agent navigating, attuning, and responding to the world. This intensified awareness seems to be why these memories imprinted as lasting memories available for recall throughout my life. It is not merely the vividness of their perceptual features but their meaning, the sense that they constitute a kernel or seed of insight that grew over time to define my conscious experience, personhood, and life.

These memories sometimes contradict storied views about consciousness. One example is that they suggest that consciousness is not as selfless as Buddhism sometimes implies in the doctrine of *anatta* or no-self (or no-soul). Instead, consciousness seems to come with an intensified self-awareness, often through an encounter with discrepant, threatening, or stimulating social messages and environments. Another insight is that consciousness seems to gather and intensify intentions as potential actions much the way matter amasses potential energy. These "intentions" and their potential are stored as memories and meaning that resurface to energize agency, empowerment, readiness, and a will-to-manifest. This active, energetic, and engaged nature of consciousness is poorly represented in popular tropes of mindfulness, whether in images of the seated Buddha in meditative equipoise or contemporary images of young women seated passively on yoga mats gazing longingly at the sun rising on the horizon.

In one of my earliest memories, I am 2.5 years of age (I guess). My older brother and I are playing outside when we hear an ice-cream truck coming down the road. My brother runs ahead to the house to get a dime from my mother so he can buy an ice-cream, while I struggle to run behind him. I am still a toddler, so I can't run well. By the time I get to my mother in the kitchen, she laughs and says she has no more coins. I cry hysterically, convinced that she is choosing to favour my brother. Although I read into the moment more than was probably justified - a prejudice or injustice that I vaguely sensed would continue on. Yet, my mother did mirror in that moment, unwittingly or not, the privileging of boys and later men that became the backdrop of my life.

The second memory came a few months later after the birth of my baby sister. My mother is in her bedroom, resting on her bed as she nurses my sister, while I am seated on the top stair of the staircase watching through the open door. I turn and notice a bottle of baby aspirins on a nearby windowsill: pink, sweet, and candy-like. I reach up and grab the bottle. My younger brother then appears and asks me to give him some, but I refuse. In the end, I give him two, while I continue to eat the rest of the bottle. Overcome with shame and fear, I go into the bedroom and interrupt my mother. I tell her what I've done. She becomes agitated and alarmed as she arranges to take me to the hospital. She orders a taxi and, once inside the cab, she continuously slaps my face to prevent me losing consciousness. At the hospital, doctors insert tubes down my nose and throat and proceed to pump my stomach empty.

The final memory is from grade 2, as I am entering school after lunch. After crossing the threshold in a throng of children, I realize that I am still chewing bubble gum. Gum is verboten inside the school, so before a teacher can see it, I place it in my hand to hide it. When I reach the garbage bin, I realize with horror that the gum has melted to the skin of the palm of my hand. I slip away to the bathroom but still can't scrape off the gum. When I then return to class and reluctantly tell my teacher, she ridicules me and leads me down the hall to the grade 1 class. She takes me in front of the grade 1 students and proceeds to humiliate me as a punishment for chewing gum. She announces that I don't deserve to be in their grade 1 class, let alone in grade 2. Ashamed, I start to cry and soon hyperventilate, so the school calls my mother to pick me up. At home, my mother is gentle and kind, helping to scrub the gum off my hand with soap.

So, why do these memories recur in my awareness of all the many events of my childhood? It's helpful to begin by considering what they have in common. First, they carry a negative affective valence. They occur in key sites of socialization: namely, home and school. They all involve shame, humiliation, or my belief that I was being discriminated against. They involve food and navigating adults for food intake, though they all concern candy or treats. Finally, in each instance, other children, siblings or peers, play a critical role in setting the social context that made shame possible.

There is a distinctive group of other, more positive and reflective, memories that seem quite different in purpose and properties. Presented below, these experiences all involved a heightened experience of meta-awareness that arose in the juncture between home and school. This brings to mind differences between "learning" as socialization, which is really more conditioning than learning, and "learning" as reflection, which involves the cultivation of intention, agency, and autonomy. In this respect, learning both at home or in school often involves more conditioning and socialization than learning as knowing. Much learning in adulthood, on the other hand, is to reclaim autonomy and agency against conditioning and socialization and so involves more reflection. In this respect, some adult learning is about learning *against* conditioning and socialization, such as the unlearning of oppression.

In one of these early memories, I am 6 years old and walking home alone from the last day of kindergarten. As I turn the corner onto my street, I become aware of the pleasant sensation of the sun on my face. With the intense light, I squint and shift my gaze inside, where I become aware of my feet walking, and this, too, brings pleasure. My feet become my body become my life moving in time, and I feel pride, confidence, and wonder at what it is to grow older. Aware of myself, I remind myself to remember this moment in the future, to recollect this moment as I turn this same corner six years later when I walk home after graduating from grade 6. I focus my intention to remember this moment into the future, to remind my future self that these feet are the very same feet that I experienced on this final day of kindergarten six years earlier. If I can just remember, I tell myself, then I will be there, too, my six-year-old self will be there, as will this pleasure, this capacity for pleasure, this insight; it will be there, too.

In another memory, I am in grade 2, again hovering in the liminal space between home and school. Though technically at home, I am alone in the living room after lunch waiting to leave for school. I usually leave the house at 12:30, but it is only 12:20. Not wanting to suffer the boredom of waiting, I begin examining the clock with the intention of discerning time. Concentrating on the second hand, I search for the basic unit of time that surely must exist in the clock. The second hand remains still for a while, despite events transpiring in the world and in my mind. Then, suddenly, it jolts forward a full minute and a half. I realize that the movement of the clock doesn't match the unfolding of time on the ground OR in the mind. I realize that time doesn't exist in the clock. So, I turn my attention inside to examine time in my mind, searching for time as a singular event, but I can't find it. Instead, I find a continuum of unstable present moments dissolving into the past as soon as they arise, while the future then replaces them. I realize time is not at all what I am being told it is in school. I feel excitement, as if I have discovered a secret. Just then, the clock reads 12:30, and I leave for school.

Together, these memories tell a story of consciousness. First worth noting is how affective tones mark memories and consciousness as negative, positive, or neutral. What this affective marking accomplishes is unclear, but together they contribute to the framing of *what it is to be me*. These tones seem connected to associated emotional tones of fear, hope, calm, and anticipation. On the one hand, consciousness becomes constrained through shame arising from even minor traumas, yet finds sanctuary through self-reflection to grow between and beyond limiting social conditions. For me, these memories contradict inflated views about the value of social environments and their role in human development. Social institutions (e.g., families, schools) are not just nurturing and essential but often constraining and even hostile to consciousness and its potentials. Navigating social and physical environments place real limits on the person, their agency, and how they are able to express themselves. Pressures to adapt and conform may override the internal motives to realize autonomy and so flourish with a more authentic self and way of being, leading to what existentialists called *bad faith*. What comes to mind here is the etymology of "to educate," which derives from the Latin word for "to lead out," distinguishing education from mere socialization or conditioning. Optimally, at its best, education, and mindfulness-based education in particular (MacPherson & Rockman, 2023), can help to "draw out" this potential of consciousness within or even against the constraints of socialization.

Considering oppression as a problem of consciousness and its constraining conditions raises a number of lingering questions. For example, if oppression constrains consciousness, then what different limitations are placed on the oppressed and how? What is the cost to their experience of personhood and their quality of life? Is it reasonable to expect living systems like human beings, occupying a range of social and physical environments, to be able to realize or express their potential relatively free of constraints? Is this a biological "right"? If so, how would such equality even be approached let alone secured. If we invoke wellbeing as an ultimate end, then we need to consider the ways in which an expanded consciousness benefits wellbeing and quality of life. How does a particular type of expanded consciousness promote *eudaimonic* wellbeing, for example, where flourishing can be understood as the fulfilment of biological and phenomenological *potential*? Yet before we do that, we need to consider consciousness itself, and what makes it distinctive from biological material structures and processes.

## Distinctive Features of Consciousness

Communicating what consciousness is and why it matters using objective language beyond what it *feels like to be something* brings to mind the story of five blindfolded people trying to describe an elephant using information from touching one part of the elephant's body: The person at its leg swears it's a tree trunk; the person touching the snout swears it's a snake; the person at the ear, a great fan. Like the elephant, consciousness can be "seen" through a range of perspectives as well. I have organized some of these perspectives into five clusters to help represent consciousness. They are as follows: two qualities (2Qs); three dimensions (3-Ds); four inputs (4-Is); five capacities (5-Cs); and most significantly for the psychology of oppression and mindfulness, seven attributes (7-As). Table 5.1 aligns these features of consciousness. These features derive from a range of sources, including mindfulness theory (especially 2Qs); cognitive science (e.g., Seth, 2021, especially 3-Ds, and Hutto & Myin, 2017, especially 4-Is); Buddhist mind

*Table 5.1* Characterizing Consciousness

| *2-Qualities (2+/-Qs)* | *3-Dimensions (3-Ds)* | *4-Inputs (4-Is)* | *5-Capacities (5-Cs)* | *7-Attributes (7-As)* |
|---|---|---|---|---|
| Savouring or Dissociating (+/-Q1) | Self | Integration | Constructing | Awareness/ Attention |
| | Contents | | Controlling | Affect Attunement |
| Meaning or Indifference (+/-Q2) | | Information | Clarifying (Unobstructed) | Anticipation |
| | Levels | | Cognizing (Knowing) | Agency |
| | | Impulses | Creating | Autonomy |
| | | Intentions | | Affiliation |

science (e.g., Wallace, 2018 – especially 5-Cs); and mindfulness research (especially 7-As).

### Two (+/-) Qualities: Savouring and Meaning

Consciousness contributes significantly to our "quality of life," arguably even more than its objective contexts. These contributions can be represented as falling into two overall categories: savouring (via sensory experience) and meaning (via conceptual appraisal), with each organized into positive and negative qualities. These qualities derive from Garland et al.'s (2015a, 2015b) MMT framework, which was designed to explain empirical evidence showing that mindfulness increases wellbeing. They operationalized wellbeing using the two variables of savouring and meaning. Most directly, mindfulness regulates attention, leading to a reduction in habitual responses and decentring, which facilitates cognitive reappraisal and the increase in positive emotions. These culminate in improved abilities to savour experience and to derive meaning. They conclude that these downstream effects on the capacities to savour and find meaning explain why mindfulness enhances wellbeing and quality of life.

As a *felt* condition, savouring and meaning are attributable to consciousness itself rather than mere contents of consciousness. By logical extension, the absence of wellbeing would imply the absence of the experiences of savouring and meaning. The inability to savour experience would suggest being unable to attune to and engage sensory experience with sufficient attention, positive affect, and appreciation, which in extreme cases suggests states of clinical or nonclinical depression (anhedonia) and dissociation. Likewise, in its more extreme versions, the inability to find meaning in experience is signalled by excessive cynicism or indifference. This indifference could be moral indifference, as with cynicism or nihilism, or an emotional or empathic indifference when remaining unresponsive to suffering in yourself or others. So, while meaning reinforces agency and affiliation, the capacity to savour experience reinforces attunement, positive affect, and affiliation with the world, broadly.

### Three Dimensions of Consciousness (3-Ds): Self, Contents, and Levels

Seth (2021) identified three features of consciousness that I describe here as: *self*, *contents*, and *levels*. I refer to these as "dimensions" as they confer depth, breadth, and degree to conscious awareness, much like a "3-D" image does. Also, the three interconnect: the *self* integrates the *contents* of consciousness to give us the sense of integrated experience, but it also regulates and transcends itself to generate new and emerging degrees or *levels* of conscious experience.

### *Self*

The *self* is a gateway for becoming aware of consciousness itself. Experienced alternatively as an observer, narrator, or active agent, the self gives us to capacity for reflectivity and meta-awareness that enables consciousness to look back on itself. Without a cultivated self-awareness, consciousness eludes us; it remains obscured by the illusion it is designed to create: that is, that the world *out there* is detached from this world *in here* that we master. Under the spell of this illusion, we are captivated by, and captive to, the world as if it were a direct representation of an *a priori* objective reality that exists outside and independent of our existence. However seemingly solid and fixed reality may appear to be, the insight afforded by the *self* as it gazes back on itself and on consciousness opens up what is possible, thereby enhancing agency and choice.

The self appears in consciousness naively as more powerful (i.e., responsible), ubiquitous, stable, and uniform than it is. It is no wonder we tend to deny death when it implies the death of this self that is so entangled in our experience of the world! Contributing to these illusions of the self, consciousness seems to be a private domain located in a personal body and private "space" occupied exclusively by the self. When thoughts, feelings, or emotions arise, we tend to attribute them to this putative sole occupant of the house of consciousness: that is, the self or *soul*. In contrast, we experience the world, including its objects, the body, and other living beings, as "out there," independent of our mind and so largely beyond our influence or control. Both of these misapprehensions of the self and of phenomena are distortions – in one case overstating the role of the self and in the other overstating the power and fixity of the world. Scientifically, the question of the privacy of consciousness needs further investigation. Many people in non-modern cultural contexts, for example, don't experience consciousness as private; instead, they attribute their personal experience and consciousness to their interconnection with other human, sentient, or spiritual life forms, as the expression of a shared or distributed intelligence or awareness.

Evidence suggests that the self is not as unitary or integrated as we tend to believe, but rather something we impose like a story or narrative on variout functions and parts. As evidence, Farb et al. (2007) used *f*MRI data from people learning to meditate to identify two brain regions, usually coupled, which progressively became uncoupled through mindfulness: the *experiential self*, the self-as-observer of experience, and the *autobiographical self*, the self-as-author of the ongoing story of life. With this decoupling, the *experiential self* expanded while the *autobiographical self* contracted. In other words, the self become less about the story of our identity and more about our direct experiences interacting in the present.

Expanding on these distinctions between the narrative and experiential self, Seth (2021) identified five phenomenological selves: three *experiential selves* (embodied, perspectival, and volitional) and two *autobiographical selves* (narrative and social). He further attributed these differentiated selves to the need for self-regulation and control: "We do not perceive ourselves in order to know ourselves, we perceive ourselves in order to control ourselves" (p. 177). This goes to the tricky question of the function of the sense of self in consciousness.

In Vago and Silbersweig's (2012) S-ART theory, the self is proposed to support the growth of consciousness through the dynamics of self-awareness, self-regulation, and self-transcendence. Meta-awareness arises from self-awareness, as the self gazes back on the mind to become aware of consciousness. Denton (2006) argues that this "inward turning of consciousness" is the highest experience of awareness or consciousness (p. 15). As Sui and Humphreys (2015) demonstrate, this self-awareness is not merely an autobiographical or narrative rendering of the self nor of episodic events in time so much as an integrative process that binds disparate components of experience together, including sensorimotor, perception, memory, and decision-making. In this role, the self is "gluing" parts into the appearance of integrated wholes in consciousness. This integrative self-referential process leads to "self-expansion." Consciousness expands as the self learns to incorporate more complex identities and identifications from new in-groups into itself, including new skills and attributes from expanding social groups.

This theory of the expanding self and its relationship to consciousness is critical to understanding the challenges of oppression, whether arising from childhood traumas or lifelong social stigma and isolation. Historically, women have endured social isolation limits to their agency. Social identity scripts further impaired the expression of their agency, scripts reinforced by structural inequities within patriarchal institutions that limited their participation in aspects of work, education, play, and politics. For some women, degrees of social isolation persist, whether through marital or child-rearing inequities or, even with admission to non-traditional roles or activities, via misogynistic sanctions when they directly or indirectly challenge patriarchal norms.

This role of the self in expanding consciousness may also explain why people who are oppressed can identify with oppressors. Identifying with oppressors may seem to offer increased opportunity for self-expansion. It may also explain the imposter phenomenon, when previous forms of exclusion are removed and the oppressed enter new environments yet continue to encounter micro-aggressions and intrinsic biases and other covert forms of discrimination. Experiencing themselves as "infiltrators" in the new social context, their "self-expansion" may become inhibited or constrained by an internalized sense of social exclusion experienced as the feeling of being an imposter or not belonging (Nadal et al., 2021).

### *Contents*

Contents of consciousness, left unexamined, reinforce the appearance of concrete, objective, and factual worlds outside and private, subjective, and introspective spaces inside, giving rise to a mistakenly rigid dualistic divide. Seth (2021) dubbed this apparently concrete world that we all experience as a "controlled hallucination." In this sense, consciousness translates past experiences into pre-conscious probabilities as anticipated experiences, which we experience, in turn, as if they were reality, representing and misrepresenting inferred bodies, selves, and worlds as "out there" when they are actually manufactured "in here" by consciousness.

Consciousness is responsible for containing and generating the contents of all experience and knowing. These contents include sensations, affective associations, thoughts (as language or images), memories, emotions, empathy, compassion, dreams, and intuition. The sense of self is also itself a content, and recent theories suggest that an even subtler or more primordial sense of self may be implicit in consciousness itself (Denton, 2006; Denton et al., 2009; Panksepp, 1998; Seth, 2021). The idea that consciousness is distinguishable from its contents means that consciousness itself is knowable directly, in the absence of its contents, and that such knowing of a basic mind has value. Though contested within cognitive science, radical embodied or enactive/ecological cognition (REC) pre-supposes that such basic minds – that is, consciousness itself – are free of contents (Hutto & Myin, 2017).

### *Levels*

*Levels* of consciousness refer to degrees of cognitive awareness rather than to physiological states of wakefulness or sleep. This is important as being asleep does not mean we have no consciousness, nor does being physiologically awake mean that we are conscious. For example, we can "wake up" in a dream or, in a coma, be unconscious despite the body cycling through daily physiological states of wakefulness. *Levels* of consciousness can be measured using physiological indicators – fMRIs and EEGs. Patterns detected by these technologies indicate if a person is conscious (as an on/off state) as well as changes in consciousness. They can examine changes in consciousness associated with the use of hallucinogens, for example, aligning profound subjective changes in consciousness with brain patterns showing the decoupling of key brain regions and decreased and more random connectivity across brain regions (Carhart-Harris et al., 2012). This led researchers to conclude that changes in the underlying neurobiology of neural networks could signal levels of consciousness, with implications for the contents of consciousness and the sense of self. In this respect, levels of consciousness have interconnected and simultaneous biological and phenomenological expressions and sets of conditions.

Phenomenologically, we experience levels of consciousness on a spectrum from unconscious to semi-conscious (or liminal) to fully conscious to meta-cognitive awareness, signifying shifts from lower to heightened levels of conscious awareness. Smith and Neumann (2005) describe this spectrum as falling into two basic processing systems: one preconscious and the other conscious. Preconscious processes are those that are relatively automatic but whose results are nonetheless accessible to conscious awareness. In contrast, fully conscious processes "involve effortful, controlled search for and use of appropriate information, with the process itself as well as its result being available to awareness" (p. 288). According to Smith and Neumann (2005), pre-conscious and fully conscious distinctions align with the dual processing model of cognition, which they characterize as a combined *associative* and *rule-based* process, respectively. Deutsch (2016) describe these two systems as impulsive (associative) and reflective (rule-based) processing systems. Kahneman (2000, 2013) referred to them as system 1 (intuitive, fast) and system 2 (rationale, slow) forms of judgement.

### *Addendum: Mindfulness and Dual Systems*

Mindfulness can be said to engage these dual processes simultaneously rather than in isolation. The practice emphasizes training attention on what is *perceived* (i.e., form) and away from conceptual elaboration, prediction, judgement, and rumination; however, the reflective system is still intact in *recognizing* (i.e., naming) what is being experienced using self- or meta-cognitive awareness. Therefore, mindfulness is the practice of paying attention without judgement to what is perceived, principally in pre-conscious experience, thereby making possible direct insights into how consciousness constructs experience. Likewise, it fosters the reflective capacity to recognize and name what is being experienced. As Analayo (2020) concludes: "The two qualities occur together as essential components of formal mindfulness practice by way of its four establishments" (i.e., mindfulness of the body, feeling tones, mind, and phenomena) (p. 870).

Collaborating across the two systems, as outlined in the MMT, mindfulness begins with attention regulation. This regulated attention reduces habitual processing pathways to increase the decentring of consciousness, thereby broadening awareness and enhancing cognitive reappraisal, which increase positive emotions. This culminates in improved wellbeing by enhancing the capacities to savour and derive meaning from experience (Garland et al., 2015a, 2015b, 2017). In this way, mindfulness brings to the study of consciousness evidence that consciousness can be intentionally transformed. As the Dalai Lama says (Wallace, 2018): "A great Tibetan teacher once remarked that one of the mind's most marvellous qualities is that it can be transformed" (p. 19).

In Buddhist psychology, mindfulness is only the first step to recovering consciousness in the wake of suffering (such as oppression). It is not the end, just the first step in this recovery process. As discussed elsewhere in this book, the path of mindfulness is depicted as having seven steps or factors to wake-up consciousness, as described in the *Seven Factors of Awakening* theory. The seven steps begin with mindfulness (*sati*), followed by investigation (*dhamma vicaya*) and energy (*viriya*), which together constitute interest or interest-taking. The collaboration between the dual systems is characterized throughout these first three: *Mindfulness*, as attention regulation, deploys subtle names to *recognize* what is being experienced. *Investigation* deliberately engages reflective or slow processing using questions and curiosity. *Energy* is persistence, accomplished by intensifying the intention and resolve needed to sustain attention and engagement over time, eventually ripening in a change in consciousness itself.

This change in consciousness is indicated by the final four steps or factors: joy (*piti*), tranquillity (*passaddhi*), concentration (*samadhi*), and equanimity (*upekkha*). These final four factors are the natural effects of efforts to practise *interest-taking* more intentionally in the first three steps. Importantly, the final quality of equanimity develops with joy, tranquillity, and concentration, cumulatively, and is not a state of indifference. The Buddha describes this state of equanimity as infused with an ecstatic form of joy (Wallace, 2018):

> Being thus detached from hedonic craving, detached from unwholesome states, one enters and remains in the first dhyana, which is imbued with coarse investigation and subtle analysis, born of detachment, filled with delight and joy. And with this delight and joy born of detachment, one so suffuses, drenches, fills, and irradiates one's body that there is no spot in one's entire body that is untouched by this delight and joy born of detachment.
>
> (p. 8)

## Four "Inputs" of Consciousness (4-Is): Integration, Information, Impulses, and Intentions

The next, third column in Table 5.1 depicts the four inputs or operations that consciousness performs on phenomenal experience: *integration*, *information*, *impulses*, and *intentions*.

### *Integration*

Consciousness *integrates* experiences to give the impression that the world is more cohesive, consistent, and concrete than it actually is. As mentioned previously, this integration appears to be linked to the sense of self (Sui & Humphreys, 2015), which integrates sensations, perceptions, interpretations, and memories to convey the semblance of a coherent world. Seth (2021) suggests that this integration enacts the control needed for the world to appear to persist as its *controlled hallucination*. So, rather than being a direct window into the world, consciousness creates a snapshot of the world based on best-case probabilities.

Because oppression weakens the sense of self, it interferes with this integrative function of consciousness. For example, de Beauvoir's (2011/1949) theorized the ways in which women's identities are distorted in being objectified as an *Other* to men so as to restrict their autonomy and consciousness. Manne (2018) illustrated, in turn, how women can identify with patriarchy and collude in misogyny. Key to the problem in her view is the social construction of a "good woman" as one who is subservient to the needs of others. Such subservience is often focused on supporting *others'* autonomy rather than her own, thereby limiting or constraining her autonomy and increasing tendencies to externalize regulation and motivation (Ryan & Deci, 2000).

For women, the impact of oppression on identity can restrict their ability to integrate experiences through self-awareness, self-regulation (autonomy), and self-transcending processes (S-ARt). This may be at the heart of gender differences in mental wellbeing that are paradoxically lower in economically developed and more gender equal countries. Campbell et al. (2021) analysed mental health data from 73 countries involving 566,829 adolescents, finding that girls reported lower levels of wellbeing and higher levels of psychological distress than boys, a gap that was significantly *greater* for girls living in countries with higher GDPs and greater gender equality. The authors explain this perplexing finding as a possible case of "frustrated achievers," whereby formerly discriminated people with access to new wealth and opportunities report negative perceived mobility and happiness because of ongoing barriers and discrimination. They conclude:

> Thus, women or girls attempting to achieve the same successes as men and boys will look to them as their reference group and this may highlight the inequalities between them, producing lower life satisfaction and mental health, while in less gender equal countries reference groups might be limited to their own sex.
>
> (p. 7)

Ussher (2011) argued differences in women's *madness* are related to sexual objectification and its internalization: "Indeed, there is incontrovertible evidence that the objectification of women is a problem of epidemic proportions, which significantly contributes to distress and the diagnosis of psychiatric disorders on the part of women and girls" (p. 112). Added to this challenge is the expectation that women sacrifice personal autonomy and growth for the sake of others, including the sexual satisfaction of men (Saez et al., 2019). Too often, women and girls are exposed to threatening messaging that their identities should be subverted to the needs of others so as to conform to patriarchal feminine ideals or face the sanctions of misogyny

(Manne, 2018). As Ussher (2011) concluded, "Rejecting the mantle of the 'good woman,' the fantasy of idealised femininity, which is internalized from childhood, is thus central to women's recovery and resistance" (p. 193).

Within standardized mindfulness programmes like MBSR and MBCT, participants learn to interrupt the appearance of integration-as-fixity. Whether pleasant, unpleasant, or neutral, experiences are parsed and labelled as bodily sensations, sensory experience, thoughts and images, emotions, or behavioural reactions or responses. In deconstructing experiences in this way, practitioners witness more directly how experiences are also constructed or reconstructed by consciousness. Interrupting the illusion of integration can foster creativity instead of a passive acceptance of the world. This is *decentring*, a key mechanism by which mindfulness is theorized to reduce clinical depression and its relapse (Segal et al., 2019).

### *Information*

The second key input of consciousness is its *information* function, wherein various sensory and conceptual pathways organize and coordinate adaptively significant information and knowledge. This "information" is not only processed through the slow System 2 as rule-based symbolic or abstract information *about* something, but also via the faster and more associative and implicit System 1 processing. This latter information has more to do with intuitive and poetic (associational) meaning than information in the scientific or computing systems (rule-based) sense.

Gender expectations that girls and women should serve others can conflict with introspective information about desires, emotions, perceptions, and physical sensations associated with self-care. Ussher and Perz (2013), for example, found that girls' menstrual distress was relieved by escaping relational demands and responsibilities by caring for the self. This dissonance between social and embodied information can cause stress, confusion, and distress, leading some to suppress evidence coming to them via affective tones, emotions, and bodily responses. Suppressing such introspective and interoceptive "information" about the state of the self/body-mind removes it from consideration by the slow System 2 processing and leaving it to instead to more automatic, habitual, and conditioned pre-conscious processing.

### *Impulses*

Consciousness is not a passive, empty receptacle for sensory imprints; it is actively engaged in decision-making and action, much of which happens pre-consciously. A principal insight of the enactivist (embodied, ecological) turn in cognitive science is the recognition of the degree of integration of sensory inputs and motor responses. Rather than a seeming linear sequence of cause and effect, perception emerges through motor action as the brain attempts to interpret the world into meaningful phenomenal experiences. Perception and motor systems coinhere to generate the world, whereby the motor systems do not just respond to but also help to create the perceived world. We might say that we redesign our worlds to align with our needs and expectations.

As embodied minds, we function principally through habits, relying on previous experiences to anticipate the present and future. So, consciousness orchestrates this life through fast decision-making using habitual responses; however, such decisions are not deliberative but more impulsive, reactive, and automatic. These impulses safeguard survival without needing to engage the slow, rule-based processes of language, thought, and intentions. Deriving from preconscious processing, these habitual actions transpire in a state likened to sleep walking, signifying the reduction of consciousness through habitual action. Therefore, shifting from fast System 1 impulses to more deliberative, slow System 2 thinking or awareness, with its heightened intention and choice, is some of what it means to be more conscious. With respect to oppression, given its internalized, preconscious enactment, the problem of impulsive, fast thinking reactivity is crucial to understanding its problem and solutions. No one is oppressed by choice, but they need to make a choice to be free from it.

### *Intentions*

*Intention* is the most important of inputs to consider in the psychology of oppression. For girls and women facing intergenerational legacies of oppression, intention provides a way to incrementally but steadily enact change. As Hutto and Myin (2017) argue, even a basic mind or consciousness *has* rudimentary intention. Buddhist psychology refers to such rudimentary intention as *desire*, an intrinsic link in the 12 links of dependent origination characterizing consciousness. Intention is also the defining nature of "Buddha" nature described in the Mahayana school. This natural mind is likened to a seed nascent in all living beings that catalyses the intention to "wake up" consciousness in the interests of the betterment of (all) sentient life. So, consciousness is not merely a discrete and passive thing that *integrates information*, it is future-directed in its intentionality, moving in coordination with personal agency to grow and flourish. In this sense, consciousness and intention partake of the same nature, which makes intention both a dimension and an input of consciousness. As an inclination, *intention* becomes an intrinsic impulse or motivation within the fast System 1, yet it is also amenable to being fostered and developed through the slow thinking, reflective deliberations and choices of System 2 processing.

For women, internalized social scripts and misogyny can hack their intention, leading girls to adopt and so *become* feminine gendered ideals that view the intentions of others as their own. In this way, as Simone de

Beauvoir famously stated, "one is not born, but rather becomes, woman." Just as a woman learns to "other" herself by diverting her intentions to fulfilling the intentions of others, so does a man "other" woman by making her the object of his desire and intention. In the process, women become, according to de Beauvoir, the object of the intention of the male gaze: "The very concept of 'women,' de Beauvoir argues, is a male concept: woman is always 'other' because the male is the 'seer:' he is the subject and she the object – the *meaning* of what it is to be a woman is given by men" (Joseph, 2008). So, while his intentions become hers, she becomes his intention, that is, the object of his agency, thereby displacing and subverting her intention and agency in the process.

Although these identity dynamics have shifted in the ensuing 75 years, women continue to struggle to internalize and lay claim to intentionality. Her biological facticity as a *woman* continues to be used to justify her oppression; however, her oppression is not biological but an identity dysfunction that is social in nature. As Joseph (2008) carried on to considerpoints out:

> De Beauvoir argues that it is not the biological condition of women *per se* that constitutes a handicap: it is how a woman construes this condition which renders it positive or negative. None of the uniquely female experiences – the development of female sex organs, menstruation, pregnancy, menopause – have a meaning in themselves; but in a hostile or oppressive society they can come to take on the meaning of being a burden and disadvantage, as women come to accept the meanings a patriarchal society accords them.

### Five Capacities (5-Cs): Constructing, Controlling, Clarifying, Cognizing, and Creating

The five capacities (5-Cs) of consciousness are its objective features viewed from a 3rd person perspective. These capacities describe what consciousness *does*, specifically: *constructing, controlling, clarifying, cognizing*, and *creating*. The first and primary capacity of consciousness is to *construct* experience. This implies, in turn, that it can *deconstruct* experience as well. In this sense, consciousness is constituted of component parts – sensory, feeling tones, thoughts, etc. The second capacity of consciousness is its capacity to *control* the self and how the world appears – that controlled hallucination that Seth (2021) referred to. These controlling functions transpire on a spectrum from pre-conscious (bare perception) processes to self-regulation to executive decision-making exercised by slow and deliberate contemplative and phenomenological reflection.

The next two capacities derive from Buddhist psychology in which consciousness is distinguished from matter by being "unobstructed." This unobstructive quality is linked to its capacity to clarify and reflect clearly what is presented to it as an object of awareness. Where matter obstructs, consciousness *clarifies*. Consciousness is thus equated to light or, more specifically, luminosity, perhaps relating to the use of the term "enlightenment" for the realization of the potential of consciousness to flourish. According to Wallace (2018), even in the earliest Pali canon, the Buddha is said to have depicted the fourth stage of mindfulness – self-illuminating mindfulness – "as brightly shining (Pali *pabhassara*) and naturally pure (Pali *Pakati-pariduddha*)" (p. 7). Added to clarifying (as illuminating) is the *cognizing* capacity of consciousness. In Vajrayana Buddhism, for example, the nature of primordial consciousness is often defined as *clear* and *knowing*, whereby cognizing is *knowing*. From a cognitive science perspective, Seth (2021) describes the knowing of a chair as its *chairness* to distinguish its independent existence as an object from the perceiving or *knowing* of it in consciousness:

> It is because our perceptions have the phenomenological character of "being real" that it is extraordinarily difficult to appreciate that, in fact, perceptual experiences do not necessarily – or ever – directly correspond to things that have a mind-independent existence. A chair has a mind-independent existence; *chairness* does not.
>
> (p. 144)

Culminating from these previous four is the *creating* capacity of consciousness. Although related to constructing, *creativity* refers to the fundamentally creative work of mind. If we grasp this new understanding that all experience is a grand hallucination of consciousness (Seth, 2021), then appreciating consciousness-as-creative becomes paramount to working with consciousness as a path of healing and wellbeing. As I described elsewhere, in the oral tradition that I was first exposed to, the first line of *the Dhammapada* made this view of mind clear almost 2,300 years ago: "Mind is the source of all things: Great mind. Creative mind."

## The Seven Attributes (7-As)

I use the term "attributes" to avoid the notion that these are "functions," though the attributes are activities enacted by consciousness. They refer to the key ways consciousness enacts our sense of self, the world, and our actions within it. If something were said to be conscious, it would need to have these attributes or abilities. Framed as nouns, the seven attributes are as follows: awareness/attention, affect, attunement, anticipation, agency, autonomy, and affiliation. As attributes of consciousness, they are irreducible to matter or biological processes. Mounting scientific evidence suggests mindfulness has a positive effect on each of these seven attributes. Understanding the seven as constituting consciousness itself paves the way to explaining the often far-reaching and wide-ranging impacts of mindfulness in the scientific literature. When we understand mindfulness as a tool to empower and improve consciousness itself, it is easier to understand why it might impact so many other components of wellbeing.

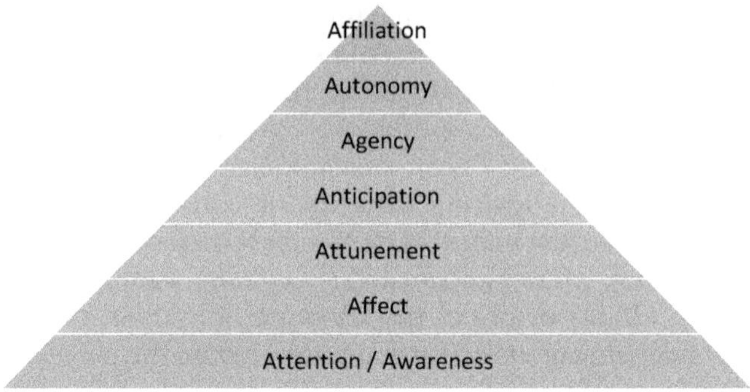


*Figure 5.1* The Seven Attributes of Consciousness.

The seven attributes appear in Table 5.1 and in Figure 5.1. They are distinctive from the other descriptors of consciousness as they map most directly to consider the role of mindfulness on consciousness and, therefore, in the psychology of oppression (see Chapter 6). These seven attributes move through: attention/awareness, affect, attunement, anticipation, agency, autonomy, and affiliation.

Breaking consciousness into seven components in this way allows us to consider how consciousness contributes to, supports, and sustains a life of flourishing and wellbeing, or alternatively how it might restrict a life. I define here a consciousness able to sustain wellbeing as having the capacity to *savour* and to derive *meaning* from experience. The absence of these capacities to savour and find meaning implies consciousness is somehow constrained and impaired in one or more of these seven attributes. Absences in these two qualities are associated with the tendency to *dissociate*, in the absence of savouring, or to display *indifference* or *moral resignation*, in the absence of meaning. This lack of meaning is the condition of *bad faith* or *false consciousness* described in earlier oppression scholarship. It is worth considering a literary depiction of the experience of consciousness, curtailed.

In Sarah Bernstein's (2023) novel, *Study for Obedience*, the narrator chronicles the emergence of her own subservient, oppressed consciousness within a patriarchal family living in the aftermath of a history of persecution. She describes her own agency being suppressed through her childhood and later in the interests of the males in her family, principally her eldest brother. As an adult, she travels to serve him after his family breaks down and his wife and children leave. To this oppressive situation is added her relative isolation as a foreigner returning to a region where her family had been historically persecuted in the past, suggestive of a Jewish woman returning to Eastern Europe a generation after the Holocaust. In these ways, she is an iconic literary figure to consider the psychology of oppression and its internalization as "obedience."

No proper nouns or names are used in the novel – for people or places. The obliteration of names contributes to the sense of the reduced awareness and stunted consciousness of the narrator. Isolated when her brother leaves and unable to speak the language, she retreats into this false consciousness that mistakenly interprets the natural and social worlds she moves in and the threats posed to her by the situation. Unnamed through the novel, she lives in a dissociated state, incapable of savouring or engaging life except by serving those who don't really deserve or merit her attentions and labour. Boundaries are violated in the process. She describes, for example, brushing her brother's back while he bathes, a man she described as abusive to his wife and children yet without seeming to judge him for it. Prior to going to live with this brother, she transcribed legal documents for a firm representing an exploitative and corrupt oil company, yet exonerated herself from any moral responsibility or culpability, priding herself instead for her copy-editing skills. In these ways, she exemplifies the effects of oppression on consciousness when left unchallenged or unaddressed: dissociation, indifference, and moral resignation, a "moral" resignation extending to passivity in the face of real threats to her own safety and wellbeing.

*Study for Obedience* is *absurdist fiction* in which the main character is unable to find meaning or purpose. This becomes integral to her oppressive condition of "obedience," a state in which she has subverted her agency and self to the purposes of others. Through her narration, she documents her dissociated states and inability to live in the present. In the process, she denies her own capacity for a quality life of savouring and meaning, suppressing even nascent impulses to savour sensory experiences in the garden or forest where she walks. Her agency became narrowly focused instead on being obedient to self-denial and meeting the needs and demands of others, her abusers:

> And so I lived in the historical rupture of the present, in the historical aberration of my life, and I submitted to those that had me at their mercy in an effort to soften their hearts. ... If in the preceding weeks I had loved too well my walks among the budding trees of the forest, if I had felt the smallest temptation to withdraw my obedience, I knew that once again I had to gain mastery over myself, over the motions of my spirit, various and vain.
>
> (p. 104)

In the protagonist's world, oppression was "obedience." In the foregoing passage, she describes a distinctive, mindful way of attending to the world that began to loosen the grip of that obedience – that is, her internalized oppression. Attending to trees and he forest and the ensuing distancing from the social world as the source of her oppression began to subdue her conditioned obedience; however, it was her own agency in the end, acting in *bad faith*, that opted to turn away from this promise of freedom, described as her "spirit, various and vain," by asserting "mastery" over herself and so restoring submissive obedience to her oppressors. In the end, she too becomes an oppressor. This is the predicament of the oppressed that reminds us why consciousness is a critical consideration in the path out of oppression.

**Attention/Awareness**

Attention is an action; awareness is a state of mind. With persistent application, attention broadens and expands awareness. Although awareness is borne of attention, attention doesn't necessarily alter awareness if not sufficiently mindful. For example, attention can be fleeting, ephemeral, scattered, or superficial. When it does alter awareness, it is because what is attended to is recognized, deepened, and held in the mind as something to be ultimately "known." In this respect, it is not the result of a passive or fleeting attention but the "realization" of what is attended to as a form of knowing, in which perception and conception, fast and slow thinking, cooperate to generate a qualitative state of awareness.

The story of the awakening of the Buddha reflects the potential harms of self-doubt and desire on awareness and, ultimately, consciousness itself. Having held attention for some time in meditation, he began to recognize its source: "I have found you, O Builder, you will build no more." Just prior to this transformational moment of enlightenment, Mara and his daughters were said to have appeared before the seated Siddhartha Gautama. Mara was a demonic figure in Buddhism associated with temptation and death. First deploying his daughters to tempt Siddhartha with desire, when that didn't work, he resorted to instilling self-doubt, telling Siddartha that his wish for freedom was a conceit. Mara asked him by what right he could claim such freedom, to which the Buddha responded by touching the ground and calling on the "earth to bear witness to my right to be, unmoved by desire or fear." The earth responded with a tremor. This gave rise to the now iconic image of the Buddha doing the earth touching mudra (with the three fingers of his right hand touching the earth).

Mindfulness self-regulates attention, which expands awareness through the combined activities of observing, describing, applying, non-judging, and not reacting (to) experience (the operationalized five facets of mindfulness or FFMQ, Baer et al., 2006). From a Buddhist perspective, this is accomplished not only by mindfulness in isolation but in tandem with investigation and perseverance (i.e., "interest-taking"), from which joy, calm, concentration, and equanimity ensue. This final equanimity *(upekkha)* is associated with wisdom (i.e., "unmoved by desire and fear") and compassion (i.e., equal consideration for self, loved ones, enemies, and strangers). Yet there are many forms of awareness that arise from mindful attention, and none are sought in themselves. What is sought is the expansion of awareness and consciousness itself, that is, to "know" what is present in any moment. This includes parsed sensory experiences that combine to construct the illusion of integration but also the affect that accompanies them, the interpretation, the emotions, memories, and associations that build them, and the ways these impel us to react in one way rather than another or not at all.

In oppression, attention and awareness are suppressed through emotions like shame and self-doubt, fear and exposure to sustained threats. Such a suppressed condition places constraints on what is attended or noticed, limiting the possibilities of self-regulated attention that would enable one to resist more effectively the external imposition of social scripts and identities arising from the external regulation of attention. Mindfulness, on the other hand, recovers attention to the present and interrupts habitual ways of perceiving the self or world, thereby broadening awareness (Garland et al., 2015a, 2015b).

## Affect

Affect (aka feelings, feeling tones, affective tones) refers to the valence associated with sensed or mental experience via the fast-thinking System 1 impulse processing. Affective tones are how preconscious processes condition more conscious experiences of feeling attraction (i.e., pleasant affective tone), repulsion or aversion (i.e., unpleasant affective tone), or indifference (i.e., neutral affective tone). This tri-valence affective spectrum is described with remarkable consistency across the contemporary psychology of emotions (Barrett, 2018) and the classical Buddhist psychology of *vedana* (Peacock & Batchelor, 2020). Although it contributes to emotion, affect is distinct from them; affective tones are valences that become associated preconsciously with every sensed or mental event so as to condition our experiences of self, people, and things, rather than being themselves mental formations like emotions. This is reflected in the word for affect, *vedana*, which is closer to the word *sensation*.

In mindfulness, affective tones are noticed in ways that distinguish them from the sensed experiences to which they are attached. So, in being mindful of the sound of a drill, for example, the qualities of the sound are untangled from the affective tone attributed to it, perhaps a negative affective tone. Even the sound itself is parsed out in attention to notice how it is constructed out of volume, intensity, persistence (or intermittence), and pitch. The affective tone is discerned by recognizing if the sound is experienced as wanted, unwanted, or neutral, and how that affective tone *feels* or is experienced in the body-mind. What might have begun as aversion or avoidance or distress, for example, may become interest and curiosity as a positive affective tone arising from mindfulness itself sets in.

Affective tones are part of the fast-thinking System 1 processing, giving rise to implicit biases and their impulses. For the oppressed, the harmful negative associations they internalize about their identities and communities are formed through implicit affective associations. This is also true of oppressors and the implicit biases driving their oppressing behaviours. So, working with affective tones – recognizing them and then broadening awareness to experience them without habitual reactions – is critical for anti-oppressive work. Mindfulness, therefore, offers a kind of desensitization process to first see these affective associations in awareness, expose them to slow System 2 reflection, and to replace the negative associations with the more positive affect that naturally arises through mindful curiosity.

### Attunement

Consciousness is a defining feature of the ecological niche of living organisms (at least animals). By coordinating experience as the *feel* of things, consciousness enhances our capacities to self-regulate (control ourselves) and to reorganize the environment to support survival, if not flourishing. This ability to relate experiences across internal and external conditions is a fundamental attribute of consciousness: *attunement*. Consciousness is attuned to both internal and external situations, sustaining and coordinating thow we interpret and respond to these situations over time. Furthermore, this attunement exists on a spectrum from non-conscious to preconscious to more intentional observations and relationships. For example, attunement is a term used to describe mother-infant instinctive or preconscious bonding and attachment processes and their role in the emergence of social cognition (Bornstein, 2022) as well as to more intentional forms relationships such as pedagogical or therapeutic (Gallese et al., 2007). With respect to the physical environment, attunement describes how consciousness adapts and grows in embodied relationship to natural and built environments, including as shared patterns or "rhythms" (Charalambous and Djebbara, 2023).

Mindfulness is associated with "third wave" psychotherapies, all of which rely on mindfulness to varying degrees. These therapies developed from the "broaden and build theory," which posits that positive emotions broaden awareness and build cognitive resources associated with meaning. As Garland & Fredrickson (2013) describe, "The broaden-and-build theory … asserts that positive emotions broaden individuals' thought-action repertoires, enabling them to draw flexibly on higher-level associations and a wider-than-usual array of sensory information, ideas, and behaviors; in turn, broadened cognition engenders behavioral flexibility" (p. 33). This was an early iteration of the mindfulness-to-meaning theory or MMT (Garland et al., 2015a, 2015b).

To extricate oneself from the shadow of oppression, it is critical to develop the capacity to discern the self and world more objectively based on what is present rather than on pre-existing ideas about ourselves and the world. The process of broadening and building describes the effects of mindfulness on the attuning attribute of consciousness, whereby through more detailed attention and awareness through mindfulness training, it becomes possible to decentre from the storied view of ourselves and our situation to allow a more positive affective tone that enables the broadening or attunement to take place. In this way, mindfulness can foster the first three attributes of consciousness – attention/awareness, affect, and attunement – to enact the broadening of awareness and building of cognitive resources associated with wellbeing.

### Anticipation

The "new science" of consciousness theorizes that consciousness presents us with a world derived from probability rather than representation (Seth, 2021). In other words, what we experience as an *a priori* world "out there" is in fact a best-guess scenario. This probability assessment is constructed from previous sensory and cognitive experiences and habits among other things. In this way, consciousness is *anticipatory* in nature, anticipating and predicting what is or will be present in any given subsequent moment. Consciousness does not provide an objective window into the world, despite appearing to do so. It reconstructs experience into forms suited to serve our senses, expectations, and, ultimately, survival. To bring home this point, Seth (2021) suggests that consciousness needs to be understood to be writing as much as reading the world through sensory experiences. What it is writing, furthermore, is fiction or what he refers to as a neuronal fantasy and collective hallucination:

> The entirety of perceptual experience is neuronal fantasy that remains yoked to the world through a continuous making and remaking of perceptual best guesses, of controlled hallucinations. You could even say that we're all hallucinating all the time. It's just that when we agree about our hallucinations, that's what we call reality.
>
> (p. 92)

These perceptual best guesses underlie the anticipatory attribute of consciousness to describe how consciousness is predicting what is about to happen as a safeguard to support survival. As a practice, mindfulness slows down and magnifies our powers of observation to enable us to witness more directly this anticipatory process. Sometimes, the ensuing awareness allows us to see consciousness projecting itself on the present moment as a mirror or screen rather than a window gazing out on the world. We are intentionally attending to the fast-thinking mind to witness how strands of memory, anticipation, interpretation, and perception are combining to form the semblance of integrated experience. This process is explicit in the secular-scientific context of teaching mindfulness, where post-meditative practices parse experience and describe such parsed experiences, separating outs in some cases accounts of bodily sensations, affect, thoughts, emotions, and behavioural inclinations.

## Agency

The next two attributes of consciousness – agency and autonomy – originate more from the scientific rather than Buddhist study of consciousness. Agency begins with intention and with the sense of self that is implicit in consciousness and intention. Yet is it not merely a passive observing or experiential self but an active decision-maker enacting intention within particular situations. Consciousness develops as a manifestation of agency, suggested by title of Anil Seth's popular book on consciousness, *Being You*.

In Buddhist psychology, the sense of self is presented as an illusion reinforcing ignorance, and therefore *anatta* or no-self is a focus of investigation and insight alongside the other two characteristics of mind, impermanence (*anicca*) and suffering *(dukkha)*. Insights into these three characteristics of mind are said to bring liberation from the suffering of conscious existence. The idea that there is no-self, however, is misleading in that consciousness is propelled and grows on the basis of more subtle manifestations of agency and meta- or self-awareness. This over-emphasis on "no" self may have led to a devaluation of agency and explain, in part, why Buddhism continues to be critiqued for generating passivity in the face of social and political injustices and harms, and why corrective movements like socially engaged Buddhism have emerged in recent decades.

In secular-scientific mindfulness programmes and practices, notably in MBSR, awareness is cultivated so as to shift from *doing* to *being*, which is operationally defined as moving from reacting to responding to stressful situations (Woods & Rockman, 2021). In MBCT, this shift is operationally defined as correcting a naive belief in the facticity of thoughts – "thoughts are not facts" (Woods et al., 2019) – to encourage instead a decentred state of broadened awareness and openness enabling cognitive reappraisal and more positive emotions (Garland et al., 2017). Although these could be misconstrued as encouraging passivity in the encounter with injustice, that would be a misreading. Instead, these themes and associated practices are inviting an unrealistic burden placed on the self and on thought to manage stress and mood disorders. Rather than cultivating expressions of agency based on the desire to control or manage a situation, mindfulness fosters a decentred awareness to invite more specific responses to complex situations. Furthermore, rather than relying excessively on System 2 rule-based thinking, mindfulness invites a form of agency empowered through intention to act across the fast System 1 and slow System 2 processing.

## Autonomy

Autonomy is a characteristic of biological organisms that extends to consciousness itself. Within closed or semi-closed systems like eco-systems, how is that life forms distinguished themselves out of chaos to sustain order (organizations) despite ongoing structural change and dissipation? Self-organizing systems begin by closing boundaries or partially closing them, a notable example being cells with semi-permeable membranes that permit the entry of only necessary materials or nutriments without allowing toxins or harmful material to pass with them and then discard waste with equal discernment. This basic principle of life is echoed in the way consciousness functions, too, wherein awareness operates with its own equivalent of a semi-permeable "membrane" that filters through what is experienced consciously based on survival needs and the pursuit of wellbeing (as flourishing).

Autonomy is disrupted when external controlling agents or systems hijack this semi-closed system by posing a sustained threat to survival (imagined or real). Given the strong, natural impetus for autonomy, this relinquishing of autonomy happens for the most part preconsciously. Autonomy requires a semi-closed system in which information is taken from the environment, including the internal environment, and then processed in relation to intentions. The organism then acts to change or respond so as to fulfill the intention. The most fundamental intention is survival, then wellbeing (as flourishing or the expression of potential). A real threat to survival will usually, but not always, trump the motivation for wellbeing, more broadly construed; however, heroic people show us how the motivation for personal or collective wellbeing (flourishing) can override even the basic motivation to survive. As the Dalai Lama pointed out in 1990 at the inauguration of a human rights monument in Ottawa, human rights abuses tend to sacrifice the most courageous among us.

For the oppressed, the task of reclaiming autonomy is critical to overcoming oppression. The internalization of the negative social scripts and narratives create a condition in which it is easy for their agency and autonomy both to be hacked and undermined. The key here is not the loss of autonomy or agency so much as the possibility of wellbeing (as flourishing). Mindfulness has been strongly associated with autonomous forms of motivation, for example, but not with externally controlled and introjected (self-controlling or suppressing) forms of motivation (Ryan & Bradshaw, 2021).

### Affiliation

It would be a mistake to misinterpret autonomy as independence. Consciousness comes with a strong motivation for autonomy, but the metaphor of a semi-permeable membrane is critical – external information and socialization are critical to the formation and functioning of consciousness. Indeed, I would go so far as to say that consciousness is fundamentally affiliative. The sense of independence, including the privacy of consciousness, seems to be part of our collective hallucination. In this sense, I would venture to guess that the full extent of the affiliative bases of consciousness is hidden or obscured.

What does this suggest? For one, it suggests that consciousness is more distributed and less personal than we tend to assume in ordinary experience. Second, it suggests that motivations to act on behalf of collective, not merely personal, wellbeing (as flourishing) may be as natural a motivation as autonomy is for the organism. This clarifies the value of empathy and compassion in the cultivation of consciousness. When we imagine another's experience, our consciousness expands accordingly to inhabit their worlds, however marginally. This also implies the importance of communication to consciousness, and not merely between humans but across sentient life forms. In this respect, "my" consciousness may be a misnomer, and "our" consciousness may be more accurate. Consciousness may well prove to store, contain, intersect, and even constitute the collective experiences of life on Earth. Mindfulness naturally extends self-awareness to awareness of others, including non-human life forms.

I wrote of my own deep encounters with non-human "teachers" during solitary silent meditation retreats and how they fostered, not merely an appreciation of nature but an expansion of consciousness. So, I close here with those same conclusions about mindfulness (MacPherson & Rockman, 2023):

> As powerful as the study of scientific ecology has been for raising awareness of the human impacts on global systems, it has proved wholly inadequate in fostering in human beings a sense of a shared welfare and belonging across species and with life on Earth. Mindfulness, as an experiential ecology process, offers a promising way to en-flesh otherwise conceptual ecological principles, to render them lived and embodied ways of knowing cultivated through direct contact with wild things.
>
> (p. 345)

## References


Analayo, Bikkhu (2018). In the seen just the seen: Mindfulness and the construction of experience. *Mindfulness*, *10*, 179–184. https://doi.org/10.1007/s12671-018-1042-9

Analayo, Bikkhu (2020). Clear knowing and mindfulness. *Mindfulness*, *11*, 862–871. https://doi.org/10.1007/s12671-019-01283-8

Baer, R., Smith, G., Hopkins, J., Krietemeyer, J., & Toney, L. (2006). Using self-report assessment method to explore facets of mindfulness. *Assessment*, *13*(1). https://doi.org/10.1177/1073191105283504

Barrett, L.F. (2018). *How emotions are made: The secret life of the brain*. Mariner Books.

Bernstein, S., (2023). *Study for Obedience*. Alfred A. Knopf Canada.

Bornstein, M. (2022). Mother-infant attunement: A multi-level approach via body, brain, and behavior. In M. Borstein, *Parenting: Selected writings of Marc Bornstein*, Ch. 12, 36 pages. Routledge.

Campbell, O., Bann, D., & Patalay, P. (2021). The gender gap in adolescent mental health: A cross-national investigation of 566,829 adolescents across 73 countries. *SSM–Population Health*, *13*, 100742, https://doi.org/10.1016/j.ssmph.2021.100742

Carhart-Harris, R. L., Erritzoe, D., Williams, T., Stone, J. M., Reed, L. J., Colasanti, A., Tyacke, R., Leech, R., Malizia, A., Murphy, K., Hobden, P., Evans, J. Feilding, A., Wise, R., & Nutt, D. J. (2012). Neural correlates of the psychedelic state as determined by fMRI studies with psilocybin. *Proceedings of the National Academy of Sciences*, *109*(6), 2138–2143. https://doi.org/10.1073/pnas.1119598109

Charalambous, E., & Djebbara, Z. (2023). On natural attunement: Shared rhythms between the brain and the environment. *Neuroscience and Biobehavioral Reviews*, *155*. https://doi.org/10.1016/j.neubiorev.2023.105438

Crick, F., & Koch, C. (1990). Towards a neurobiological theory of consciousness. *Seminars in the Neurosciences*, *2*, 263–275.

de Beauvoir, S. (1948). The ethics of ambiguity.

de Beauvoir, S. (2011/1949). *The second sex* (C. Borde & S. Malavany-Chevallier, Trans.). Vintage. (Originally published in 1949).

Denton, D. (2006). *The primordial emotions: The dawning of consciousness*. Oxford University Press.

Denton, D., McKinley, M., Farrell, M., & Egan, G. (2009). The role of primordial emotions in the evolutionary origin of consciousness. *Consciousness and Cognition*, *18*, 500–514.

Deutsch, R. (2016). Associative and propositional processes from the perspective of the reflective–impulsive model. In R. Deutsch, B. Gawronski, & W. Hofmann (Eds.), *Reflective and impulsive determinants of human behavior* (pp. 63–80). Routledge. https://doi.org/10.4324/9781315523095

Fanon, F. (1961). *The wretched of the earth*. Francois Maspero.
Farb, N., Segal, Z., Mayberg, H., Bean, J., McKeon, D., Fatima, Z., & Anderson, A. (2007). Attending to the present: Mindfulness meditation reveals distinct neural modes of self- reference. *Social, Cognitive, and Affective Neuroscience*, 2(4), 313–322. https://doi.org/10.1093/scan/nsm030
Firestone, S. (1970). *The dialectic of sex: The case for feminist revolution*. Farrar, Straus, Giroux.
Freire, P. (1970). *Pedagogy of the oppressed* (M. B. Ramos, Trans.). Herder & Herder.
Gallese, V., Eagle, M., & Migone, P. (2007). Mirror neurons and the neural underpinnings of interpersonal relations. *Journal of the American Psychoanalytic Association*, 55(1), 131–175. https://doi.org/10.1177/00030651070550010601
Garland, E., Farb, N., Goldin, P., & Fredrickson, B. (2015a). Mindfulness broadens awareness and builds eudaimonic meaning: A process model of mindful positive emotion regulation. *Psychological Inquiry*, 26(4), 293–314. https://doi.org/10.1080/1047840X.2015.1064294
Garland, E., Farb, N., Goldin, P., & Fredrickson, B. (2015b). The mindfulness-to meaning theory: Extensions, applications, and challenges at the attention-appraisal-emotion interface. *Psychological Inquiry*, 26(4), 377–387. https://doi.org/10.1080/1047840X.2015.1092493
Garland, E., & Fredrickson, B. (2013). Mindfulness broadens awareness and builds meaning at the attention-emotion interface. In T. Kashdan & J. Ciarrochi (Eds.), *Mindfulness, acceptance, and positive psychology: The seven foundations of well-being*, Ch. 2 (pp. 30–67). Context Press.
Garland, E., Kiken, L, Faurot, K., Palsson, O., & Gaylord, S. (2017). Upward spirals of mindfulness and reappraisal: Testing the mindfulness-to-meaning theory with autoregressive latent trajectory modelling. *Cognitive Therapy and Research*, 41(3), 381–392. https://doi.org/10.1007/s10608-016-9768-y
Griffin, D. (1976). *The question of animal awareness: Evolutionary continuity of mental experience*. Rockefeller University Press.
Hutto, D., & Myin, E. (2017). *Evolving enactivism: Basic minds meet contents*. MIT Press.
Joseph, F. (2008). Becoming a woman: Simone de Beauvoir on female embodiment. *Philosophy Now*, 69, September/October 2008. Accessed at: https://philosophynow.org/issues/69/Becoming_A_Woman_Simone_de_Beauvoir_on_Female_Embodiment
Kahneman, D. (2000). A psychological point of view: Violations of rational rules as a diagnostic of mental processes. *Behavioral and Brain Sciences*, 23(5), 681–683. https://doi.org/10.1017/S0140525X00403432
Kahneman, D. (2013). *Thinking fast and slow*. Anchor Canada.
MacPherson, S., & Rockman, P. (2023). *Mindfulness-based teaching and learning: Preparing mindfulness specialists in education and clinical care*. Routledge.
Manne, K. (2018). *Down girl: The logic of misogyny*. Oxford University Press.
Nadal, K., King, R., Sissoko, G., Floyd, N., & Hines, D. (2021). The legacies of systemic and internalized oppression: Experiences of microaggressions, imposter phenomenon, and stereotype threat on historically marginalized groups. *New Ideas in Psychology*, 63. 100895. https://doi.org/10.1016/j.newideapsych.2021.100895
Nagel, T. (1974). What is it like to be a bat? *The Philosophical Review*, 83(4). 435–450.
O'Regan, J.K. (2011). *Why red doesn't feel like a bell*. Oxford University Press.
Panksepp, J. (1998). *Affective neuroscience: The foundations of human and animal emotions*. Oxford University Press.
Peacock, J. & Batchelor, M. (Eds.) (2020). *The definition, practice, and psychology of vedana: Knowing how it feels*. Routledge.

Ryan, R., & Bradshaw, E. (2021). Mindfulness and motivation: A process view using self-determination theory. *Current Directions in Psychological Science*, *30*(4), 300–306. https://doi.org/10.1177/09637214211009511

Saez, G., Valor-Segura, I., & Esposito, F. (2019). Interpersonal Sexual Objectification Experiences: Psychological and Social Well-Being Consequences for Women. *Journal of Interpersonal Violence*, *34*(4), 741–762. https://doi.org/10.1177/0886260516645813

Schlanger, Z. (2024). *The light eaters: How the unseen world of plant intelligence offers a new understanding of life on Earth*. Harper.

Segal, Z., Anderson, A., Gulamani, T, Dinh Williams, L., Desormeau, P., Ferguson, A., Walsh, K., & Farb, N. (2019). Practice of therapy acquired regulatory skills and depressive relapse/recurrence prophylaxis following cognitive therapy or mindfulness based therapy. *Journal of Consulting and Clinical Psychology*, *87*(2), 161–170. https://doi.org/10.1037/ccp0000351

Seth, A., (2018). Consciousness: The last 50 years (and the next). *Brain and Neuroscience Advances*, 2, 1–6. https://doi.org/10.1177/2398212818816019

Seth, A. (2021). *Being you: A new science of consciousness*. Dutton.

Simard, S. (2021). *Finding the mother tree: Discovering the wisdom of the forest*. Penguin Random House.

Smith, E., & Neumann, R. (2005). Emotion processes considered from the perspective of dual-process models. In L.F. Barrett, P. Niedenthal, & P. Winkielman (Eds.), *Emotion and consciousness*, (pp. 287–311). The Guilford Press.

Sui, J., Humphreys, G. (2015). The integrative self: How self-reference integrates perception and memory. *Trends in Cognitive Science*, *19*(12), 719–728. https://doi.org/10.1016/j.tics.2015.08.015

Ussher, J. (2011). *The madness of women: Myth and experience*. Routledge.

Ussher, J. & Perz, J. (2013). PMS as a process of negotiation: Women's experience and management of premenstrual distress. *Psychology & Health*, *28*(8), https://doi.org/10.1080/08870446.2013.765004

Vago, D., & Silbersweig, D. (2012). Self-awareness, self-regulation, and self-transcendence (S-ART): A framework for understanding neurobiological mechanisms of mindfulness. *Frontiers of Human Neuroscience*, *6*. https://doi.org/10.3389/fnhum.2012.00296

Wallace, A. (2011). *Stilling the mind: Shamatha teachings from Dudjom Lingpa's "Vajra Essence"*. Wisdom Publications.

Wallace, A. (2018). *Fathoming the mind: Inquiry and insight in Dudjom Lingpa's "Vajra Essence"*. Wisdom Publications.

Woods, S., & Rockman, P. (2021). *Mindfulness-based stress reduction: Protocol, practice, and teaching skills*. New Harbinger Publications.

Woods, S., Rockman, P., & Collins, E. (2019). *Mindfulness-based cognitive therapy: Embodied presence and inquiry in practice*. New Harbinger Publications.

# 6 Mindfulness as Anti-Oppressive Practice

So far, I have focused on presenting rationales and evidence for the deployment of mindfulness as an anti-oppressive practice. In this final chapter, I consider specific mindfulness methods and techniques that make it well suited for this purpose. In secular-scientific contexts, mindfulness is defined as intentionally paying attention in the present without judgement. The non-judging component concerns not judging experiences as good (correct, wanted), bad (incorrect, unwanted), or neutral (boring, irrelevant). In contrast, traditional Buddhist definitions of mindfulness emphasized mindfulness as *remembering*. Rather than alluding to memory per se, this is closer to the sense of "remembering yourself and your intention." This reference to memory is close to the literal term for mindfulness in Pali, *sati* (Dreyfus, 2011). Operationally defined, mindfulness is both a dispositional trait and a state. These two are related insofar as practising mindfulness as a state increases trait or dispositional mindfulness. This chapter considers how mindfulness can be taught and learned to optimize anti-oppressive outcomes.

Throughout my career as an educator, I have resisted presenting "how to" recipes for teachers and learners alike. In my view, the art of teaching and learning is for thoughtful and creative educators, clinicians, and learners alike to interpret and choose relevant contents based on learner needs and contexts. Therefore, this chapter does not present a programme or set of prescriptions so much as bridging principles, strategies, and sample practices to link anti-oppressive intentions to pre-existing and emerging practices in the teaching and learning of mindfulness. This requires that I highlight what is essential to include, alter, or introduce to make mindfulness a meaningful response to oppression.

## Contexts for Learning Mindfulness

One challenge in identifying strategies to introduce anti-oppressive praxis in mindfulness-based teaching and learning (MBTL) is that there are so many contexts in which mindfulness is taught or learned: preK-12 schools, post-secondary institutions, healthcare contexts, religious contexts, community-based programmes, apps, Internet videos, and ad hoc self- or peer-taught (MacPherson &

DOI: 10.4324/9781003449355-6

Rockman, 2023). Many such programmes are not even labelled as "mindfulness" but instead as resilience, social-emotional learning, compassion, or wellness programmes. The value of learning mindfulness by whatever name, with the support of an expert teacher, peers, and an evidence-based programme cannot be overstated. This makes both accessibility and availability key challenges.

Accessibility and availability are critical considerations when the purpose is to address oppression. Many people – women or otherwise – who suffer from the aftermath of oppression or oppressive conditions are marginalized from the more affluent, often white upper middle-class contexts in which mindfulness emerged in the West (MacPherson & Rockman, 2023). Until recently, connecting with established mindfulness teachers or programmes required paying rather steep tuitions or accepting religious contents than may be unwanted, unhelpful, or unnecessary. Standardized and evidence-based eight-week secular-scientific programmes like MBSR, MBCT, and Mindful Self Compassion (MSC) commonly have tuition rates in excess of $500 in non-subsidized community-based programmes. While not prohibitive, these rates can be a significant investment, which would most likely only be made if mindfulness were valued and endorsed within one's communities.

To address this, some teachers or clinicians have piloted or designed outreach programmes to improve access for more vulnerable populations, such as homeless women with PTSD in the USA (Gannon, 2018) and vulnerable youth in the UK (Abdullahzadeh, 2017). These programmes are expanding globally as well to serve poor and vulnerable women in the developing world, such as sex workers and addicts in Iran (Adelian et al., 2021) and women in socially vulnerable communities in Chile (Araya-Veliz et al., 2018) and Brazil (Kolchraiber et al., 2025). To serve more vulnerable populations, mindfulness trainers need skills to specify and adapt programmes to ensure they are culturally appropriate and trauma-informed (Liu et al., 2024; Spears, 2019). Added to these, mindfulness programmes for professionals and paraprofessionals have expanded, both to teach empathy and compassion towards their clients and to reduce compassion fatigue, ultimately to avoid fuelling oppression with vulnerable populations (Kolchriaber et al., 2025; Sanchez-Flores, 2017).

I implemented strategies myself to expand accessibility to mindfulness training. These included an MBTL graduate certificate to support people working with vulnerable populations in healthcare, education, and social work to develop skills in teaching mindfulness. This "teach the teacher" approach was designed to help professionals introduce mindfulness in sectors where services were accessible at low or no cost, so as to reach the most vulnerable. I also adapted standardized mindfulness (MBSR and MBCT) courses for students to take as upper-level university credits so it was integrated and covered as part of their programme rather than as an additional extra-curricular task and expense. As part of the graduate certificate programme, I instituted a community-based teaching and research project to place MBTL graduate students on practica in sectors directly serving vulnerable children, youth, or adults. The placements included teaching mindfulness as part of a career course for high school students to to prepare them for placements in early childhood centres serving vulnerable populations; integrating mindfulness as part of an Indigenous community wellbeing programme with the local health authority; and teaching mindfulness in a resilience programme at a high school that was in recovery from a serious fatal shooting. The motive in all of these placements was to build programming and expertise to serve vulnerable and oppressed populations through transdisciplinary practices across multiple institutions and stakeholders.

## Anti-Oppressive Mindfulness-Based Teaching and Learning

In an earlier book, my co-author and I developed the term MBTL to refer to the integration of mindfulness techniques to teaching and learning across clinical and educational contexts (MacPherson & Rockman, 2023). We developed a model to represent the distinctive approach of mindfulness in both clinical and educational practice. Minimally, all MBTL begins with attention training. This then can be extended to address social-emotional learning outcomes, and from there broader inquiry-based outcomes in a wide range of disciplines (see Figure 6.1).

This same model applies to adaptations of MBTL to serve anti-oppressive outcomes. As the MMT suggests, the attention regulation of mindfulness leads to significant downstream effects on wellbeing (via broadening awareness, reappraisal, positive emotion, and savouring) and the capacity to engage the world and experience in a more meaningful way (Garland et al., 2015). As anti-oppressive praxis, the attention and cognitive reappraisal processes

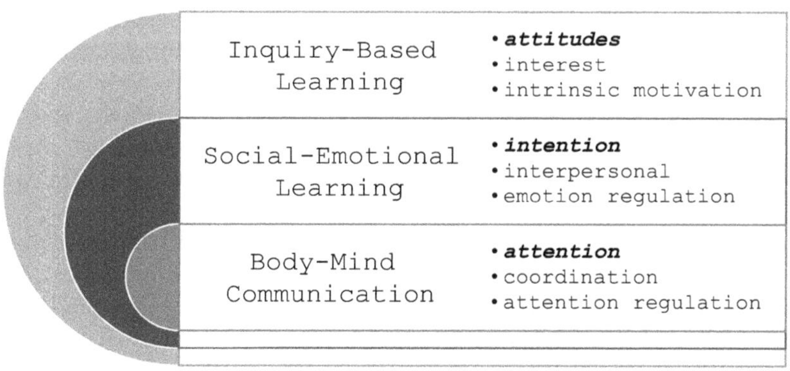


*Figure 6.1* An Integrative Model of MBTL (Adapted from MacPherson & Rockman, 2023).

extend to experiences arising from oppressive conditions, the social-emotional impacts of those experiences (e.g., emotions like shame, humiliation, anger), and inquiry with curiosity into the phenomena of oppression and liberation from oppression.

Three prevailing MBTL frameworks seem particularly relevant to anti-oppressive ends: (i) the three engagements of intention, attention, and attitudes; (ii) the three wisdoms of hearing, thinking, and meditating; and (iii) the four foundations of mindfulness of body, of feeling tones, of consciousness, and of phenomena.

## Three Engagements: *Intention, Attention, and Attitudes*

Shapiro et al. (2006) proposed three key mechanisms or forms of engagement to explain how mindfulness effects positive changes: intention, attention, and attitudes. These are not typically included in formal teaching and learning in the modern context and are only partially present in therapeutic contexts. The three derive from the standard definition in secular-scientific mindfulness originating with the founder of MBSR, Kabat-Zinn (2017): "Mindfulness is awareness that arises through paying attention, on purpose, in the present moment, non-judgementally."). Shapiro et al. operationalize this definition into the three axioms of *intention* ("on purpose"), *attention* ("paying attention … in the present moment"), and *attitude* ("non-judgementally").

Shapiro et al. (2006) propose *reperceiving* as an additional meta-mechanism or form of meta-engagement arising from the engagement of the other three. They liken reperceiving to the psychological concepts of *decentring, deautomization*, and *detachment*. Like decentring, it involves the capacity to stand outside of experience with less identification and habitual reactivity. Likewise, it is related to cognitive reappraisal, another common concept in clinical psychology, but reperceiving involves perception not just interpretation or cognition. The authors, however, point out that it is quite different from detachment, the separation or distancing from experience arising from apathy or numbness. The authors identify four subsequent mechanisms that arise from reperceiving as a meta-mechanism that help explain the positive impacts of mindfulness: self-regulation and self-management; emotional, cognitive, and behavioural flexibility; values clarification; and exposure. Exposure is the holding in the mind of an experience that might otherwise be avoided.

Segal et al. (2019) provided evidence of decentring (aka reperceiving) as a mechanism explaining how mindfulness reduces relapse in clinical depression. For two years, the researchers followed a group of formerly diagnosed clinical depressive participants on completion of a standardized MBCT or, alternatively, cognitive therapy (CT) programme. They found decentring and distress tolerance continuing to increase following the training, in particular among those who continued to practise mindfulness or CT practices.

Furthermore, and most critically, decentring negatively predicted the risk of relapse over that period.

What does this mean for applying mindfulness as an anti-oppressive praxis? One important perspective is potential of reperceiving or decentring reduce the deleterious effects of oppression on a harmful form of detachment. In previous research on the impacts of mindfulness and compassion on the legacies of race-related racism, many participants reported this kind of alienated detachment as a key feature of oppression (Munjee & MacPherson, 2025):

> Most participants described internalized oppression as a gradual alienation from a sense of authenticity to an internalization of White values or cultures in which they felt themselves an "Other." An Asian participant described learning to deny what she called her "true identity" in adapting to a dominant White professional workplace. By acquiring a disciplined professional "tone" and exactingly code of conduct, her alienation intensified as she placed increasing pressure on herself to self-monitor or "police" her behaviour, leading to self-censorship and emotion suppression.
>
> (p. 99)

Mindfulness cultivates the meta-awareness needed to stand back and observe these self-suppressing legacies of oppression though decentring or reperceiving. This is critical for healing from the aftermath of the trauma and self-diminishing narratives that come to define women and other oppressed people. The process of finding a more "authentic" self may be most about discovering more authentic intentions and the agency to enact them, which are the cornerstones of autonomy. So, I will now turn to the question of how intention, attention, and attitudes are nurtured through mindfulness and the implications for mindfulness as an anti-oppressive practice.

### *Intention*

Identifying and refining intentions in mindfulness are critical in the beginning, middle, and end. In teaching, it is common to scaffold students from more extrinsic to more intrinsic intentions to practise. In her study of the progression of mindfulness practitioners' intentions over time, Shapiro (1992) found an initial orientation on *self-regulation* gave way to a focus on *self-exploration* and later on *self-liberation*. Furthermore, whichever intention dominated reflected the outcome of the practice. This fits well with mindfulness as an anti-oppressive praxis. Initially, the motivation to practise would probably orient on correcting emotional dysregulation through self-regulation, but this orientation would soon be replaced by an interest in the investigation of the wounded self and its origins, and from there to the motivation to liberate from oppression itself.

As Stoljar (2022) argues, oppression diminishes women's autonomy principally by undermining her intentions. This happens as oppressive social scripts pre-empt her own intentions, thereby displacing her autonomy and self-determination. Her capacity to identify her intrinsic intentions and self-interest, and to cultivate the will and determination to act on them, is critical to her ability to overcome or resist oppression.

Oppression can lead women to devalue the intrinsic intention for self-care. Because oppression minimizes, conceals, and inhibits the self through shame and self-doubt, in the aftermath of oppression, women may feel that they are unworthy recipients of care and attention, even from themselves. Compounding this are internalized gender scripts that lead these same women to orient instead on the welfare and care of others. Such self-abnegation is misconstrued as a virtue. While it may cultivate a more compassionate orientation, such virtue cuing, humility, and self-denial may mask a subservience to oppressive social norms and a willingness to engage in the misogynistic sanctioning of other women who violate these same norms.

### *Attention*

Most directly, mindfulness educates attention. To engage in mindfulness as a practice is to begin to intentionally direct, redirect, hold, and release attention with increasing agency, flexibility, and choice. In the context of MMT, Garland et al. (2015) investigated how the education of attention could lead to such widespread downstream effects such as increased positive emotions and wellbeing. They concluded that paying attention in this way shifted consciousness out of automatic, habitual processing through decentring and broadened awareness a more accurate appraisal of self and world. This shift from habitual to present-moment experience enhanced wellbeing through two main effects: increased savouring (pleasure from experience) and meaning (significance ascribed experience).

As an anti-oppressive practice, mindfulness training begins by self-regulating attention in ways that are consistent across all forms of mindfulness practices and MBTL (MacPherson & Rockman, 2023). The downstream effects of such attentional training bring liberation from oppressive habits and conditioning. Throughout, the orientation is on the direct evidence of suffering, such as oppression, as it directly presents itself in the psyche of the practitioner and not on theories about its origins or therapeutically motivated war stories from the past. However horrific or benign one's personal history may seem, it does not negate or attest to the ongoing presence or absence of oppression. Indeed, revisiting stories of oppression may retraumatize or re-oppress those freeing themselves from oppressing conditions (Treleaven, 2018). False narratives may further reinforce avoidance strategies and the denial that oppression or the tendencies to oppress others continue to operate in one's habits of mind and behaviour.

### *Attitudes*

The dominant attitude cultivated in mindfulness is a *non-judgemental attitude* (Shapiro et al., 2006). This does not refer to suspending judgements about others or the world so much as suspending judgements about the self and one's experiences as a form of self-doubt. The first act of mindfulness is to recognize what is present; however, there are many avoidance strategies that may interfere with and prevent such recognition and knowing, and non-judging is aimed at removing these. In this way, as an attitudinal factor of mindfulness, non-judging is associated with openness to, and acceptance of, experience.

As anti-oppressive practice, mindfulness addresses the conditioned, habitual ways the oppressed view themselves and the oppressors view others. This suggests that for the oppressed, the emphasis is on cultivating a broadened and more open and accepting awareness of themselves, whereas for oppressors it is about broadening their awareness of others. For oppressors, research suggests that their close-mindedness is accompanied by a lack of empathy and compassion towards those they are oppressing.

In her study of masculine entitlement in boys, Keddie (2021), proposed three anti-oppressive mind-sets or attitudes to reduce such entitlement: (i) pedagogic discomfort, (ii) mutual vulnerability, and (iii) strategic empathy and ethical self-reflection. To cultivate these mind-sets involves openly discussing uncomfortable topics or investigating vulnerability as it arises, both in oppressors and the oppressed alike. Cultivating empathy towards the other and practising these in a safe environment may help, too (Munjee & MacPherson, 2025). Evidence suggests, however, that the need for empathy is greater for oppressors, especially under the influence of collective narcissism (Montoya et al., 2020). For oppressed women, it is important than an emphasis on empathy doesn't focus on cultivating empathy for men in ways that reinforce *himpathy* and so further fuel misogynistic and oppressive stances towards other women (Manne, 2021).

## The Three Wisdoms – Hearing, Thinking, and Meditating

Buddhism developed distinctive theories about epistemology, learning, and the relationship between conceptual and direct perceptions (MacPherson & Rockman, 2023). In Buddhist psychology, each source of knowing – conceptual and experiential – is considered to offer a valid source of knowing or *wisdom* with an interconnected pathway to insight (Analayo, 2021). Valid conceptual knowing on its own, however, is viewed as weaker than valid direct perceptual knowing (Cabezon, 1994). These two epistemic processes underpin the Buddhist view of learning, which is broken down into three forms or stages of inquiry. Hearing (including reading and viewing) and thinking or *contemplation* (including writing and reflection) are both more conceptual, while the third, meditation or *cultivation*, is a more direct perceptual way of knowing. Together these are said to offer the the *realization* of the nature of phenomena, including their ultimate nature as both form and emptiness (Cabezon, 1992). Such realization goes beyond accumulating inert facts or information and aims instead at transforming the person through the deepening of knowing (Vokey, 2007).

Analayo (2021) investigated the historical development of these three wisdoms in Buddhism, how they relate to one another and how each develops, "at first sight somewhat unexpectedly," through the cultivation of mindfulness. He compared the earliest canonical *Abhidharma* to later exegetical works to determine a consistent indication that all three – hearing, contemplation, and meditation—can all contribute to the cultivation of the seven awakening factors arising from mindfulness and so lead to awakening (transformative insight). This suggests that a strict opposition between theory (as conceptual) and practice (as direct knowing) would misrepresent the relationship between these three sources of wisdom and their relationship to mindfulness. In this, we might consider mindfulness as an anti-oppressive *praxis* rather than practice, whereby theory and practice are intimately and continuously related and interacting through mindfulness. Analayo is arguing here that, although mindfulness is associated with meditative practice and direct perception, it is also important in the development of theoretical or conceptual ways of knowing accessed through hearing and thinking. He concludes:

> Stepping out of the limitations that can come from excessive reliance on a sharp opposition between theory and practice toward instead viewing these as interrelated dimensions of mindfulness practice would also do better justice to the statement, made particularly in the context of the awakening factors, that mindfulness is always useful.

### *Hearing*

Hearing refers to a receptive process of learning from expert-others using reasoned facts, evidence, accounts of their direct experiences, and/or theories. Although it is called "hearing," reflecting the predominance of oral instruction in Buddhism, it includes reading or viewing. Engaging in hearing (including viewing and reading) provides roadmaps for novices. As DeRoche (2019) explains: "Listening to a teacher or studying texts can be seen as the first input of relevant information from outside, which begins to reorient one's own priorities, interests, and attention through learning from the wisdom accumulated by past generations" (p. 283).

In anti-oppressive mindfulness, hearing strategies offer ways to expose the oppressed to alternative narratives, scripts, and norms. These alternative are helpful to counteract fear and internalized misogyny and, in the process, harmful, oppressive norms. These need not be theories or analyses either; narrative accounts of people who faced and overcame oppression can be very valuable in supplanting oppressive norms. To know that someone countered oppression, how they did so, and that they were victorious can increase bravery in the face of fear.

### *Thinking*

Analayo (2021) cites an early Buddhist text, the *Petakopadesa*, to demonstrates how the more receptive wisdom from hearing deepens through more active analytical thinking and contemplation (referred to below as *reflection*):

> The teacher or some companion in the holy life, who takes the standing of a teacher, teaches someone the Dharma. Having heard this Dharma, one gains confidence. Herein, any investigation, application, gauging, and examining is wisdom produced from hearing. In reliance on having heard, any investigation, application, gauging, and examining is wisdom produced from reflection.

This connection harkens back to the first two of the seven factors of awakening, wherein mindfulness gives rise to investigation. In this case, based on mindfulness arising from hearing, investigation arises. Citing a Buddhist text, the *Samyukta-agama* (T 99), Analayo (2021) clarifies this link between mindfulness from hearing and investigation:

> From time to time one gets to hear profound and sublime teachings. Having heard profound teachings, one accomplishes the twofold proper behavior, bodily propriety and mental propriety. At that time, one cultivates the awakening factor of mindfulness. Having cultivated the awakening factor of mindfulness, the awakening factor of mindfulness becomes fulfilled. The awakening factor of mindfulness having been fulfilled, one investigates the teaching, analyzes the teaching, and examines the teaching. At that time, one diligently cultivates the awakening factor of investigation-of-dharmas.
>
> (SA 723)

Thinking or *contemplation* arises in its aftermath, deepening mindfulness through investigation (i.e., questioning) and critical inquiry (i.e., examining evidence more sceptically). Thinking is part of investigation, the second factor of seven factors of awakening, *following* mindfulness and followed *by* energy, culminating in a state of interest (or interest-taking). In this way, thinking is often referred to as *contemplation*, distinct from discursive thought or negative rumination (associated with depression). As contemplation, such investigation persists and deepens over time through *energy*.

In anti-oppressive mindfulness, such contemplation involves aligning concepts and indicators of oppression derived from research and others' experiences and applying them to one's own memories, experiences, and behaviour. This kind of self-examination and self-reflection is critical to cultivate anti-oppressive intentions and practice. Such inquiry need not be done in isolation but may be even more effective within a sympathetic group of peers, where the new supportive social context may help members overcome internalized shame with its tendencies to inhibit and conceal.

And just as hearing includes reading, thinking includes writing. Therefore, journaling or writing can foster contemplative reflection on oppression. The added benefit of this is that writing can bridge private introspection with more social engagement with sympathetic peers in group inquiries. Establishing probes to direct contemplation may help, but so too may free writing that allows self-organizing contents and themes from experience to emerge. Another possibility is to draw rather than write or, even more challenging, to draw with the left hand to withdraw even more controls and so invite the peripheral or liminal contents of consciousness to become more apparent.

### *Meditating*

Meditating or *cultivating*, the third wisdom, leads most directly to mindfulness and liberatory insight (Nairn et al., 2019). This process is most associated with mindfulness as it is conventionally understood. As meditation, mindfulness directly perceives the phenomenon under investigation. It directly perceives in the present, free of judgement. This practice of direct attention involves noticing or observing experiences rather than thinking about them; however, both scientific and Buddhist psychologies are quick to point out that such an observing mind includes subtle forms of naming or conceptual designation (Analayo, 2018a; Lupyan, 2012).

When meditating on oppression, the key is to observe and meditate on the aftermath of oppression as it appears in present-moment experience rather than on memories of past events. No matter how distanced we may be from the causes of oppression, if it remains unresolved it will continue to resurface until it is healed. The promise of mindful inquiry (i.e., meditation) as *purposeful, present-centred awareness free of judgement* is to enable one to recognize unwanted or avoided memories or experiences, to accept them, and to adapt so as to enhance wellbeing through mindfulness as a self-organizing process.

DeRoche (2021) refers to these three wisdoms as memory (via study), judgement (via reflection), and attention (via cultivation), all of which involve mindfulness. Together, by whatever name, these three wisdoms heal the mind from being captive to dysfunctional views of the self or identity arising from oppression. In this way, the path of transformative learning through mindfulness is a therapeutic path, just as the therapeutic path of mindfulness is a path of learning, both progressing through the effects of mindfulness on self-knowledge. As DeRoche concludes:

> Mindfulness, applied successively at the levels of study, reflection and cultivation, generates and sustains the presence of awareness that becomes the center around which the entire system of psychophysiological functions can be reorganized, and the personality reintegrated, overthrowing narrative self-reference or egological consciousness in the process. Memory, judgment, and attention are reorganized and redirected by a sense of presence, alignment, embodiment, and integrity. The deep interrelations of mindfulness with the constructs of self-control, self-regulation, and executive functions, especially executive attention, all emphasize that mindfulness is at the core of self-knowledge.

## The Four Foundations of Mindfulness

The four foundations of mindfulness *(satipatthana)* are a cornerstone of both Buddhist (Analayo, 2018a) and secular-scientific (MacPherson & Rockman, 2023) mindfulness praxes. The four foundations of mindfulness on the body, feeling tones, mind, and phenomena establish optimal objects for attention in the cultivation of mindfulness, which enable it to serve as a liberatory (anti-oppressive) praxis. Practised sequentially and additively, they enable the practitioner to broaden awareness and expand mindfulness to more subtle and complex objects.

### *Mindfulness of the Body*

Learning to practise mindfulness begins by anchoring attention to the body. There are many reasons for this, the most important being that attending to the body is relatively easy and naturally brings attention to the present moment. Also, the body is a familiar anchor or refuge for the mind. The distressing experience of being submerged in thoughts with little control or sense of agency is an existential state common to depression, anxiety, obsession stress, and oppression. To reign in and exercise more control and agency over attention and the mind are easiest to enact by attending to the body rather than to the more elusive mind with its abstracting tendencies.

In a commentary on one of the oldest mindfulness practice texts in Buddhism on mindfulness of breathing (the *Anapanasati Sutta*), Namgyal Rinpoche (2019/1992) elucidates how mindfulness of the breath proceeds. After anchoring attention on the breath by discerning if it is short or long, the meditator extends attention to mindfulness of the whole body (of breath). In the wake of this attention to the calming of the physical body, physical bliss or rapture arises. He points out how this link between the physical body and bliss may be surprising in light of mistaken presumptions that mental factors drive emotions:

> Perhaps you are more accustomed to an emotional or mental state producing rapture, like listening to Beethoven or having a beautiful thought and then experiencing physical-bliss. The instruction given in this text reverses that order of unfoldment. Here you are watching what is

> happening with each breath and, from this watching, physical calm is established. Once physical calm is present, physical rapture springs up, hence emotion, as if the physiology would release itself.
>
> (p. 27)

Common practices used to cultivate mindfulness of the body are mindfulness of breathing and mindfulness of the body (itself). Mindfulness of the breath is used to tether attention to the experiences of the natural (vs. controlled) process of breathing in one location in the body. Attention is directed to noticing the inbreath, outbreath, and the pause between the two and in noticing other features of breathing, such as its duration, its balance, its associated sensations, and releasing impulses to control the breath. When the mind moves away from paying attention to the breath to ruminate or notice other sensations or experiences, practitioners are instructed to gently return the mind to the breath using curiosity rather than judgement. The notion of the mind "wandering" is discouraged given that to notice the mind moving away is itself mindfulness. The key is to notice how the mind and attention work rather than controlling them to conform to some ideal standard or expectation (via judging).

Mindfulness of the body involves a broad awareness of the entire body and specific bodily sensations. It can be cultivated by attending to the stationery body in the body scan practice, the flexing body in progressive relaxation (used often with insomnia sufferers), or moving body during yoga or walking (Woods & Rockman, 2021). Specific areas of the body commonly used as anchors for attention include the hands, the feet, or the backside as it presses against the seat. Although the breath was recommended as an anchor for the mind in the past, because it can lead to highly introspective states, teachers have begun to recommend shifting the bodily locations of anchors to the hands, feet, or entire body or to the senses and their objects (Treleaven, 2018). Trauma aside, the interoceptive orientation can make it difficult to hold attention on the breath while functioning in a busy world. Namgyal Rinpoche recommended that mindfulness of breathing be reserved for formal (sitting) meditation rather than the informal anchoring practices one might use to move about the world while working, driving, and navigating interpersonal relations (2019/1992).

As an anti-oppressive practice, mindfulness of the body cultivates autonomy and self-determination (Ryan et al., 2021). "Self-possession," Rhys David's original English translation for *sati* before using "mindfulness" (Gethin, 2011), conveys this sense well of how mindfulness enhances agency not only in the mind but in the body as well. Oppression often involves the loss of autonomy and control over one's own body and, with it, the self and identity. Women's bodies and personhood are subsumed in oppression as the means to the happiness and welfare of others. Therefore, reclaiming bodily autonomy – including the choice to attend to different parts of the body, the choice to move (or not move) specific parts of the body, and the ability to know pleasure through the body are important steps to liberating oneself from oppression. For women, oppression involves internalized expectations to serve others' ends rather than one's own happiness and wellbeing. Recovering from oppression requires reclaiming our bodies (as life) and the capacities for both personal flourishing and pleasure as ends in themselves.

Exteroceptive experiences arising from the five senses appear to be related to mindfulness of the body, but they are classified as mindfulness of affect or feeling tones. Science has added three additional senses associated with body awareness. These are *interoception*, the awareness of the body or specific body parts; *proprioception*, the awareness of the position of the body in space; and *kinesthesia*, awareness of muscles and movement of the body through sensory systems embedded in muscles and joints. These three sources of internal bodily sensations locate our sense of ourselves and our minds in our physical bodies.

### *Mindfulness of Feeling Tones*

The focus of the second foundation of mindfulness is the least familiar to most readers. *Vedana*, the original Pali term translated here as feeling (or affective) tones, is closer to the English word *sensation*; however, it doesn't refer to a sensed object but rather to the process of sensing itself. In particular, it refers to the process of affixing an affective tone or valence to what is sensed, thereby giving "the taste of experience" (Peacock & Batchelor, 2019). These tones, preconsciously ascribed, condition and distort what is sensed and perceived to habitually affect both perception and behavior (Brewer, 2019; Grossman, 2019; Gupta, 2019).

The three valencies acribed as feeling tones are positive, neutral, or negative, which generate the experiences of wanting (desiring), disregarding (ignoring), or not wanting (avoiding or aversion), respectively. The valence is associated preconsciously, and so automatically, to sensory experiences so as to condition our perceptions and reactions to the world. In the process, they eclipse the perception of the uniqueness of the present moment by distorting it as a generalization.

Analayo (2018b) describes in detail how and why it is important in mindfulness to be aware of feeling tones and why the second foundation of mindfulness is dedicated to it:

> The recognition task described here requires a practitioner to be clearly aware of the feeling tone of the present moment as pleasant, unpleasant, or neutral. In a way, this brings down the complexity of mental experience to a fundamental level, focusing on a clear appreciation of the main driving forces in the mind. These are as follows:

> - to like and crave for an increase of what is pleasant;
> - to dislike and crave for a reduction or even vanishing of what is unpleasant;
> - to be bored and crave for a more entertaining alternative to what is neutral.
>
> Training oneself in recognition of these three feeling tones and the type of reaction they tend to trigger enables an honest recognition of what really motivates one's behaviour, of the how and why of one's reactions to the ups and downs of life.
>
> In practical terms, insight into the working mechanism of craving requires staying with mindful awareness at the level of the affective tonality of experience and thereby come to note the push that feeling can exercise on the mind.
>
> (p. 49)

Even single-celled, self-propelling amoebas in a petri dish have feeling tones, moving towards nourishment, repelling away from toxins, and remaining indifferent to what is neither food nor threat. In mindfulness, feeling tones (*vedana*) are investigated as they arise in experience as wanted (pleasant), unwanted (unpleasant), or ignored (neutral) feelings associated with sensations or memories. Such awareness does not necessarily remove the affective tones or conditioning directly but rather enhances the capacity to make choices beyond their automatic or habitual impulses. In this respect, awareness of feeling tones is the most direct path to becoming liberated from social and behavioural conditioning.

This practice of mindfulness of feeling tones is critical for anti-oppressive mindfulness given that affective tones form the bases of implicit biases. For example, their operationalization as labels of "good" or "bad" is used to measure implicit biases in Project Implicit (see https://implicit.harvard.edu/implicit/Registration to try yourself). As with all implicit biases, the internalization of oppression involves affective tones – positive, negative, and neutral – becoming preconsciously associated with generalized classes of people. These associations derive from a range of social sources, including media, the family, and school. For the oppressed, these associations become internalized as negative (unwanted) views towards their own identity and identity group and as positive (wanted) views towards members of dominant oppressing groups. These automatic associations can lead to negative self-perceptions, self-doubt, and shame or, alternatively, to identifying with oppressors. Likewise, these same affective tones can operate in oppressors, affixing implicit biases to make them feel entitled to exceptional treatments and to believe that they have been unfairly denied social goods they feel (wrongly) they deserve. Again, mindfulness doesn't directly remove these feeling tones so much as raise them from their preconscious processing into the light of conscious awareness. In the process, they diminish through slow attrition. Analayo (2018b) describes this process in detail:

> If mindfulness is established at the initial stage when feeling arises, it becomes possible to recognise an unwholesome reaction when it is still just about to come into being and thus before it has acquired full force. In other words, mindfulness of feelings can lead to becoming aware of mental reactivity when it is still in its incipient stage. As long as unwholesome thoughts and associations have not yet acquired full force, it is considerably easier to nip them in the bud.
>
> Once the mind has proliferated into various unwholesome perceptions and thoughts related to what happened, however, it is much more difficult to change the course of events. Having gotten caught up in what has happened for some time, the degree of identification with the thought processes that have arisen (following the course set by the initial input provided by feeling) has become stronger. This makes it more difficult to let go and change the course of the mind.
>
> (p. 51)

Mindfulness of feeling tones is seldom taught explicitly. For example, in Buddhism, affective tone tends to be presented theoretically by differentiating sukha (pleasure) from dukkha (suffering) or in the theory of interdependent origination. Within secular-scientific MBSR or MBCT programmes, feeling tones are introduced in an activity called pleasant or unpleasant events calendars. These calendars involve identifying a daily incident over two successive weeks, first week of a daily pleasant event and then a week of a daily unpleasant event (Woods et al., 2019; Woods & Rockman, 2021). Many teachers don't even realize that these calendar activities are to increase awareness of feeling tones, nor do some necessarily even know the theory of feeling tones. Indeed, some students mistakenly believe that the point is to experience positive things and avoid distress, leading them to focus on whether or not they like the various mindfulness practices or other experiences. Good teachers correct this misunderstanding, but it is a common mistake of novices. Because feeling tones are assigned preconsciously, it is difficult to notice them in fast-thinking System 1 processing in the midst of everyday experiences. Therefore, learning to identify them in the slowed-down and more deliberative processes of formal practice is important. Below I describe two mindfulness exercises I use to teach mindfulness of feeling tones explicitly.

## Feeling Tones in Bodily Sensations

One technique to enhance awareness of feeling tones involves touching the body in three spots with two finger tips (along one cheek and the lips; in the indentation of the suprasegmental knot between the clavicles; and on the outside of the leg at the knee). I invite participants to touch these areas with varying degrees of pressure – with light, strong, and ordinary pressure, respectively. I instruct them to look for the experience of wanting (pleasure; positive), not wanting (subtle pain; negative), or indifference (neutral), respectively, but I don't tell them what to expect so they can investigate themselves. Students may experience affect in the body differently based on trauma histories (Treleaven, 2018) or difficulty in discerning affect. I believe we are conditioned to discern affective tones (pleasure, pain, and neutrality, respectively) in these specific areas of the body – as infants, the mouth is linked to the sucking reflex, for example, the natural gagging response to dangerous pressure being placed on the suprasegmental knot, and indifference to the outer side of the knee when touched unavoidably by strangers' knees in auditoriums, for example. Distortions in these feeling tone responses, however, can indicate a degree of confusion or disassociation from the body rooted in trauma or mental disturbances.

### Feeling Tones in Seeing

An alternative and perhaps less threatening (for some) and safer approach that I use on occasion is an adapted mindfulness of seeing practice. As Treleaven (2018) points out in his study of trauma-informed mindfulness, exteroceptive sensory tasks that direct attention outside of oneself can be less threatening than interoceptive attention to the body. So, during this 10- to 20-minute-guided seeing practice, I ask participants to notice objects to which their eyes (or minds) are drawn (i.e., lingering or captivating their gaze); objects they avoid looking at (i.e., deflecting or averting their gaze), and objects they don't even notice (i.e., "overlooked"). Students are then encouraged to scan the room again to try to see all objects with equal interest and curiosity. In guiding the practice, I direct practitioners to notice feeling tones (as noticing if an experience is "wanted," "unwanted," or "ignored.")

#### *Mindfulness of Consciousness*

The third foundation of mindfulness is of mind or consciousness itself, both its contents (thoughts, emotions, and mental states) and contexts (mind and meta-consciousness). Such mindfulness involves paying attention to contents such as thoughts, emotions, imagery, and the sense of self as well as to meta-awareness. As the third foundation of the four, mindfulness of mind or consciousness is more subtle and tricky, building on the prior foundations that prepare practitioners to regulate attention, to anchor mindfulness in the body, and to recognize feeling tones. These are important preliminaries to becoming aware of the more nuanced movements of the mind itself. Mindfulness of consciousness requires some awareness of the constructed nature of all experience and the capacity to *decentre* from habitual, self-centred ways of thinking or perceiving. On this basis, mindfulness of mind involves paying attention to what pays attention – a recursive gesture underpinning meta-awareness.

### Thoughts and Images

To be mindful of thoughts and images is not merely to engage in thinking or imagining but rather to stand outside and notice the experience of thinking and images as contents of consciousness. One sense of this comes from MBCT, which uses the theme "thoughts are not facts" to foster decentring and deflate the hypnotic power of thoughts (Woods et al., 2019). We might begin this process with some analytical meditation, questioning whether or not a thought is even "ours" in the first place. We might instead see thoughts as lingering social narratives and scripts ingested and then regurgitated over time, seeming to come from the self at the centre of awareness despite originating with someone (or somewhere) else. "Whose thoughts are those, anyway? Whose words?" This can help to decentre from the hypnotic sense that thoughts are more concrete and determinant than they are.

There are different types of thinking, of course, ranging from (negative) rumination to (critical) investigation to (transformative) insight. These distinctions become clarified as we step aside and view thoughts from a distance. Mindfulness doesn't use conceptual thought to mediate experience as is done in analytical meditation or contemplation. Of course, there is a subtle process of conceptualizing in mindfulness that enables a practitioner to recognize or know what they are experiencing. It is not enough to merely experience the breath or body; it is important also to *know* that one is experiencing it (Analayo, 2019).

Imagery is also a form of conceptualizing, though different from thought. Images have more embodied and less explicit meanings. For example, in Buddhism images may arise predictably in practice as *nimitta*, signs of milestones in the achievement of calm or jhana states. Dreams and memories arise as images, often coded to be deciphered to understand. Given it is also "coded," metaphoric or figurative language is rarely used either in guiding or inquiry in secular-scientific mindfulness. The one exception is with thoughts and emotions, where an image is deployed to help practitioners to decentre by experiencing thoughts and emotions as less concrete. A common example is to equate thoughts and emotions with clouds forming, transforming, and dissipating in the sky.

To apply mindfulness of thoughts in anti-oppressive approaches requires recognizing the negative internalized scripts that re-present themselves in ongoing narratives (ruminative thoughts) about the self, one's community, and oppressors, while not accepting or believing them. This can be done by combining mindfulness with cognitive behavioural therapeutic techniques or through mindfulness directly. In the latter case, it is enough to recognize the thoughts as epiphenomena and not as truth statements or fact. Whether positive, negative, or neutral, they are observed without attachment or reacting. The key is the decentring of belief in the veracity of the thought, thereby fostering reappraisal and a broadening of awareness to attune to what is present rather than to habitual, inherited, or harmful perspectives.

## Emotions

In my experience, both with myself and with students, emotions can be difficult to discern, which may be why practices like Open Awareness encourage labelling them. Emotions hover in the liminal zones of consciousness, where they pervade and colour consciousness without necessarily being sufficiently clear to recognize and name. They often only become clearer when we react to them, when it is difficult to reverse their effects. In Buddhism, some emotions are often referred to as "afflictive," with qualities to be corrected or mysteriously transmuted in the case of Tantra (with mixed results).

As an anti-oppressive process, mindfulness needs to cultivate emotional awareness, that is, the capacity to notice, name, and transform emotions. To foster the recognition and identification of emotions in mindfulness, I developed a method using visualization within a mindfulness technique. This practice derives from holistic clearing meditation practice that I learned in a retreat at Shawnigan Lake, BC, in 1986 with the late Namgyal Rinpoche (n.d.). In the retreat, we were instructed to identify states of mind associated with strengths, weaknesses, and blocks. To identify these states, Rinpoche suggested that we first search our mind for an associated image and texture – that is, a visualized tangible object in the imagination with particular qualities associated with touch – and then to extrapolate from that texture to identify states of mind and associated memories. He was suggesting that to recognize a "state of mind" consciousness it was helpful to identify it first as an analogous embodied texture.

Realizing that emotions pervade consciousness like dye dissolving in water, I adapted this practice of to cultivate awareness of emotions in my own teaching. I recognized that, like mind states, emotions could be distilled into textures or derivatives of textures. So, I developed the following method, embedded within the Opening Awareness practice that I present later:

Step 1 First, try to discern what emotions are present without visualizing; however, in my case, on most days, I can't identify more than the vague sense of a mood.

Step 2 Then imagine your left hand reaching into the imagined space to your left. When I do it, what I find there are imagined objects (of one kind or type) with distinctive textures. (NB: They seem to occupy a kind of limit or boundary of consciousness with nothing beyond them).

Step 3 Focusing on the object(s), imagine touching them, and explore the (imagined) sensations of their textures, which, in my case, come quickly and vividly to mind (see Table 6.1, column 1).

Step 4 Then invite a word or several words to ariseto describe the texture. These descriptors appear effortlessly from the sensation of the texture itself (Table 6.1, column 2).

Step 5 Translate the texture descriptors to name the associated emotion(s) (Table 6.1, column 3).

Step 6 Returning to the opening awareness practice, check in to see if the labelled emotion accurately names your current emotional state, which it usually does. Table 6.1 documents the daily record of my practice during morning Open Awareness practices for a few weeks.

*Table 6.1* Identifying and Labelling Emotions Using Imagined Textures (of Mind)

| *Image* | *Texture/Quality* | *Emotion* |
|---|---|---|
| molten lava, flowing | burning<br>obliterating | mild anxiety |
| walking in forest – tree trunks, leaves, underbrush – light muted as if at dusk | haunted | mild fear<br>backdrop of fear |
| red brick aqueduct or mote – image of bricks on one side and water on other-dark water | murky<br>dank | mild depression<br>subdued |
| holding the long, sturdy stem of a bright yellow tulip in sunny field with other tulips | refreshed<br>ready | vigilant<br>diligent<br>upright |
| touching a spiky cactus in the desert and seeing blood trickling from finger. | prickly | mildly stressed<br>touchy |
| duck's yellow-orange beak (intact on its head) | hard | effortful (trying "hard")<br>motivated |
| holding wet pebbles that are lying at the bottom of a spring or stream | slimy<br>weighted down | restrained |
| petting hide of living deer in a forest with streaming light | (intense) pleasure<br>alive | stimulated |
| hand touching pink sticky candy floss | sticky<br>soft | sticky mind<br>mild anxiety |
| hand reaching into a mass of small, coloured plastic balls in a children's ball pit. | playful | easeful |
| finger in holes of honeycomb then of a natural sponge | absorbent<br>porous | saturated |
| touching shards of broken glass | broken<br>sharp | wounded<br>vulnerable |
| fingers pressing into bright orange jello | gooey, resistant<br>bright | mild resistance<br>buoyant |
| hand resting in layers of raw silk batten | soft, melting<br>pleasure | content<br>savouring |

For the oppressed, using mindful emotion regulation techniques corrects potential harms arising from more controlling forms of emotion regulation, such as suppression or unregulated expression. While suppression leads to indifference and passivity, unregulated expression leads to increased marginalization or social exclusion. In contrast, mindful emotion regulation conserves autonomy and empowers agency to strengthen the consciousness and adaptability of the oppressed. In tracking emotions through these anti-oppressive mindfulness techniques, the capacities to identify and attend to emotions associated with oppression, oppressing, and liberating are all enhanced (see Table 4.5 in Chapter 4). In this way, monitoring and investigating emotions become a way to assess oppression, making emotional literacy a critical resource in anti-oppressive practice.

## Consciousness Itself

As difficult as it may be to notice and identify emotions, the ability to identify consciousness is even more challenging. As Chapter 5 presents, oppression inhibits the flourishing of consciousness itself, not just its contents as body image, self-confidence, identity, thoughts, memories, or emotions. Table 6.2 revisits the seven attributes of consciousness (7-As) (column 1) to provide an

*Table 6.2* A Rubric to Assess Consciousness (and to Guide Mindfulness Practice)

| *7 Attributes* | *Sample Practices* | *(-) Indicator* | *(+) Indicator* |
|---|---|---|---|
| **Attention / Awareness** | *mindfulness of breath*<br>*mindfulness of body*<br>*mindfulness of sensing* | • worry and rumination<br>• restlessness and agitation<br>• avoidance, procrastination<br>• compulsive thoughts, acts<br>• dullness or distractibility | • noticing attention moving<br>• placing, holding, moving attention with intention<br>• broadening attention<br>• open, receptive attention |
| **Affect** | *mindfulness of sensing*<br>*mindfulness of feelings* | • excess aversion, repulsion<br>• numb, dull, disassociated<br>• impulse to control | • recognizing affective tone<br>• curious w/out judging<br>• equanimity |
| **Attunement** | *mindful movement*<br>*mindfulness of sensing*<br>*mindfulness of emotion* | • not noticing physical, social environments<br>• dull, habitual perceptions<br>• lack of particularity | • noticing focal, periphery<br>• details in noticing<br>• noticing patterns<br>• noticing change |
| **Anticipation** | *thoughts and emotions*<br>*visualization practice* | • dullness, habitual thinking<br>• dread, conspiracy thinking<br>• hope (w/certainty) | • recognizing mind when predicting, creating futures<br>• hope (w/ uncertainty) |
| **Agency** | *visualization practice*<br>*mindful movement*<br>*3MRB+action* | • not doing what you say you will do<br>• passivity, resignation<br>• blaming others (falsely)<br>• self-doubt | • following through with commitments or offers<br>• active, responsive<br>• accepting responsibility<br>• self confidence |
| **Autonomy** | *body scan*<br>*3MRB+action* | • externalized motivation<br>• externalized control<br>• sense of loss of control or of little or no control | • intrinsically motivated<br>• acting on bases of choice<br>• using feedback from mind states to make choices |
| **Affiliation** | *loving-kindness practice*<br>*compassion practice* | • lack of empathy or burnout<br>• non-response to suffering<br>• isolated; seeing bodies-minds as discrete, separate | • empathic; motivated<br>• assume responsibility for suffering of self/ others<br>• seeing mind as distributed |

assessment rubric for tracking indicators of the diminishment (column 3) and expansion (column 4) of consciousness, including some associated sample mindfulness strategies (column 2).

More holistic emotional indicators of oppression and its effects on consciousness are also important to track. Oppression inhibits and restricts consciousness and its capacity to promote flourishing. Oppressing others, on the other hand, closes the mind towards out-group members such as the oppressed and is characterized by a distinctive lack of empathy towards them and others. Liberation from oppression is characterized by wellbeing (flourishing), including being empowered, open, and compassionate (and empathic) towards self and others. These offer more global indicators of the quality of consciousness as impacted by the presence or absence of oppression.

### *Mindfulness of Phenomena*

The fourth foundation of mindfulness is mindfulness of phenomena. Phenomena refer to all things as they appear to consciousness. This is rarely properly presented or interpreted in my view, something I've discussed at length elsewhere (MacPherson & Rockman, 2023). As the fourth foundation or object domain for mindfulness, it is the culmination of the practice of the other three foundations. Thus prepared, a practitioner can now turn their inquiring minds towards any topic for significant, valid, and enlightening insights. In this respect, it implies that now that the preliminary work is completed, we can turn our attention to the real work of consciousness, which is to know itself and the world. Applying mindfulness in this way brings increased clarity, curiosity, equanimity, and intelligence to mind, thereby augmenting the capacity of knowing itself. In this respect, it is similar to science, but a science in which one is prepared through mindfulness to then investigate the world.

As anti-oppressive practice, the mindfulness of phenomena include inquiring into oppression itself and investigating the impacts of oppression on the body, feeling tones, and mind, including emotions and consciousness. With respect to the oppression of women, it means considering the rich scholarship and studies associated with feminism. Yet it would not be restricted to ideas but to observing oneself, others, and the world as part of a contemplative mindfulness of phenomena process. Consistent with feminist therapies, this also suggests the need to build communities of practice in which women come together to read, discuss, and engage in mindfulness on the path to liberation as they see it unfolding in their own lives: a path of consciousness raising through community.

## Mindfulness Practices

Below I introduce three meditational (mindfulness) practices I use personally and teach to others. They include secular-scientific and Buddhist practices, including one that is exclusively (Tibetan) Buddhist and not technically mindfulness (White Tara, a visualization or deity yoga practice).

## Opening Awareness Practice

As the gold standard practice of secular-scientific mindfulness, taught in both MBSR and MBCT, opening awareness practice builds on traditional Buddhist practices in a very skilful way. The practice involves scaffolding attention in succession on the breath, body, senses (feeling tones), mind (thoughts and emotions), and opening awareness (decentring), this practice can be effectively done in 20–50 minutes a day to provide an excellent foundation in mindfulness for anti-oppressive ends (Woods et al., 2019; Woods & Rockman, 2021). It is explicitly designed to extend and broaden awareness from a narrow focus on the breath in the body to a broad and open awareness of whatever appears in the mind. There is little presented in this book about mindfulness that isn't integrated in this practice and capable of being developed through doing it on a daily basis.

Below, I outline this practice in six steps of three to eight minutes each in duration. At the end of each step, that focus becomes the background awareness for the next focus, making the practice cumulative and expanding. A guided audio recording or script may be helpful, but here it is described:

1 ***Posture*** – The practice begins, as do all formal mindfulness practices, with attention to the position of the body. In this case, the body is positioned in specific ways to optimize an alert yet relaxed mind and body. This practice is usually done in a seated position, which can be on a cushion, a meditation bench, or in a chair. The back is erect, eyes closed or partially shut and gazing down, and, if on a cushion, the posterior should be elevated by a small cushion and the knees fall below the hips (or be supported by small cushions if they don't). If in a chair, straight-backed varieties are optimal but others are fine so long as the back is erect and the feet can rest flat on the floor.
2 ***Mindfulness of Breathing*** – Now, bringing attention inside the body, notice breathing in one salient place in the body: at the end of the nostrils, along the back of the throat, in the chest, or in the lower abdomen, wherever the breath feels most readily available. Holding attention there, notice breathing in the body. (Specific cues are used to guide participants at this point).
3 ***Mindfulness of the Body*** – Allowing the breath to move into the background, on an in-breath, inviting attention now to extend to the entire body. Beginning with the outer perimeter of the body, where the skin meets the air or clothing, attention moves inwards to hold the entire body in awareness. This awareness of the entire body alternates with the awareness of specific sensations that come to attention.
4 ***Mindfulness of Sound*** – Inviting the body now to move into the background, on an in-breath, attention extends to sound: sounds coming from the body and sounds from the surrounding environment are all held in awareness withoutstruggling to identify the source but rather noticing their qualities – intensity, frequency, and duration. Noticing feeling tones

that appear with the sound – wanting, not wanting, or indifference with curiousity and noticing sounds you haven't yet noticed or silence, perhaps, begin to notice communicate information about space: location, direction, and distance.

5 ***Mindfulness of Thoughts and Emotions*** – Now letting sounds move into the background, invite attention to shift to noticing thoughts and emotions, not intentionally engaging thoughts so much as noticing them when they happen to arise, as they inevitably do. Notice particular types of thoughts, perhaps. Also notice emotions and label them. [Perhaps using the texture practice and technique here to help identify emotions that are present.] Consider thoughts and emotions like clouds in the sky [or alternative metaphor], forming, unforming, and dissipating, fleeting and changing, taking this or that shape before dissolving again into molecules of air.
6 ***Opening Awareness*** – Now, letting thoughts and emotions move into the background open awareness to whatever appears in the field of attention. Here, there is no right or wrong, focus or distraction, or correct or incorrect object to pay attention to. All phenomena are welcomed and greeted with curiosity and interest as worthy of our attention. Just as they appear, they disappear with time, without our effort or intervention.

### Three-Minute Responsive Breathing Practice

This is a shortened version of the opening awareness practice taught in MBCT. This three-minute (though not strictly timed) practice is intended as an informal practice to use in the midst of challenging and potentially reactive situations. There are three key steps in this practice:

1 ***Step 1: Checking in*** – Bringing attention inside the body, begin to notice what is present without trying to change it: body and sensations, thoughts, and emotions, merely noticing with curiosity, without judging and seeing whatever is here as the aftermath of what came before, lingering still.
2 ***Step 2: Abdominal Breathing*** – Gathering attention in the belly, begin to notice breathing, including the rising of the lower abdomen with the in-breath and falling with the out-breath.
3 ***Step 3: The Body and Beyond*** – Returning attention to the entire body, begin to notice what is present here, both as the entire body and as particular sensations that come to our attention. Expanding from the body, begin to notice what else is discerned – sounds, sensations, thoughts, and emotions.

Once the 3MRB practice is completed, an action-step can be taken, where choices can be made on how to respond to the challenge: continue being mindful without deciding right not how to respond; choose to leave it alone and let it go; or choose to act by expressing or addressing the challenge directly.

**White Tara Practice**

I would be remiss not to introduce a Tibetan Buddhist practice, given its prominence in my own development. That said, it is not technically a mindfulness practice but a visualization practice. Unlike mindfulness, which is oriented on paying attention to what is present in experience in the immediate moment, visualization practices in the Tibetan tradition – also known as *deity yoga* – are oriented on imagining the mind, the body, and the world transformed into archetypal, often blissful, manifestations and qualities that are simultaneously recognized as empty (decentred) (Dalai Lama et al., 1982).

White Tara is a practice I do daily, which is why I chose it. The Tibetan tradition requires that people are initiated in a deity yoga practice in order to recite the mantra alongside the accompanying visualization (Dalai Lama et al., 1982). The secrecy is very strict for practices categorized as Highest Yoga Tantra, which this is not. That said, to honour the role this kind of practice has had on my own liberation from oppression without violating its trust, I will present an overview but omit the mantra. Otherwise, such practices will continue to be overlooked and poorly represented within enriching Buddhist-secular-scientific dialogues. Although they are referred to as *deity yoga* practices, they aren't technically deities in the way we are accustomed to thinking of deities. The encapsulate perfections that we can assume ourselves by meditating on them, which is signalled by calling them a form of *yoga*, which shares the same Indo-European root with the word *yoke* – meaning to harness or bind.

There are many emanations of Tara, including a set of 21 Taras (with multiple colours and forms); Cittamani Tara (Highest Yoga Tantra); and White Tara (Wooten, 2020). Green Tara is particularly beloved by Tibetans, who know her by her Tibetan name, *Dolma*. Although all Taras are associated with liberation, Green Tara is most directly believed to bring liberation from suffering. White Tara is a peaceful emanation of Tara associated with longevity and protection (Beyer, 1973).

There are three aspects to these deity yoga practices: mantra recitation (mind, vibration); assuming the emanation body (appearing as White Tara); and viewing the mandala, the divine abode of the deity. In this way, the imagination is deployed to transform thoughts and mind into the purified and blissful mantra, body, and home of White Tara. The mantra is visualized as a seed syllable ("Tam") in the heart and surrounded by the seed mantra of Tara (ten syllables). The longer mantra (with ten additional syllables) particular to White Tara is first visualized atop a white wheel with the seed syllable at its hub. This white, radiant wheel spins both counterclockwise and clockwise on its periphery in a gesture of protection, vanquishing potential harms at the periphery or liminalities of consciousness. The mantra is recited alongside this visualization, giving a certain resonance or vibration in the body to the visualized images. Then the meditator imagines themselves in the form of White Tara, radiant white with two hands and two feet. She has seven eyes (of wisdom), one on each of her forehead, eyes, hands (palms), and feet (soles). She is adorned in white silks and pearls. Her legs are crossed and she sits on a white lotus with her right arm stretched out with her right palm open in a gesture of offering. Her left arm is bent, while her left hand holds the stem of a lotus flower in bloom (along with a bud and old bloom to suggest the three times of past, present, and future). Around her emanate circles of protective, coloured lights in sequence: white, yellow, red, blue, green, and mauve (Beyer, 1973).

I do this practice after opening awareness. I include it to show how using such visualization can help to reduce oppression in self-affirming and peaceful ways. For example, a keystone of deity yoga practice is said to be assuming the "pride of the deity," which is considered to be a non-afflicted pride based on manifesting their virtues. The Dalai Lama et al. (1982) use a passage from the *Vajrapani Initiation Tantra* to show how such divine pride depends on combining deity and emptiness yogas with a foundation of virtuous conduct:

> When a practitioner of the Bodhisttva deeds engaging in the Secret Mantra approach causes himself (*sic*) to have the form of his own deity and with a mind free from doubt generates the pride [of being a deity] whether going, standing, or sitting is always immovable [in this clear appearance and pride of a deity] though moving about. O Shantimati, he is endowed with the ethics of a great Bodhisattva who is practicing the Bodhisattva deeds of the Secret Mantra approach.
>
> (p. 59)

As a woman, White Tara lends us her confidence and liberation from shame when we yoke ourselves to her imagined form (Wooten, 2020). This practice is a refuge for me, personally, and for my mind. Tara offers to fill a gap for me that I don't find in routine mindfulness practices, which is this need for a refuge or sanctuary in the struggle to resist oppression. The symbolic violence of oppression and its targeting of our sense of self can be threatening and even terrorizing to those subjected to it. So, of course, removing the fear and providing sanctuary is part of the remedy.

## Anti-Oppressive Integrated Mindfulness Programme Features

The above are meditations. What is also needed, however, is to engage in hearing (including reading and viewing) and thinking (including contemplation andwriting) about oppression as forms of mindfulness. One symptom of the internalization of oppression is to over-attribute hardships to personal shortcomings and under-attribute social barriers and bias. So, it is crucial to develop a critical awareness of the interaction between psychological, social, and political factors to assess more accurately one's situations and their causes. This is accomplished largely through reading, contemplation, and discussion. And it should end with concrete action in the situations that define our experience and identity. Anti-oppressive mindfulness doesn't end with introspection, it just begins there. It ends with the world, as one comes to radiate compassionate actions to liberate others on the bases of one's own liberation.

## Conclusion

As it so happens, I am finishing reading a book as I am finishing writing this one. That book is *Finding the Mother Tree: Discovering the Wisdom of the Forest* by Suzanne Simard (2021). In this combined personal and professional account, the author documents her scientific discoveries regarding cooperation within and across species in forest ecosystems. As resident and forest ecology professor at the University of British Columbia in the province in which I live – that is, British Columbia, Canada – she invokes my own memories of meditating and hiking through wild corners of this province, including during silent solitary retreats (MacPherson & Rockman, 2023). I see other alignments as well, notably that Simard's account highlights three important messages: (i) as a scientist, she practised mindful investigation to arrive at her discoveries about nature; (ii) as a woman, she navigated marginalization and misogyny successfully to persist and even triumph in her profession; and (iii) as a conveyer of knowledge, her life exemplifies what is at stake in overcoming misogyny and the marginalization of women within human societies and science.

With respect to the first point, Simard embodies dispositional or trait mindfulness in her detailed descriptions of her observations and experiences as a forest ecologist and naturalist. She describes in detail what it is to engage in mindful observation followed by persistent contemplative investigation, thereby deriving significant and creative insights about the world (in this case, the world of forests.).

With respect to the second point, although the narrative is focused on Simard's discovery of communicative networks between trees, mediated by fungi, it also documents her experience being marginalized and subjected to misogynistic micro-aggressions directed at her as a woman in male-dominated professionaland research situations in the context of governmental forestry management. Despite her research being vetted via rigorous peer-review processes and published in top-tier journals like *Nature*, some male peers responded to her data and theories with unreasonable scepticism, subjecting her instead to ridicule and denigrating comments. In response, she recounts feeling inhibited and silenced and nearly giving up.

Finally, with respect to the third point, her discoveries challenge a distinctively masculine approach to nature that has dominated both science and industrial practices. By showing the value of cross-species cooperation and communication in forest ecology and health, she exposed the errors and excesses of the then prevalent assumption that nature functioned exclusively through competition and so required extreme controls to exploit it (e.g., herbicides; clearcutting).

Simard's testimonial speaks to what may be at stake in tolerating the misogyny and oppression against women in science may be the suppression of more valid holistic, cooperative, and compassionate perspectives about nature, humanity, and our inter-relations. In this respect, misogyny does not merely suppress women, it suppresses forms of knowledge and ways of life that women may contribute, disproportionately, to this world. In this, I think there is considerable truth to the idea that the oppression of women echoes the suppression of nature itself by humanity. Yet women face a choice as well, to stand by their sisters against such suppression or to align themselves with patriarchal systems and so become agents of misogyny. I am confident that mindfulness offers a corrective and resource to make us braver and more able to meet this challenge.

## References

Abdullahzadeh, A. (2017). *Investigation of the effectiveness of a mindfulness-based intervention with vulnerable young people.* Doctoral thesis (PhD), Manchester Metropolitical University. Available at: https://e-space.mmu.ac.uk/618689/

Adelian, H., Shahraki, S.K., Miri, S., & Farokhzadian, J. (2021). The effect of mindfulness stress reduction on resilience of vulnerable women at drop-in centers in the southeast of Iran. *BMC Women's Health*, *21*, 255. https://doi.org/10.1186/s12905-021-01390-6

Analayo, B. (2018a). *Satipatthana meditation: A practice guide.* Windhorse publications.

Analayo, B. (2018b). Why be mindful of feelings? *Contemporary Buddhism*, *19*(1), 47–53. https://doi.org/10.1080/14639947.2018.1450958

Analayo, B. (2019). *Mindfulness of breathing: A practice guide and translations.* Windhorse Publications.

Analayo, B. (2021). Hearing, reflection and cultivation: Relating the three types of wisdom to mindfulness. *Religions*, *12*(441). https://doi.org/10.3390/rel12060441

Araya-Veliz, C., Mocada, L., Becerra, M., Alberto, G., Acosta, C., Medina, Pl, Ramos, D., Alfaro, M., Araya, P., Concha, L., Cerda, J., Musa, G., Fernandez, Pl, & Munoz, S. (2018). Intervention based on mindfulness and self-compassion with Chilean women in a social vulnerability context: A qualitative study. *Revista Argentina de Clinica Psicologica*, *28*(4), 501. https://doi.org/10.24205/03276716.2019.1107

Beyer, S. (1973). *The cult of Tara: Magic and ritual in Tibet.* University of California Press.

Brewer, J. (2019). Feeling is believing: The convergence of Buddhist theory and modern scientific evidence supporting how the self is formed and perpetuated through feeling tone (*vedana*). In J. Peacock & M. Batchelor, (Eds.), *The definition, practice, and psychology of vedana: Knowing how it feels* (Ch. 9), Routledge.

Cabezon, J. (1992). *A dose of emptiness: An annotated translation of the sTong thun chen mo of mKhas grub dGe legs dpal bzang.* SUNY Press.

Cabezon, J. (1994). *Buddhism and language: A study of Tibetan scholasticism.* SUNY Press.

Dalai Lama, H.H., Tsongkapa, & Hopkins, J. (1982). *Deity yoga: In action and performance tantra.* Snow Lion Publications.

DeRoche, M. (2019). Buddhist philosophy as a way of life: Perspectives of the "Three Wisdoms; from Tibet and Japan". In D. Arnold, C. Ducher, & P. Harter (Eds.), *Reasons and lives in Buddhist tradition: Studies in honour of Matthew Kapstein*, (pp. 277–292), Wisdom Publications.

DeRoche, M. (2021). Mindful wisdom: The path integrating memory, judgment, and attention. *Asian Philosophy 31*, 19–32.

Dreyfus, G. (2011). Is mindfulness present-centred and non-judgmental? A discussion of the cognitive dimensions of mindfulness. Contemporary Buddhism, 12(1), 41–54. https://doi.org/10.1080/14639947.2011.564815

Gannon, B. (2018). *Trauma-Informed brief mindfulness training: A new adaptation for homeless women with PTSD*. Open Access Thesis, Doctor of Nursing Practice, Yale University School of Nursing. Available at: https://elischolar.library.yale.edu/ysndt/1063/

Garland, E., Farb, N., Goldin, P., & Fredrickson, B. (2015). Mindfulness broadens awareness and builds eudaimonic meaning: A process model of mindful positive emotion regulation. *Psychological Inquiry*, *26*(4), 293. https://doi.org/10.1080/1047840X.2015.1064294

Gethin, R. (2011). On some definitions of mindfulness. *Contemporary Buddhism*, *12*(1), 263–279. https://doi.org/10.1080/14639947.2011.564843

Grossman, P. (2019). Serious illness: Overwhelmingly unpleasant feeling tone of life, and how even incipient mindfulness training may sometimes help. In J. Peacock & M. Batchelor, (Eds.), *The definition, practice, and psychology of vedana: Knowing how it feels* (Ch. 10), Routledge.

Gupta, A. (2019). *Vedana* of bias: Latent likes and dislikes fuelling barriers to human connection. In J. Peacock & M. Batchelor, (Eds.), *The definition, practice, and psychology of vedana: Knowing how it feels* (Ch. 9), Routledge.

Kabat-Zinn, J. (2017). Jon Kabat-Zinn: Defining mindfulness. *Mindful: Healthy Mind, Healthy Life*, Jan 11, 2017. Accessed on Jul 2025 at: https://www.mindful.org/jon-kabat-zinn-defining-mindfulness/

Keddie, A. (2021). Engaging boys in gender transformative pedagogy: Navigating discomfort, vulnerability, and empathy. *Pedagogy, Culture & Society*, *30*(3), 401–412. https://doi.org/10.1080/14681366.2021.1977980

Kolchraiber, F., Tanaka, L., Negi, L., Nunes, R., deSouza, E., & deSouza, K. (2025). Vulnerability, compassion meditation and well-being: Community-based participatory research. *Physis*, *35*(01). https://doi.org/10.1590/S0103-7331202535 0114en

Liu, V., Nelson, L., & Shorey, S. (2024). Experiences of women receiving trauma-informed care: A qualitative systematic review. *Trauma, Violence, & Abuse*, *25*(4), 3054–3065. https://doi.org/10.1177/15248380241234346

Lupyan, G. (2012). Linguistically modulated perception and cognition: The label-feedback hypothesis. *Frontiers of Psychology: Cognition*, *3*, https://doi.org/10.3389/fpsyg.2012.00054

MacPherson, S., & Rockman, P. (2023). *Mindfulness-based teaching and learning: Preparing mindfulness specialists in education and clinical care*. Routledge.

Manne, K. (2021). *Entitled: How male privilege hurts women*. Crown Publishing.

Montoya, M., Pittinsky, T., & Rosenthal, S. (2020). A multidimensional model of collective narcissism. *Journal of Theoretical Social Psychology*, https://doi.org/10.1002/jts5.71

Munjee, R. & MacPherson, S. (2025). Mindfulness and compassion in response to racism. *Diaspora, Indigenous, and Minority Education*, *19*(2), 91–107. https://doi.org/10.1080/15595692.2023.2254873

Nairn, R., Choden, Regan-Addis, H. (2019). *From mindfulness to insight: Meditations to release your habitual thinking and activate your inherent wisdom*. Shambhala Press.

Peacock, J. & Batchelor, M. (Eds.) (2019). *The definition, practice, and psychology of vedana: Knowing how it feels*. Routledge.

Rinpoche, N. (2019/1992). *The breath of awakening: A guide to liberation through Anapanasati mindfulness of breathing*. Bodhi Publishing.

Rinpoche, N. (n.d.). *Holistic clearing meditation: An anti-paralytic practice for human liberation*. Bodhi Publishing.
Ryan, R., Donald, J., & Bradshaw, E. (2021). Mindfulness and motivation: A process view using self-determination theory. *Current Directions in Psychological Science*, *30*(4), https://doi.org/10.1177/09637214211009511
Sanchez-Flores, M. (2017). Mindfulness and complex identities in equity training: A pilot study. *European Review of Applied Sociology*, *10*(14), 20–33.
Segal, Z., Anderson, A., Gulamani, T., Dinh Williams, L., Desormeau, P., Ferguson, A., Walsh, K., & Farb, N. (2019). Practice of therapy acquired regulatory skills and depressive relapse/recurrence prophylaxis following cognitive therapy or mindfulness based cognitive therapy. *Journal of Consulting and Clinical Psychology*, *87*(2), 161–170. https://doi.org/10.1037/ccp0000351
Shapiro, D. (1992). A preliminary study of long term meditators: Goals, effects, religious orientation, cognitions. *Journal of Transpersonal Psychology*, *24*(1), 23–39.
Shapiro, S., Carlson, L., Astin, J., & Freedman, B. (2006). Mechanisms of mindfulness. *Journal of Clinical Psychology*, *62*(3), 373–386. https://doi.org/10.1002/jclp.20237
Simard, S. (2021). *Finding the mother tree: Discovering the wisdom of the forest*. Penguin Random House.
Spears, C. (2019). Mindfulness-based interventions for addictions among diverse and underserved populations. *Current Opinion in Psychology*, *30*, 11–16. https://doi.org/10.1016/j.copsyc.2018.12.012
Stoljar, N. (2022). Ineffective intentions: How oppressive scripts undermine autonomy. In B. Colburn (Ed.), *The Routledge Handbook of Autonomy*, Chapter 23 13 pages], https://doi.org/10.4324/9780429290411
Treleaven, D. (2018). *Trauma-sensitive mindfulness: Practices for safe and transformative healing*. W.W. Norton & Co.
Vokey, D. (2007). Hearing, contemplating, and meditating: In search of the transformative integration of heart and mind. In C. Eppert & H. Wang (Eds.), *Cross-cultural studies in curriculum: Eastern thought, educational insights*, Chapter 12 [26 pages]. Routledge.
Woods, S., Rockman, P., & Collins, E. (2019). *Mindfulness-based cognitive therapy: Embodied presence and inquiry in practice*. New Harbinger Publications.
Woods, S., & Rockman, P. (2021). *Mindfulness-based stress reduction: Protocol, practice, and teaching skills*. New Harbinger Publications.
Wooten, R. (2020). *Tara, the liberating power of the female Buddha: 22 meditations to heal ourselves and repair our world*. Sounds True.

# Index

Pages in *italics* refer to figures and pages in **bold** refer to tables.

For Product Safety Concerns and Information please contact our EU representative GPSR@taylorandfrancis.com
Taylor & Francis Verlag GmbH, Kaufingerstraße 24, 80331 München, Germany

www.ingramcontent.com/pod-product-compliance
Ingram Content Group UK Ltd.
Pitfield, Milton Keynes, MK11 3LW, UK
UKHW020705121225
465993UK00022B/2169
*9781032582665*